Third Joint SIGHUM Workshop on Computational Linguistics for Cultural Heritage, Social Sciences, Humanities and Literature (LaTeCH-CLfL-2019)

Minneapolis, Minnesota, USA
7 June 2019

ISBN: 978-1-5108-8779-4

NAACL HLT 2019

The Joint SIGHUM Workshop on Computational Linguistics for Cultural Heritage, Social Sciences, Humanities and Literature

Proceedings of the Third Workshop

June 7, 2019
Minneapolis, MN, USA

Preface

Welcome to the third edition of LaTeCH-CLfL—which also is the thirteenth edition of LaTeCH and eighth of CLfL. We have had fun preparing the workshop, and we will be happy if you have fun attending (or at least reading the workshop papers -:). Please visit the website at https://sighum.wordpress.com/events/latech-clfl-2019/ where you will find the workshop presentations, among other things.

The papers cover, as usual, topics which you will not easily find at regular NLP conferences. The authors take on literary texts, including drama and poetry, and more generally literary study; historical texts; ancient or otherwise old languages; government documents; code switching; and more.

Last but certainly not least, we will have an invited talk. Ian Milligan, a historian, has a deep interest in Digital Humanities, and understands the role on Natural Language Processing in his discipline.

It is our pleasant duty to thank the authors: there would be no workshop without you. Nor without the program committee, to whom we are ever so grateful for their thorough and helpful reviews.

Beatrice, Stefania, Nils, Stan, Anna

Invited Talk

Working with Cultural Heritage at Scale: Developing Tools and Platforms to Enable Historians to Explore History in the Age of Abundance

The rise of the Web as a primary source will have deep implications for historians. It will affect our research — how we write and think about the past — and it will change how humanists and social scientists make sense of culture at scale. Scholars are entering an era when there will be more information than ever, left behind by people who rarely entered the historical record before. Web archives, repositories of archived websites dating back to 1996, will fundamentally transform scholarship, requiring a move towards computational methodologies and the digital humanities.

The talk explores this dramatic shift — and what is to be done about it — by arguing that historians will have to understand how to work with textual (and other) data at scale. Historians will soon need to become familiar, at the very least, with NLP techniques. This is not just a marginal problem: the need to explore the big data of the Web (and other digitized repositories) strikes to the core of our discipline.

All Historians Have to Begin to Work with Data

Initial moves towards digital methods have been very promising, as historians begin to study the 1990s. Even so, they will discover sooner than they think that one cannot write most histories of the 1990s or later without reference to web archives. They must be ready, but they are hamstrung. The profession has largely turned away from statistics and from quantitative methodologies more generally; and the web archiving analysis ecosystem is largely based on tools that require a high level of technical expertise. Access to web archives at scale requires, more often than not, fluency with command-line interfaces, access to high-performance computing, and storage at the terabyte scale. Historians need to analyze web archives to write histories, yet that requires skills and infrastructure beyond what one can reasonably expect of them. What, then, can be done?

Tools and Platforms: The Archives Unleashed Project

The talk introduces this problem, and discusses the process of developing tools and platforms to enable historians to explore this "age of abundance". It does so by highlighting the Archives Unleashed Project, an interdisciplinary initiative funded by the Andrew W. Mellon Foundation. The project's goal is to "make petabytes of historical Internet content accessible to scholars and others interested in researching the recent past", and brings together a historian, a computer scientist, and a librarian to lead a team to develop such infrastructure. The project will achieve it in three main ways.

- The Archives Unleashed Toolkit is an open-source platform for analyzing web archives with Apache Spark. It is a scalable toolkit, based upon a process cycle that we have developed; we call it the Filter-Analyze-Aggregate-Visualize cycle. To use the Toolkit, a scholar first filters down a large web (a particular range of dates, a domain, or only pages with certain keywords present); analyzes (finds links, or named entities, sentiment, topics); aggregates (summarizes the output); and visualizes (either through various data tools or tabular data). The Toolkit, based on a command-line interface, is unfortunately very difficult to use.

- The Archives Unleashed Cloud is a web-based front-end for working with the Toolkit. It takes data from the Internet Archive and processes it into formats familiar to researchers: network diagrams, filtered text files, and other statistical information about a collection. We also provide all of this data for download with a bundled Jupyter Notebook. This allows scholars to use a web-based interface to perform basic data science operations on the data: draw on popular computational linguistics or data science Python libraries to process data and find answers. Suddenly, working with web archives is not so terrifying, and the users have been connected to the mainstream of the Natural Language Processing world.

- We run a series of datathons (three to date, as part of the Mellon grant). They bring together domain experts, researchers, and others to work with web archive data at scale and so help lower barriers; connect people interested in the topic and build community; and help develop a body of practice around web archiving collection and analysis practices.

Conclusion

The talk explores ways in which we can help historians move into an age when working with cultural heritage at scale is no longer a "nice to have" but a necessary component of studying periods from the 1990s onwards.

About the speaker

Ian Milligan is an Associate Professor of History at the University of Waterloo, where he teaches Canadian and digital history. He is currently the principal investigator of the Archives Unleashed project, which seeks to make web archives accessible to humanities and social sciences researchers. Ian has published several books: the forthcoming *History in the Age of Abundance? How the Web is Transforming Historical Research* (April 2019), the *SAGE Handbook of Web History* (co-edited with Niels Brügger, 2018), *Exploring Big Historical Data: The Historian's Macroscope* (co-authored with Scott Weingart and Shawn Graham, 2015), and *Rebel Youth: 1960s Labour Unrest, Young workers, and New Leftists in English Canada* (2014). In 2016, Ian was named the Canadian Society for Digital Humanities's recipient of the Outstanding Early Career Award.

Program Committee

JinYeong Bak, KAIST, Republic of Korea
Gosse Bouma, University of Groningen, Netherlands
Paul Buitelaar, Insight Centre for Data Analytics, National University of Ireland Galway, Ireland
Gerard de Melo, Rutgers University, United States
Thierry Declerck, DFKI GmbH, Germany
Stefanie Dipper, Ruhr-University Bochum, Germany
Jacob Eisenstein, Georgia Institute of Technology, United States
Micha Elsner, The Ohio State University, United States
Mark Finlayson, FIU, United States
Serge Heiden, ENS de Lyon, France
Graeme Hirst, University of Toronto, Canada
Mika Hämäläinen, University of Helsinki, Finland
Adam Jatowt, Kyoto University, Japan
Mike Kestemont, University of Antwerp, Belgium
Dimitrios Kokkinakis, University of Gothenburg, Sweden
Stasinos Konstantopoulos, NCSR Demokritos, Greece
John Lee, City University of Hong Kong, Hong Kong
Chaya Liebeskind, Jerusalem College of Technology, Lev Academic Center, Israel
Rada Mihalcea, University of Michigan, United States
Borja Navarro-Colorado, University of Alicante, Spain
John Nerbonne, Albert-Ludwigs Universität Freiburg, Germany
Pierre Nugues, Lund University, Sweden
Petya Osenova, Sofia University and IICT-BAS, Bulgaria
Michael Piotrowski, Université de Lausanne, Switzerland
Andrew Piper, McGill University, Canada
Thierry Poibeau, LATTICE-CNRS, France
Georg Rehm, DFKI, Germany
Martin, Reynaert, Tilburg University, Netherlands
Pablo Ruiz, LINHD, UNED, Spain
Marijn Schraagen, Utrecht University, Netherlands
Eszter Simon, Research Institute for Linguistics, Hungarian Academy of Sciences, Hungary
Elke Teich, Universität des Saarlandes, Germany
Sara Tonelli, FBK, Italy
Thorsten Trippel, University of Tübingen, Germany
Ted Underwood, Univ of Illinois, United States
Menno van Zaanen, Tilburg University, Netherlands
Kalliopi Zervanou, Eindhoven University of Technology, Netherlands
Heike Zinsmeister, Universität Hamburg, Germany

Invited Speaker

Ian Milligan, Department of History, Faculty of Arts, University of Waterloo, United States

Organizers

Beatrice Alex, School of Informatics, University of Edinburgh
Stefania Degaetano-Ortlieb, Department of Language Science and Technology, Universität des Saarlandes
Anna Kazantseva, National Research Council of Canada
Nils Reiter, Institute for Natural Language Processing (IMS), Stuttgart University
Stan Szpakowicz, School of Electrical Engineering and Computer Science, University of Ottawa

Table of Contents

Conference Program

Friday, June 7, 2019

08:55–10:30   *Session 1*

08:55–09:00   *Welcome*

09:00–09:30   *Modeling Word Emotion in Historical Language: Quantity Beats Supposed Stability in Seed Word Selection*
Johannes Hellrich, Sven Buechel and Udo Hahn

09:30–10:00   *Clustering-Based Article Identification in Historical Newspapers*
Martin Riedl, Daniela Betz and Sebastian Padó

10:00–10:30   *Poster Teasers*

11:00–12:30   *Session 2*

11:00–11:30   *The Scientization of Literary Study*
Stefania Degaetano-Ortlieb and Andrew Piper

11:30–12:00   *Are Fictional Voices Distinguishable? Classifying Character Voices in Modern Drama*
Krishnapriya Vishnubhotla, Adam Hammond and Graeme Hirst

12:00–12:30   *Automatic Alignment and Annotation Projection for Literary Texts*
Uli Steinbach and Ines Rehbein

14:00–15:00   *Invited Talk*

14:00–15:00   *Working with Cultural Heritage at Scale: Developing Tools and Platforms to Enable Historians to Explore History in the Age of Abundance*
Ian Milligan

15:00–15:30   *Poster Session*

Inferring missing metadata from environmental policy texts
Steven Bethard, Egoitz Laparra, Sophia Wang, Yiyun Zhao, Ragheb Al-Ghezi, Aaron Lien and Laura López-Hoffman

Stylometric Classification of Ancient Greek Literary Texts by Genre
Efthimios Gianitsos, Thomas Bolt, Pramit Chaudhuri and Joseph Dexter

A framework for streamlined statistical prediction using topic models
Vanessa Glenny, Jonathan Tuke, Nigel Bean and Lewis Mitchell

Revisiting NMT for Normalization of Early English Letters
Mika Hämäläinen, Tanja Säily, Jack Rueter, Jörg Tiedemann and Eetu Mäkelä

Graph convolutional networks for exploring authorship hypotheses
Tom Lippincott

Semantics and Homothetic Clustering of Hafez Poetry
Arya Rahgozar and Diana Inkpen

Computational Linguistics Applications for Multimedia Services
Kyeongmin Rim, Kelley Lynch and James Pustejovsky

Correcting Whitespace Errors in Digitized Historical Texts
Sandeep Soni, Lauren Klein and Jacob Eisenstein

16:00–17:35   *Session 3*

16:00–16:30   *On the Feasibility of Automated Detection of Allusive Text Reuse*
Enrique Manjavacas, Brian Long and Mike Kestemont

16:30–17:00   *The limits of Spanglish?*
Barbara Bullock, Wally Guzman and Almeida Jacqueline Toribio

17:00–17:30   *Sign Clustering and Topic Extraction in Proto-Elamite*
Logan Born, Kate Kelley, Nishant Kambhatla, Carolyn Chen and Anoop Sarkar

Modeling Word Emotion in Historical Language: Quantity Beats Supposed Stability in Seed Word Selection

Johannes Hellrich*   Sven Buechel*   Udo Hahn

{firstname.lastname}@uni-jena.de

Jena University Language & Information Engineering (JULIE) Lab
Friedrich-Schiller-Universität Jena, Jena, Germany
julielab.de

Abstract

To understand historical texts, we must be aware that language—including the emotional connotation attached to words—changes over time. In this paper, we aim at estimating the emotion which is associated with a given word in former language stages of English and German. Emotion is represented following the popular Valence-Arousal-Dominance (VAD) annotation scheme. While being more expressive than polarity alone, existing word emotion induction methods are typically not suited for addressing it. To overcome this limitation, we present adaptations of two popular algorithms to VAD. To measure their effectiveness in diachronic settings, we present the first gold standard for historical word emotions, which was created by scholars with proficiency in the respective language stages and covers both English and German. In contrast to claims in previous work, our findings indicate that hand-selecting small sets of seed words with supposedly stable emotional meaning is actually harm- rather than helpful.

1 Introduction

Language change is ubiquitous and, perhaps, most evident in lexical semantics. In this work, we focus on changes in the affective meaning of words over time. Although this problem has been occasionally addressed in previous work (see Section 2.3), most contributions in this area are limited to a rather shallow understanding of human emotion, typically in terms of *semantic*

polarity (feelings being either positive, negative or neutral). Another major shortcoming of this area is the lack of appropriate data and methodologies for evaluation. As a result, the aptness of algorithmic contributions has so far only been assessed in terms of face validity rather than quantitative performance figures (Cook and Stevenson, 2010; Buechel et al., 2016; Hamilton et al., 2016a; Hellrich et al., 2018).

To tackle those shortcomings, we first introduce adaptations of algorithms for word polarity induction to vectorial emotion annotation formats, thus enabling a more fine-grained analysis. Second, to put the evaluation of these methods on safer ground, we present two datasets of affective word ratings for English and German, respectively.[1] These have been annotated by scholars in terms of language-stage-specific emotional connotations.

We ran synchronic as well as diachronic experiments to compare different algorithms for modeling historical word emotions—the latter kind of evaluation employs our newly created gold standard. In particular, one prominent claim from previous work has been that *full-sized* emotion lexicons of contemporary language are ill-suited for inducing historical word emotion. Rather, it would be much more beneficial to select a small, *limited* set of seed words of supposedly invariant emotional meaning (Hamilton et al., 2016a). In contrast, our experiments indicate that larger sets of seed words perform better than manually selected ones despite the fact that some of their entries may not be accurate for the target language stage. Our unique historical gold standard is thus an important step towards firmer methodological underpinnings for the computational analysis of textually encoded historical emotions.

---

* These authors contributed equally to this work. Johannes Hellrich was responsible for selecting historical text corpora and training embedding models. Sven Buechel selected existing emotion lexicons and was responsible for modeling word emotions. The adaptation of polarity-based algorithms (Section 3), the creation of the German and English historical gold standard lexicons (Section 5.1), as well as the overall study design were done jointly.

[1] Publicly available together with experimental code at github.com/JULIELab/HistEmo

Proc. of the 3rd Joint SIGHUM Workshop on Computational Linguistics for Cultural Heritage, Social Sciences, Humanities and Literature, pp. 1–11
Minneapolis, MN, USA, June 7, 2019. ©2019 Association for Computational Linguistics

2 Related Work

2.1 Representing Word Emotions

Quantitative models for word emotions can be traced back at least to Osgood (1953) who used questionnaires to gather human ratings for words on a wide variety of dimensional axes including "*good* vs. *bad*". Most previous work focused on varieties of such forms of semantic polarity, a rather simplified representation of the richness of human affective states—an observation increasingly recognized in sentiment analysis (Strapparava, 2016). In contrast to this bi-polar representation, the Valence-Arousal-Dominance (VAD) model of emotion (Bradley and Lang, 1994) is a well-established approach in psychology (Sander and Scherer, 2009) which increasingly attracts interest by NLP researchers (Köper and Schulte im Walde, 2016; Yu et al., 2016; Wang et al., 2016; Shaikh et al., 2016; Buechel and Hahn, 2017; Preoţiuc-Pietro et al., 2016; Mohammad, 2018). The VAD model assumes that affective states can be characterized relative to Valence (corresponding to the concept of polarity), Arousal (the degree of calmness or excitement) and Dominance (perceived degree of control). Formally, VAD spans a three-dimensional real-valued space (see Figure 1) making the prediction of such values a multi-variate regression problem (Buechel and Hahn, 2016).

Another popular line of emotion representation evolved around the notion of *basic emotions*, small sets of discrete, cross-culturally universal affective states (Scherer, 2000). Here, contributions most influential for NLP are Ekman's (1992) six basic emotions as well as Plutchik's (1980) wheel of emotion (Strapparava and Mihalcea, 2007; Mohammad and Turney, 2013; Bostan and Klinger, 2018). In order to illustrate the relationship between Ekman's basic emotions and the VAD affect space the former are embedded into the latter scheme in Figure 1.

The affective meaning of individual words is encoded in so-called *emotion lexicons*. Thanks to over two decades of efforts from psychologists and AI researchers alike, today a rich collection of empirically founded emotion lexicons is available covering both VAD and basic emotion representation for many languages (see Buechel and Hahn (2018b) for an overview). One of the best know resources of this kind are the *Affective Norms for English Words* (ANEW; Bradley and Lang, 1999)

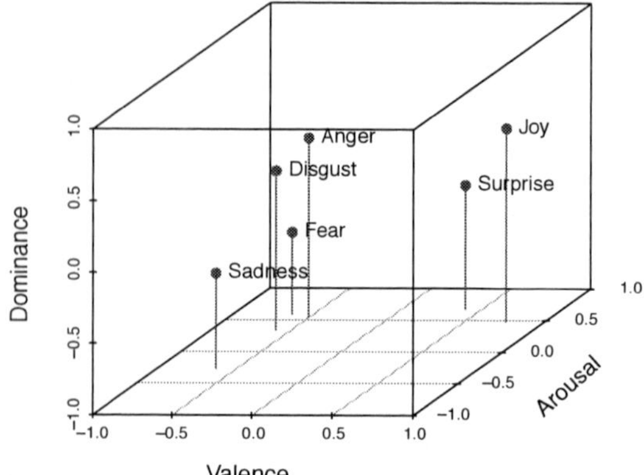

Figure 1: Affective space spanned by the Valence-Arousal-Dominance (VAD) model, together with the position of six basic emotion categories.

Entry	Valence	Arousal	Dominance
rage	2.50	6.62	4.17
orgasm	8.01	7.19	5.84
relaxed	7.25	2.49	7.09

Table 1: Sample Valence-Arousal-Dominance (VAD) ratings from the emotion lexicon by Warriner et al. (2013). The scales span the interval of $[1, 9]$ for each dimension, "5" being the neutral value.

which comprise 1,034 entries in VAD format. ANEW's popular extension by Warriner et al. (2013) comprises roughly 14k entries acquired via crowdsourcing (see Table 1 for examples).

Recently, researchers started to build computational models of the relationship between VAD and discrete categories (illustrated in Figure 1) resulting in techniques to automatically translate ratings between these major representation schemes (Calvo and Kim, 2013; Buechel and Hahn, 2018a).

2.2 Predicting Word Emotions

Word emotion induction—the task of predicting the affective score of unrated words—is an active research area within sentiment analysis (Rosenthal et al., 2015). Most approaches either rely on hand-coded lexical resources, such as WORDNET (Fellbaum, 1998), to propagate sentiment information to unkown words (Shaikh et al., 2016), or employ similarity metrics based on distributional semantics (see below). We deem the former inadequate for diachronic purposes, since almost all lexical resources typically cover contemporary language only. In the following, we focus on algorithms which have been tested in diachronic settings in previous work. An overview of recent work focusing on applications to contemporary language is given by Buechel and Hahn (2018c).

More than a decade ago, Turney and Littman (2003) introduced a frequently used and often adopted (e.g., Köper and Schulte im Walde (2016); Palogiannidi et al. (2016)) algorithm. It computes a sentiment score based on the similarity of an unrated word to two sets of positive and negative seed words. Bestgen (2008) presented an algorithm which has been prominently put into practice in expanding a VAD lexicon to up to 17,350 entries (Bestgen and Vincze, 2012). Their method employs a k-Nearest-Neighbor methodology where an unrated word inherits the averaged ratings of the surrounding words. Rothe et al. (2016) presented a more recent approach to polarity induction. Based on word embeddings and a set of positive and negative paradigm words, they train an orthogonal transformation of the embedding space so that the encoded polarity information is concentrated in a single vector component whose value then serves as an explicit polarity rating. The algorithm proposed by Hamilton et al. (2016a) employs a random walk within a lexical graph constructed using word similarities. They outperform Rothe et al. (2016) when embeddings are trained on small datasets.

Note that these algorithms differ in the kind of input representation they require. Whereas Turney and Littman (2003), Rothe et al. (2016), and Hamilton et al. (2016a) expect binary class ratings (positive or negative), Bestgen's algorithm (Bestgen, 2008) takes vectorial seed ratings, illustrated in Table 1, as input.

2.3 Historical Sentiment Information

There are several studies using contemporary word emotion information, i.e., emotion lexicons encoding today's emotional meaning, to analyze historical documents. For instance, Acerbi et al. (2013) and Bentley et al. (2014) observed long-term trends in words expressing emotions in the Google Books corpus and linked these to historical (economic) events. Another example are Kim et al. (2017) who investigate emotions in literary texts in search for genre-specific patterns. However, this contemporary emotion information could lead to artifacts, since the emotions connected with a word are not necessarily static over time. This phenomenon is known as elevation & degeneration in historical linguistics, e.g., Old English *cniht* 'boy, servant' was elevated becoming the modern *knight* (Bloomfield, 1984).

Alternatively, algorithms for bootstrapping word emotion information can be used to predict historical emotion values by using word similarity based on historical texts. This was first done for polarity regression with the Turney and Littman (2003) algorithm and a collection of three British English corpora by Cook and Stevenson (2010). Jatowt and Duh (2014) tracked the emotional development of words by averaging the polarity of the words they co-occurred with (assuming the latters' polarity to be stable). Hamilton et al. (2016a) used their novel random walk-based algorithm for polarity regression on COHA. They consider their method especially suited for historical applications.[2] This algorithm was also used by Généreux et al. (2017) to test the temporal validity of inferred word abstractness, a psychological measure akin to the individual VAD dimensions. They used both modern and historical (1960s) psychological datasets rating the same words as gold standards and found a strong correlation with predicted historical abstractness. Buechel et al. (2016) used Bestgen (2008)'s algorithm to investigate emotional profiles of different genres of historical writing. Finally, we used the Turney and Littman (2003) algorithm to induce historical sentiment information which is provided as part of `JeSemE.org`, a website for exploring semantic change in multiple diachronic corpora (Hellrich et al., 2018).

3 Methods

3.1 Word Similarity

We measure word similarity by the cosine between word embeddings, the most recent method in studies of distributional semantics. Their most popular form are Skip-Gram Negative Sampling (SGNS; Mikolov et al., 2013) embeddings which are trained with a very shallow artificial neural network. SGNS processes one word-context pair, i.e., two nearby words, at a time and learns good embeddings by trying to predict the most likely contexts for a given word.

---

[2] However, the algorithm is sensitive to changes in its training material and thus likely prone to compute artifacts, see their **README** at `github.com/williamleif/socialsent`

An alternative solution for generating low dimensional vectors is gathering all word-context pairs for a corpus in a large matrix and reducing its dimensionality with singular value decomposition (SVD), a technique very popular in the early 1990's (Deerwester et al., 1990; Schütze, 1993). Levy et al. (2015) propose SVD$_{\text{PPMI}}$, a state-of-the-art algorithm based on combining SVD with the positive pointwise mutual information (PPMI; Niwa and Nitta, 1994) word association metric.

Both SGNS and SVD$_{\text{PPMI}}$ have been shown to be adequate for exploring historical semantics (Hamilton et al., 2016b,a). A general downside of existing embedding algorithms other than SVD$_{\text{PPMI}}$ is their inherent stochastic behavior during training which makes the resulting embedding models unreliable (Hellrich and Hahn, 2016; Antoniak and Mimno, 2018; Wendlandt et al., 2018). Very recently, contextualized word embeddings, such as ELMo (Peters et al., 2018) and BERT (Devlin et al., 2018), have started to establish themselves as a new family of algorithms for word representation. Those methods achieve enhanced performance on many downstream tasks by taking context into account, both during training and testing, to generate an individual vector representation for each individual *token*. This makes them unsuitable for our contribution, since we address emotion on the *type* level by creating emotion lexicons.

3.2 Word Emotion

Our work employs three algorithms for inducing emotion lexicons, two of which had to be adapted to deal with the more informative vectorial VAD representation instead of a simple binary two-class representation (positive vs. negative polarity):

KNN — The k-Nearest-Neighbor-based algorithm by Bestgen (2008) which already supports vectorial input.

PARASIMNUM — An adaptation of the classical PARASIM algorithm by Turney and Littman (2003) which is based on the similarity of two opposing sets of paradigm words.

RANDOMWALKNUM — An adaptation of the RANDOMWALK algorithm proposed by Hamilton et al. (2016a) which propagates affective information of seed words via a random walk through a lexical graph.

KNN sets the emotion values of each word w to the average of the emotion values of the k most similar seed words. For any given seed word s, let $e(s)$ denote its three-dimensional emotion vector corresponding to its VAD value in our seed lexicon. Furthermore, let $\text{nearest}(w, k)$ denote the set of the k seed word most similar to a given word w. Then the predicted emotion of word w according to KNN is defined as follows:

$$e_{\text{KNN}}(w, k) := \frac{1}{k} \sum_{s \in \text{nearest}(w,k)} e(s) \qquad (1)$$

PARASIM computes the emotion of word w by comparing its similarity with a set of positive and negative paradigm words (POS and NEG, respectively):

$$e_{\text{PARASIM}}(w) := \sum_{p \in \text{POS}} \text{sim}(w, p) - \sum_{n \in \text{NEG}} \text{sim}(w, n) \qquad (2)$$

where $\text{sim}(\cdot, \cdot)$ denotes the cosine similarly between two embedding vectors.

Let $e(s)$ map to '1', if word $s \in$ POS, and to '−1', if $s \in$ NEG, then Equation (2) can be rewritten as

$$e_{\text{PARASIM}}(w) = \sum_{s \in \text{POS} \cup \text{NEG}} \text{sim}(w, s) \times e(s). \qquad (3)$$

For PARASIMNUM, our adaptation of PARAMSIM, we change $e(s)$ to map to a three-dimensional vector corresponding to the VAD entry of a word in our set of seed words $\mathcal{S} :=$ POS $\cup$ NEG. We also introduce a normalization factor so that the predictions according to PARASIMNUM take the form of a weighted average:

$$e_{\text{PARASIMNUM}}(w) := \frac{\sum_{s \in \mathcal{S}} \text{sim}(w, s) \times e(s)}{\sum_{s \in \mathcal{S}} \text{sim}(w, s)} \qquad (4)$$

RANDOMWALK propagates sentiment scores through a graph, with vertices representing words and edge weights denoting word similarity. Let $\mathcal{V}$ represent the set of words in this lexical graph, and let the vector $p \in \mathbb{R}^{|\mathcal{V}|}$ represent the induced sentiment score for each word in the graph. To compute word emotions, p is iteratively updated by applying a transition matrix T:

$$p^{(t+1)} := \beta T p^{(t)} + (1 - \beta)s \qquad (5)$$

Here $s \in \mathbb{R}^{|\mathcal{V}|}$ is the vector representing the seed sentiment scores and the β-parameter balances between assigning similar scores to neighbors and correct scores to seeds. The vector p is initialized so that the i-th element $p_i = 1/|\mathcal{V}|$, whereas s is initialized with $s_i = 1/|\mathcal{S}|$ ($\mathcal{S}$ being the set of seed words), if the corresponding word w_i is a seed word and 0, otherwise. Details how the transition matrix is initialized can be found in Zhou et al. (2004).

To obtain the final sentiment scores p_{final}, the process is independently run until convergence for both a positive and a negative seed set, before the resulting values p^+ and p^- are normalized by performing a z-transformation on:

$$p_{\text{final}} := \frac{p^+}{p^+ + p^-} \tag{6}$$

We now provide a simple adaptation for vectorial emotion values, RANDOMWALKNUM: p and s are replaced by $|\mathcal{V}| \times 3$ matrices P and S, respectively. All entries of P are initialized with $1/|\mathcal{V}|$. For the positive seed set, S is populated with the original VAD values of each word in the seed lexicon and 0, otherwise. For the negative seed set all values are inverted relative to the center of the numerical VAD rating scales. For instance, the valence score of *relaxed* in Table 1 is transformed from 7 to 3, because 5 is the center of the respective scale. Finally, S is normalized so that each column adds up to 1. P_{final} can then be calculated analogously to the original algorithm.

4 External Datasets

4.1 Diachronic Corpora

We rely on two well curated diachronic corpora—the Corpus of Historical American English[3] (COHA; Davies, 2012) and the core corpus of the Deutsches Text Archiv[4] ['German Text Archive'] (DTA; Geyken, 2013; Geyken and Gloning, 2015). They are smaller than some alternative diachronic corpora, especially the Google Books N-gram subcorpora (Lin et al., 2012), yet their balanced nature and transparent composition should make results more resilient against artifacts (Pechenick et al., 2015). Both corpora contain metadata in the form of automatically generated POS annotations and lemmatizations. The latter appears to be more consistent in DTA, possibly due to the inclusion of an orthographic normalization step (Jurish, 2013).

COHA is relatively large for a structured corpus (Davies, 2012, p. 122) containing over 100k long and short texts from the 1810s to the 2000s. It is conceptually centered around decades and aims at providing equally sized and genre-balanced data for each decade. The only deviations are an increase in size between the 1810s and 1830s to a then stable level, as well as the inclusion of newspaper texts from the 1860s onwards. COHA is based on post-processed texts from several pre-existing collections, e.g., Project Gutenberg (Davies, 2012, p. 125), digitized with optical character recognition (OCR) software.

DTA is the closest German equivalent to COHA and the result of an ongoing effort to create a digital full-text corpus of printed German documents from the 15th to the 19th century. It is smaller than COHA, containing only about 1.3k long texts, yet of higher quality, based on extensive manual transcription (mostly double keying, in some cases corrected OCR). It contains texts from different genres, and individual texts were chosen with an eye toward cultural (not statistical) representativeness. Balance between genres is limited for some timespans, e.g., non-fiction is strongly over-represented in the early 17th century. However, the texts used in our experiments (see below) are well balanced between fictional and non-fictional texts (101 vs. 91 texts, respectively).

For both, COHA and DTA, we selected all texts from particular timespans as basis for our experiments. Those timespans served two purposes: (a) when building our gold standard of historical word emotions (Section 5.1) the annotators were requested to rate word emotions according to the respective target language stage; (b) documents associated with the respective timespan were used to train language stage-specific word embeddings (Section 6.1) in order to model those gold ratings.

The 2000s decade of COHA was an obvious fit for our synchronic experiments in Section 6.2, as it is the most recent one. For our diachronic experiments in Section 6.3 we aimed at sufficiently sized training material (10M+ tokens) to ensure high quality word embeddings. We also wanted to use data as distant from the present time as possible. We thus picked the 1830s decade of COHA for English and combined thirty years of DTA texts (1810–1839) for German—earlier COHA decades, as well as all individual DTA decades, are of insufficient size.

---

[3] `english-corpora.org/coha/`

[4] `deutschestextarchiv.de` — we used the May 2016 snapshot.

4.2 Emotion Lexicons

We now describe the VAD lexicons which were used to provide seed words for both synchronic and diachronic experiments. Based on its size and popularity, we chose the extended version of ANEW (Warriner et al., 2013; see Section 2) for English. Concerning German emotion lexicons, we chose the *Affective Norms for German Sentiment Terms* (ANGST; Schmidtke et al., 2014) which contain 1,003 words and largely follows ANEW's acquisition methodology.

5 Historical Gold Standard

5.1 Dataset Construction

In general, native speakers fluent in the respective (sub)language are the only viable option for acquiring a gold standard lexicon of emotional meaning for any language or domain. In the case of historical language older than about a century, this option is off the table due to biological reasons—we simply lack native speakers competent for that specific language period.

As the best conceivable surrogate, we rely on historical language experts for constructing our dataset. The gold standard consists of two parts, an English and a German one, each with 100 words. We recruited three annotators for German and two for English, all doctoral students experienced in interpreting 19th century texts.

We selected high-frequency words for the annotation to ensure high quality of the associated word embeddings. The selection was done by, first, extracting adjectives, common nouns and lexical verbs from the 1830s COHA and the 1810–1839 DTA subcorpus and then, second, randomly sampling 100 words out of the 1000 most frequent ones. We manually excluded two cases of ordinal numerals misclassified as adjectives.

The actual rating process was set up as a questionnaire study following established designs from psychological research (Bradley and Lang, 1999; Warriner et al., 2013). The participants were requested to put themselves in the position of a person living between 1810 and 1839 for the German data set, or a person living in the 1830s for the English one. They were then presented with stimulus words and used the so-called Self-Assessment Manikin (SAM; Bradley and Lang, 1994) to judge the kind of feeling evoked by these lexical items. SAM consists of three individual nine-point scales, one for each VAD dimension.

	Valence	Arousal	Dominance	Mean
goldEN	1.20	1.08	1.41	1.23
goldDE	1.72	1.56	2.31	1.86
Warriner	1.68	2.30	2.16	2.05

Table 2: Inter-annotator agreement for our English (goldEN) and German (goldDE) gold standard, as well as the lexicon by Warriner et al. (2013) for comparision; Averaged standard deviation of ratings for each VAD dimension and mean over all dimensions.

Each of the 27 rating points is illustrated by an cartoon-like anthropomorphic figure serving as a non-verbal description of the scale. Moreover, these figures are supplemented by verbal anchors for the low and high end points of the scales e.g., the rating point "9" of the Valence scale represents "complete happiness". They were not provided with or instructed to use any further material or references, e.g., dictionaries. The final ratings for each word were derived by averaging the individual ratings of the annotators.

5.2 Dataset Analysis

We measure inter-annotator agreement (IAA) by calculating the standard deviation (SD) for each word and dimension and averaging these, first, for each dimension alone, and then over these aggregate values, thus constituting an error-based score (the lower the better). Results are provided in Table 2. In comparison with the lexicon by Warriner et al. (2013), our gold standard displays higher rating consistency. As average over all three VAD dimensions, our lexicon displays an IAA of 1.23 and 1.86 for English and German, respectively, compared to 2.05 as reported by Warriner et al. (2013). This suggests that experts show higher consensus, even when judging word emotions for a historical language period, than crowdworkers for contemporary language. An alternative explanation might be differences in word material, i.e., our random sample of frequent words.

Next, we provide a short comparison of historical and modern emotion ratings. This analysis is restricted to the English language, because the overlap of the historical and modern German lexicons is really small (13 words compared to 97 for English). This difference is most likely due to the fact that the English modern lexicon is more than an order of magnitude larger than the German one.

	historical			modern		
	V	A	D	V	A	D
daughter	3.5	4.0	4.0	6.7	5.0	5.1
divine	7.0	7.0	2.0	7.2	3.0	6.0
strange	2.0	6.5	1.0	4.7	3.5	5.3

Table 3: Illustrative example words with large deviation between historical and modern affective meaning; Valence-Arousal-Dominance (VAD) of newly created gold standard compared to Warriner et al. (2013).

The Pearson correlation between modern and historical lexicons is 0.66, 0.51, and 0.31 for Valence, Arousal, and Dominance, respectively. Table 3 displays illustrative examples from our newly created gold standard where historical and modern affective meaning differ strongly. We conducted a post-facto interview on annotator motivation for those cases. Explanations—which match observations described in common reference textbooks (e.g., Brinkley (2003))—range from the influence of feminism leading to an increase in Valence for *"daughter"* up to secularization that might explain a drop in Arousal and rise in Dominance for *"divine"*. The annotation for *"strange"* was motivated by several now obsolete senses indicating foreignness or alienness.[5]

In summary, we recruited historical language experts as best conceivable surrogate to compensate for the lack of actual native speakers in order to create a gold standard for historical word emotions. To the best of our knowledge, no comparable dataset is elsewhere available, making this contribution unique and hopefully valuable for future research, despite its obvious size limitation.

6 Modeling Word Emotions

This section describes how we trained time period-specific word embeddings and used these to evaluate the algorithms presented in Section 3.2 on both a contemporary dataset and our newly created historical gold standard.

6.1 Word Embedding Training

COHA and DTA were preprocessed by using the lemmatization provided with each corpus, as well as removing punctuation and converting all text to lower case.

We used the HYPERWORDS toolkit (Levy et al., 2015) to create one distinct word embedding model for each of those subcorpora. Hyperparameter choices follow Hamilton et al. (2016a). In particular, we trained 300-dimensional word vectors, with a context window of up to four words. Context windows were limited by document boundaries while ignoring sentence boundaries. We modeled words with a minimum token frequency of 10 per subcorpus, different from Hamilton et al. (2016a). For SVD_{PPMI}, eigenvectors were discarded, no negative sampling was used and word vectors were combined with their respective context vectors.

6.2 Synchronic Evaluation

Our first evaluation of lexicon induction algorithms compares the ability of the three different algorithms described in Section 3 to predict ratings of a modern, contemporary VAD lexicon, i.e., the one by Warriner et al. (2013), using two different types of seed sets (see below). For this experiment, we used word embeddings trained on the 2000s COHA subcorpus. We call this evaluation setup *synchronic* in the linguistic sense, since seed lexicon, target lexicon and word embeddings belong to the same language period. A unique feature of our work here is that we also take into account possible interaction effects between lexicon induction algorithms and word embedding algorithms, i.e., SGNS and SVD_{PPMI}.

We use two different seed lexicons, both are based on the word ratings by Warriner et al. (2013). The *full* seed lexicon corresponds to all the entries of words which are also present in ANEW (about 1,000 words; see Section 2). In contrast, the *limited* seed lexicon is restricted to 19 words[6] which were identified as temporally stable by Hamilton et al. (2016a).

The first setup is thus analogous to the polarity experiments performed by Cook and Stevenson (2010), whereas the second one corresponds to the settings from Hamilton et al. (2016a). We use Pearson's r between actual and predicted values for each emotion dimension (Valence, Arousal and Dominance) for quantifying performance[7] and a

---

[5] See the Oxford English Dictionary: `oed.com/view/Entry/191244`

[6] One of the 20 words given by Hamilton et al. (2016a), *"hated"*, is not present in the Warriner lexicon and was therefore eliminated.

[7] Some other studies use the rank correlation coefficient Kendall's τ. We found that for our experiments the results are overall consistent between both metrics. In the following we only report Pearson's r as it is specifically designed for

Induction Method	Seed Selection	SVD$_{PPMI}$	SGNS
KNN	full	**0.548**	0.487
PARASIMNUM	full	**0.557**	0.489
RANDOMWALKNUM	full	**0.544**	0.436
KNN	limited	0.181	0.166
PARASIMNUM	limited	0.249	0.191
RANDOMWALKNUM	limited	**0.330**	0.181

Table 4: Results of the synchronic evaluation in Pearson's r averaged over all three VAD dimensions. The best system for each seed lexicon and those with statistically non-significant differences ($p \geq 0.05$) are in **bold**.

Language	Induction Method	Seed Selection	SVD$_{PPMI}$	SGNS
English	KNN	full	0.307	**0.365**
English	PARASIMNUM	full	0.348	0.361
English	RANDOMWALKNUM	full	0.351	0.361
English	KNN	limited	0.273	0.153
English	PARASIMNUM	limited	0.295	0.232
English	RANDOMWALKNUM	limited	**0.305**	0.039$^\triangle$
German	KNN	full	0.366	0.263
German	PARASIMNUM	full	**0.384**	0.214
German	RANDOMWALKNUM	full	0.302	0.273

Table 5: Results of the diachronic evaluation in Pearson's r averaged over all three VAD dimensions. The best system for each language and seed selection strategy (*full* vs. *limited*) is in **bold**. Only the system marked with '$\triangle$' is significantly different from the best system ($p < 0.05$).

Fisher transformation followed by a Z-test for significance testing (Cohen, 1995, pp. 130–131).

Table 4 provides the average values of these VAD correlations for each seed lexicon, embedding method and induction algorithm. SGNS embeddings are worse than SVD$_{PPMI}$ embeddings for both full and limited seed lexicons. SVD$_{PPMI}$ embeddings seem to be better suited for induction based on the full seed set, leading to the highest observed correlation with PARASIMNUM. However, results with other induction algorithms are not significantly different. For the limited seed set, consistent with claims by Hamilton et al. (2016a), RANDOMWALKNUM is significantly better than all alternative approaches. However, all results with the limited seed set are far (and significantly) worse than those with the full seed lexicon.

Performance is known to differ between VAD dimensions, i.e., Valence is usually the easiest one to predict. For the full seed lexicon and the best induction method, PARASIMNUM with SVD$_{PPMI}$ embeddings, we found Pearson's r correlation to range between 0.679 for Valence, 0.445 for Arousal and 0.547 for Dominance.

6.3 Diachronic Evaluation

The second evaluation set-up utilizes our historical gold standard described in Section 5.1. We call this set-up *diachronic*, since the emotion lexicons generated in our experiments aim to match word use of *historical* language stages, whereas the seed values used for this process stem from *contemporary* language. This approach allows us to test the recent claim that artificially *limiting* seed lexicons to words assumed to be semantically stable over long time spans is beneficial for generating historical emotion lexicons (Hamilton et al., 2016a). We used Pearson's r correlation and the Z-test, as in Section 6.2.

Again, we investigate interactions between lexicon induction algorithms and embedding types. For English, we evaluate with both *full* and *limited* seed lexicons, whereas for German, we evaluate only using the *full* seed lexicon (ANGST, see Section 2) since most entries of the English *limited* lexicon have no corresponding entry in ANGST. Embeddings are based on the 1830s COHA subcorpus for English and on the 1810–1839 DTA subcorpus for German, thus matching the time frames featured by our gold standard.

The results of this experiment are given in Table 5. For English, using the full seed lexicons, we achieve performance figures around $r = .35$. In contrast, using the *limited* seed lexicon we find that the performance is markedly weaker in each of our six conditions compared to using the full seed lexicon. This observation directly opposes the claims from Hamilton et al. (2016a) who

---

numerical values. In contrast, Kendall's τ only captures ordinal information and is therefore less suited for VAD.

argued that their hand selected set of emotionally stable seed words would boost performance relative to using the full, contemporary dataset as seeds.

Our finding is statistically significant in only one of all cases (the combination of SGNS and RANDOMWALKNUM). However, the fact that we get the *identical* outcomes for all the other five combinations of embedding and induction algorithm strongly indicates that using the full seed set is virtually superior, even though the differences are not statistically significant when looking at the individual conditions in isolation, due to the size[8] of our gold standard. Note that this outcome is also consistent with our results from the synchronic evaluation where we did find significant differences.

German results with the full seed lexicon are similar to those for English. Here, however, the SGNS embeddings are outperformed by SVD_{PPMI}, whereas for English both are competitive. A possible explanation for this result might be differences in pre-processing between the two data sets which were necessary due to the more complex morphology of the German language.

7 Conclusion

In this contribution, we addressed the task of constructing emotion lexicons for historical language stages. We presented adaptations of two existing polarity lexicon induction algorithms to the multidimensional VAD model of emotion, which provides deeper insights than common bipolar approaches. Furthermore, we constructed the first gold standard for affective lexical semantics in historical language. In our experiments, we investigated the interaction between word embedding algorithm, word emotion induction algorithm and seed word selection strategy. Most importantly, our results suggest that limiting seed words to supposedly temporally stable ones does not improve performance as suggested in previous work but rather turns out to be harmful. Regarding the compared algorithms for emotion lexicon induction and embedding generation, we recommend using SVD_{PPMI} together with PARASIMNUM (our adaption of the Turney and

Littman (2003) algorithm), as this set-up yields strong and stable performance, and requires few hyperparameter choices. We will continue to work on further solutions to get around data sparsity issues when working with historical language, hopefully allowing for more advanced machine learning approaches in the near future.

Acknowledgments

We thank our emotion gold standard annotators for volunteering. This research was partially funded by the Deutsche Forschungsgemeinschaft (DFG) within the Graduate School *The Romantic Model* (GRK 2041/1).

References

Alberto Acerbi, Vasileios Lampos, Philip Garnett, and R. Alexander Bentley. 2013. The expression of emotions in 20th century books. *PLoS ONE*, 8(3):e59030.

Maria Antoniak and David Mimno. 2018. Evaluating the stability of embedding-based word similarities. *Transactions of the Association for Computational Linguistics*, 6:107–120.

R. Alexander Bentley, Alberto Acerbi, Paul Ormerod, and Vasileios Lampos. 2014. Books average previous decade of economic misery. *PLoS ONE*, 9(1):e83147.

Yves Bestgen. 2008. Building affective lexicons from specific corpora for automatic sentiment analysis. In *LREC 2008*, pages 496–500.

Yves Bestgen and Nadja Vincze. 2012. Checking and bootstrapping lexical norms by means of word similarity indexes. *Behavior Research Methods*, 44(4):998–1006.

Leonard Bloomfield. 1984. *Language*. University of Chicago Press. [Reprint, first published 1933].

Laura Ana Maria Bostan and Roman Klinger. 2018. An analysis of annotated corpora for emotion classification in text. In *COLING 2018, Technical Papers*, pages 2104–2119.

Margaret M. Bradley and Peter J. Lang. 1994. Measuring emotion: The self-assessment manikin and the semantic differential. *Journal of Behavior Therapy and Experimental Psychiatry*, 25(1):49–59.

Margaret M. Bradley and Peter J. Lang. 1999. Affective norms for English words (ANEW): Stimuli, instruction manual and affective ratings. Technical Report C-1, The Center for Research in Psychophysiology, University of Florida, Gainesville, FL.

Alan Brinkley. 2003. *American History. A Survey*, 11th edition. McGraw Hill.

---

[8] Typical emotion lexicons are one or even two orders of magnitude larger, as discussed in Section 2.1. Given the current correlation values, we would need to increase the size of our gold standard by a factor of about 40—a challenging task, given its expert reliant nature—to ensure $p < .05$.

Sven Buechel and Udo Hahn. 2016. Emotion analysis as a regression problem — Dimensional models and their implications on emotion representation and metrical evaluation. In *ECAI 2016*, pages 1114–1122.

Sven Buechel and Udo Hahn. 2017. EMOBANK: Studying the impact of annotation perspective and representation format on dimensional emotion analysis. In *EACL 2017, Short Papers*, pages 578–585.

Sven Buechel and Udo Hahn. 2018a. Emotion representation mapping for automatic lexicon construction (mostly) performs on human level. In *COLING 2018, Technical Papers*, pages 2892–2904.

Sven Buechel and Udo Hahn. 2018b. Representation mapping: A novel approach to generate high-quality multi-lingual emotion lexicons. In *LREC 2018*, pages 184–191.

Sven Buechel and Udo Hahn. 2018c. Word emotion induction for multiple languages as a deep multi-task learning problem. In *NAACL-HLT 2018, Long Papers*, pages 1907–1918.

Sven Buechel, Johannes Hellrich, and Udo Hahn. 2016. Feelings from the past: adapting affective lexicons for historical emotion analysis. In *LT4DH @ COLING 2016*, pages 54–61.

Rafael A. Calvo and Sunghwan Mac Kim. 2013. Emotions in text: Dimensional and categorical models. *Computational Intelligence*, 29(3):527–543.

Paul R. Cohen. 1995. *Empirical Methods for Artificial Intelligence*. MIT Press.

Paul Cook and Suzanne Stevenson. 2010. Automatically identifying changes in the semantic orientation of words. In *LREC 2010*, pages 28–34.

Mark Davies. 2012. Expanding horizons in historical linguistics with the 400-million word Corpus of Historical American English. *Corpora*, 7:121–157.

Scott C. Deerwester, Susan T. Dumais, George W. Furnas, Thomas K. Landauer, and Richard A. Harshman. 1990. Indexing by latent semantic analysis. *Journal of the American Society for Information Science*, 41(6):391–407.

Jacob Devlin, Ming-Wei Chang, Kenton Lee, and Kristina Toutanova. 2018. BERT: pre-training of deep bidirectional transformers for language understanding. http://arxiv.org/abs/1810.04805.

Paul Ekman. 1992. An argument for basic emotions. *Cognition & Emotion*, 6(3-4):169–200.

Christiane Fellbaum, editor. 1998. WORDNET: An Electronic Lexical Database. MIT Press, Cambridge/MA; London/England.

Michel Généreux, Bryor Snejfella, and Marta Maslej. 2017. Big data in psychology: Using word embeddings to study theory-of-mind. In *IEEE BigData 2017*, pages 4747–4749.

Alexander Geyken. 2013. Wege zu einem historischen Referenzkorpus des Deutschen: das Projekt Deutsches Textarchiv. In Ingelore Hafemann, editor, *Perspektiven einer corpusbasierten historischen Linguistik und Philologie*, pages 221–234.

Alexander Geyken and Thomas Gloning. 2015. A living text archive of 15th-19th-century German. Corpus strategies, technology, organization. In Jost Gippert and Ralf Gehrke, editors, *Historical Corpora. Challenges and Perspectives*, pages 165–180. Narr.

William L. Hamilton, Kevin Clark, Jure Leskovec, and Dan Jurafsky. 2016a. Inducing domain-specific sentiment lexicons from unlabeled corpora. In *EMNLP 2016*, pages 595–605.

William L. Hamilton, Jure Leskovec, and Dan Jurafsky. 2016b. Diachronic word embeddings reveal statistical laws of semantic change. In *ACL 2016, Long Papers*, pages 1489–1501.

Johannes Hellrich, Sven Buechel, and Udo Hahn. 2018. JESEME: a website for exploring diachronic changes in word meaning and emotion. In *COLING 2018, System Demonstrations*, pages 10–14.

Johannes Hellrich and Udo Hahn. 2016. Bad company—Neighborhoods in neural embedding spaces considered harmful. In *COLING 2016, Technical Papers*, pages 2785–2796.

Adam Jatowt and Kevin Duh. 2014. A framework for analyzing semantic change of words across time. In *JCDL 2014*, pages 229–238.

Bryan Jurish. 2013. Canonicalizing the Deutsches Textarchiv. In Ingelore Hafemann, editor, *Perspektiven einer corpusbasierten historischen Linguistik und Philologie*, pages 235–244.

Evgeny Kim, Sebastian Padó, and Roman Klinger. 2017. Investigating the relationship between literary genres and emotional plot development. In *LaTeCH-CLfL @ ACL 2017*, pages 17–26.

Maximilian Köper and Sabine Schulte im Walde. 2016. Automatically generated affective norms of abstractness, arousal, imageability and valence for 350,000 German lemmas. In *LREC 2016*, pages 2595–2598.

Omer Levy, Yoav Goldberg, and Ido Dagan. 2015. Improving distributional similarity with lessons learned from word embeddings. *Transactions of the Association for Computational Linguistics*, 3:211–225.

Yuri Lin, Jean-Baptiste Michel, Erez Lieberman Aiden, Jon Orwant, William Brockman, and Slav Petrov. 2012. Syntactic annotations for the GOOGLE BOOKS NGRAM corpus. In *ACL 2012, System Demonstrations*, pages 169–174.

Tomas Mikolov, Kai Chen, Gregory S. Corrado, and Jeffrey Dean. 2013. Efficient estimation of word representations in vector space. In *ICLR 2013*.

Saif Mohammad. 2018. Obtaining reliable human ratings of valence, arousal, and dominance for 20,000 English words. In *ACL 2018, Long Papers*, pages 174–184.

Saif M. Mohammad and Peter D. Turney. 2013. Crowdsourcing a word-emotion association lexicon. *Computational Intelligence*, 29(3):436–465.

Yoshiki Niwa and Yoshihiko Nitta. 1994. Co-occurrence vectors from corpora vs. distance vectors from dictionaries. In *COLING 1994*, pages 304–309.

Charles E. Osgood. 1953. *Method and Theory in Experimental Psychology*. Oxford University Press.

Elisavet Palogiannidi, Polychronis Koutsakis, Elias Iosif, and Alexandros Potamianos. 2016. Affective lexicon creation for the Greek language. In *LREC 2016*, pages 2867–2872.

Eitan Adam Pechenick, Christopher M. Danforth, and Peter Sheridan Dodds. 2015. Characterizing the GOOGLE BOOKS corpus: Strong limits to inferences of socio-cultural and linguistic evolution. *PLoS One*, 10(10):e0137041.

Matthew E. Peters, Mark Neumann, Mohit Iyyer, Matt Gardner, Christopher T. Clark, Kenton Lee, and Luke S. Zettlemoyer. 2018. Deep contextualized word representations. In *NAACL-HLT 2018, Long Papers*, pages 2227–2237.

Robert Plutchik. 1980. A general psychoevolutionary theory of emotion. *Emotion: Theory, Research and Experience*, 1(3):3–33.

Daniel Preoțiuc-Pietro, Hansen Andrew Schwartz, Gregory Park, Johannes C. Eichstaedt, Margaret L. Kern, Lyle H. Ungar, and Elizabeth P. Shulman. 2016. Modelling valence and arousal in FACEBOOK posts. In *WASSA @ NAACL-HLT 2016*, pages 9–15.

Sara Rosenthal, Preslav I. Nakov, Svetlana Kiritchenko, Saif M. Mohammad, Alan Ritter, and Veselin Stoyanov. 2015. SemEval 2015 Task 10: Sentiment analysis in Twitter. In *SemEval 2015*, pages 451–463.

Sascha Rothe, Sebastian Ebert, and Hinrich Schütze. 2016. Ultradense word embeddings by orthogonal transformation. In *NAACL 2016*, pages 767–777.

David Sander and Klaus R. Scherer, editors. 2009. *The Oxford Companion to Emotion and the Affective Sciences*. Oxford University Press, Oxford, U.K., New York, N.Y.

Klaus R. Scherer. 2000. Psychological models of emotion. In Joan C. Borod, editor, *The Neuropsychology of Emotion*, pages 137–162. Oxford University Press.

David S. Schmidtke, Tobias Schröder, Arthur M. Jacobs, and Markus Conrad. 2014. ANGST: Affective norms for German sentiment terms, derived from the affective norms for English words. *Behavior Research Methods*, 46(4):1108–1118.

Hinrich Schütze. 1993. Part-of-speech induction from scratch. In *ACL 1993*, pages 251–258.

Samira Shaikh, Kit Cho, Tomek Strzalkowski, Laurie Feldman, John Lien, Ting Liu, and George Aaron Broadwell. 2016. ANEW+: Automatic expansion and validation of affective norms of words lexicons in multiple languages. In *LREC 2016*, pages 1127–1132.

Carlo Strapparava. 2016. Emotions and NLP: Future directions. In *WASSA @ NAACL 2016*, page 180.

Carlo Strapparava and Rada Mihalcea. 2007. SemEval-2007 Task 14: Affective text. In *SemEval 2007*, pages 70–74.

Peter D. Turney and Michael L. Littman. 2003. Measuring praise and criticism: Inference of semantic orientation from association. *ACM Transactions on Information Systems*, 21(4):315–346.

Jin Wang, Liang-Chih Yu, K. Robert Lai, and Xuejie Zhang. 2016. Dimensional sentiment analysis using a regional CNN-LSTM model. In *ACL 2016, Long Papers*, pages 225–230.

Amy Beth Warriner, Victor Kuperman, and Marc Brysbært. 2013. Norms of valence, arousal, and dominance for 13,915 English lemmas. *Behavior Research Methods*, 45(4):1191–1207.

Laura Wendlandt, Jonathan K. Kummerfeld, and Rada Mihalcea. 2018. Factors influencing the surprising instability of word embeddings. In *NAACL-HLT 2018, Long Papers*, pages 2092–2102.

Liang-Chih Yu, Lung-Hao Lee, Shuai Hao, Jin Wang, Yunchao He, Jun Hu, K. Robert Lai, and Xuejie Zhang. 2016. Building Chinese affective resources in valence-arousal dimensions. In *NAACL 2016*, pages 540–545.

Denny Zhou, Olivier Bousquet, Thomas N Lal, Jason Weston, and Bernhard Schölkopf. 2004. Learning with local and global consistency. In *NIPS 2004*, pages 321–328.

Clustering-Based Article Identification in Historical Newspapers

Martin Riedl and **Daniela Betz** and **Sebastian Padó**
Institut für Maschinelle Sprachverarbeitung
Universität Stuttgart
Pfaffenwaldring 5b, 70569 Stuttgart, Germany
`{riedlmn,pado}@ims.uni-stuttgart.de,mail@danielabetz.de`

Abstract

This article focuses on the problem of identifying articles and recovering their text from within and across newspaper pages when OCR just delivers one text file per page. We frame the task as a segmentation plus clustering step. Our results on a sample of 1912 New York Tribune magazine shows that performing the clustering based on similarities computed with word embeddings outperforms a similarity measure based on character n-grams and words. Furthermore, the automatic segmentation based on the text results in low scores, due to the low quality of some OCRed documents.

1 Introduction

Historical newspapers are among the "most important" and "most often used" sources for many historians (Tibbo, 2003): Since the rise of regional and local newspaper culture in the late 18th and early 19th centuries, newspapers provide a window into national and global events and debates as well as into local everyday life (Slauter, 2015).

Traditionally, historical newspapers were stored on microfilms in local archives. Access was manual, required travel and authorization, and was often complicated by poor film quality (Duff et al., 2004). Digital availability of newspapers has scaled up the accessibility of historical newspapers tremendously and enabled large-scale analysis of phenomena like text re-use (Smith et al., 2015) or ethnic stereotyping (Garg et al., 2018).

Digital access to the full range of information in a newspaper is challenging, though. It requires (a), scanning of newspaper pages or microfilms into digital image files; (b), optical character recognition (OCR) to transfer images into text streams; and (c), identification of articles in the text stream.[1] Few historical newspapers have gone through all

steps. For example, the vast Chronicling America archive of historical newspapers at the Library of Congress[2] only underwent steps (a) and (b), providing text files at the level of newspaper pages, without manual OCR post-correction (see Figure 1).

Due to the multi-column format of almost all newspapers, each text file contain multiple articles. In addition, many articles span several pages: they are split across text files. This is an obvious obstacle to any analysis requiring complete articles. It becomes particularly pressing for articles that span multiple issues (typically days or weeks). Notable among them are *serial stories* or *serial novels*, serialization being among the most important publication strategies for literary works in the 19th and 20th centuries (Lund, 1993).

In this paper, we investigate the task of *article identification across newspaper pages*, corresponding to step (c) above. We use only textual information from OCR as input, modelling the task as a sequence of a segmentation and a clustering step. Whereas most previous work solely uses image data for similar tasks, here, we examine the performance of an approach that uses textual information only. We introduce and provide a new annotated dataset sampled from the 1912 New York Tribune magazine. We find that clustering segments works relatively well for individual issues and becomes substantially more difficult across issues. Segment similarity based on word embeddings outperforms character n-grams similarities for most cases. The major challenge of the task is mainly the inferior scan quality which results in poor OCR text output.

2 Related Work

The task tackled in this paper can be split into two sub-tasks: the detection of the different articles and the clustering of parts of the same article.

---

[1] In this paper, we ignore the issue of metadata extraction.

[2] `https://chroniclingamerica.loc.gov`

Proc. of the 3rd Joint SIGHUM Workshop on Computational Linguistics for Cultural Heritage, Social Sciences, Humanities and Literature, pp. 12–17
Minneapolis, MN, USA, June 7, 2019. ©2019 Association for Computational Linguistics

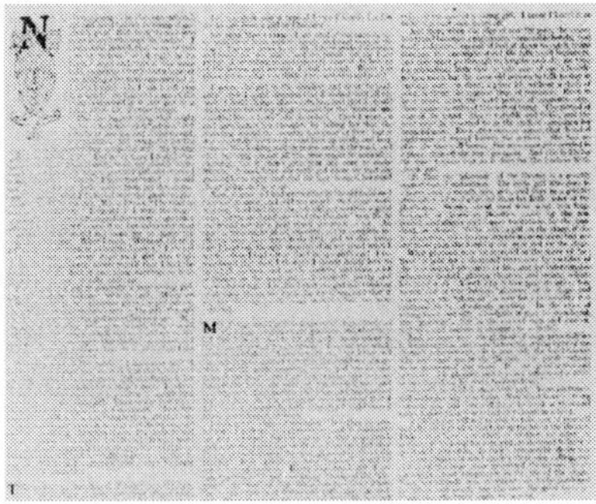

(a) newspaper page

(b) text sample

Figure 1: Historical newspaper page with OCR output

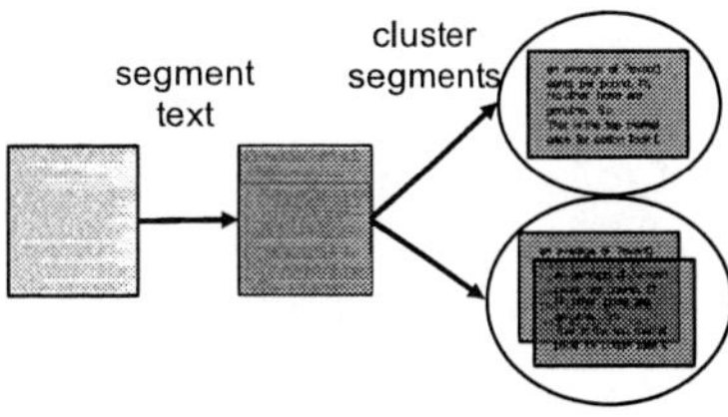

Figure 2: Overview of the method for detecting and merging serial stories

Most previous work performs the segmentation of newspaper pages directly at the image level (Hebert et al., 2014; Meier et al., 2017). This strategy avoids having to deal with spelling errors arising from OCR. However, these methods are not applicable when only textual output is available.

A different line of research addresses the detection of segments in texts. Often, contemporary newspaper texts, Wikipedia articles or novels are artificially merged (e.g. Choi, 2000; Galley et al., 2003). Most of these methods are based on similarities between adjacent sentences or segments. The similarities are mostly computed using words (Hearst, 1997; Choi, 2000) or dense vector representations like topic models (Bestgen, 2006; Riedl and Biemann, 2012) or embeddings (Alemi and Ginsparg, 2015).

Another related task is genre classification, in particular for newspaper texts. Lorang et al. (2015) present a classifier for detecting poetic content, which is however based again on images and incorporates image preprocessing techniques. Lonij and Harbers (2016) build a general genre classifier for text spans, but only for historical Dutch newspapers. A general limitation of this approach is that the articles which we want to separate may not differ in gender: this is often true (e.g., editorial content in the middle with advertisements on the side) but not always (e.g., multi-column pages such as title pages).

At the textual level, article identification is related to author identification (Stamatatos, 2009) and style breach detection (Tschuggnall et al., 2017), which group texts by author. However, these settings typically do not attempt grouping at the story level and use predefined lists of authors. Also, noisy texts are generally not considered.

3 Method

Recall that in this article we have the goal of turning a collection of (textual) newspaper pages into a collection of (textual) articles.

We follow the intuition that articles should be recoverable through *coherence* at multiple levels. Not only are articles *semantically* coherent in terms of vocabulary and names by virtue of typically covering one topic, but they are also *stylistically* coherent since they are typically written by one author. We operationalize this intuition by recovering articles through *semantic clustering* of text segments.

The most straightforward type of text segment provided by historical newspapers is the individual line. However, multi-column layouts lead to very short lines which are too information poor for reliable clustering. Therefore, we adopt a two-step procedure as shown in Figure 2: We first subdivide the pages into *segments* (stretches of text that presumably belong to the same article). Then, we cluster segments within and across pages to assign all segments of the same article in one cluster.

Text Segmentation. TextTiling (Hearst, 1997) is based on the intuition that chunks that are semantically coherent use a similar vocabulary. First the document is segmented into sentences and tokens. In the next step the lexical similarity between two neighboring blocks of $b = 10$ sentences is computed. TextTiling computes lexical similarities of pairs of adjacent blocks around the i-th gap, s_i, as the cosine similarity between the lexical distributions of both blocks. Plotting these scores, TextTiling assumes that minima within this line indicate also segmentation boundaries. In order to find segmentation boundaries, a depth score, $D_i = (s_{i-1} - s_i) + (s_{i+1} - s_i))$, is computed and local minima are selected.

Segment Clustering. Subsequently, we cluster the segments into articles. In this study, we focus on semantic similarity among segments and do not take positional information into account. We use a simple but powerful clustering method, spectral clustering (Ng et al., 2002). Spectral clustering applies k-means not to the original similarity matrix, but to a dimensionality-reduced version, increasing expressiveness and robustness of the method. Thus, we first build the matrix by computing similarity scores between all segments. Based on this matrix, we then perform the spectral clustering.

Two measures of pairwise segment similarity appear particularly appropriate for OCRed, and thus noisy, texts. The traditional one is the similarity of words or character n-gram distributions, using the Jaccard coefficient.

We hypothesize, that due to OCR errors, character n-grams might work better than using complete words. Thus, we compute the Jaccard coefficient on words as well as on character n-grams (n=2– 8). A more recent approach is using the cosine similarity between 200 dimensional embeddings defined as centroids of their fastText word embeddings (Bojanowski et al., 2017). Using fastText we benefit from the functionality that embeddings can be generated from out-of-vocabulary words.

4   Dataset

To our knowledge, there is no standard dataset for article identification in historical newspapers.[3] Thus, we created such a dataset.

We selected the five March 1912 issues of the *New York tribune* Sunday magazine[4] for annotation since this dataset contains long articles, some but not all of which are serializations that extend over multiple issues. We annotated a total of 82 pages.

The annotation was performed by three annotators so that each page was annotated by two different annotators. We annotated each segment in the OCR output, marking it either as part of an article with a unique ID, or as an advertisement.

The high number of short advertisements, combined with the low OCR quality due to very small and artistic typesetting, led to high disagreement on the segmentation annotations. Since our focus is on articles, we merged all advertisement blocks. The resulting annotation achieves a Cohen's (Cohen, 1960) kappa score of $\kappa = 0.85$, ("almost perfect" agreement). Subsequently, we manually checked the disagreements and merged the annotations.[5]

In the following experiments, we consider either all pages of one issue (BYISSUE setting), or all pages of all issues (ALLISSUES setting). The BYISSUE dataset contains an average of 37 gold segments corresponding to 12.6 articles. The ALLISSUES dataset consists of 53 different articles split among 185 gold segments — i.e., we have an average of 3 to 4 segments per article.

5   Experimental Setup

Preprocessing. We remove all non-alphanumeric characters and transform similarities exponentially for clustering. The fastText embeddings are trained on all 1912 English-language newspapers available from Library of Congress.

Design. We conduct two experiments. In the first experiment, we use our gold standard (manually annotated) segment boundaries and perform only clustering. This setup reveals the performance of the clustering method. The second experiment adopts a more realistic setting and evaluates clustering performance when using automatically predicted segments obtained by TextTiling.

Evaluation. In the first experiment, only the clustering needs to be evaluated. For the evaluation, we rely on the B-cubed measure, an adaptation of the familiar IR precision/recall/F_1 measure to the clustering setup (Bagga and Baldwin, 1998). In the second experiment, we additionally evaluate automatic segmentation, for which we report precision and recall. Using this measure is motivated as when using automatic text segmentation as a preprocessing step, we prefer high recall, resulting in fine-grained

---

Similarity	n	B-Cubed		
		Prec.	Rec.	F1
Cosine fastText		0.6983	0.6316	0.6591
Jaccard n-gram	2	0.5335	0.5349	0.5298
	3	0.5621	0.5343	0.5432
	4	0.6153	0.5595	0.5824
	5	0.6234	0.5507	0.5813
	6	0.6634	0.5698	0.6097
	7	0.6774	0.5712	0.6158
	8	0.6576	0.5510	0.5963
	word	0.6880	0.5905	0.6328

Table 1: Effect of similarity measure on clustering performance for a fixed number of clusters of 12 (BYISSUE setting, gold standard segmentation)

segments. Due to the non-deterministic nature of the spectral clustering, we perform each clustering run 5 times and report averages.

6 Results

6.1 Experiment 1: Gold boundaries

First, we inspect the effect of computing similarity in different ways for the BYISSUE setting for 12 clusters, the average number of articles per issue (cf. Section 4). The results in Table 1 show that among the Jaccard-based similarities, there is an interesting tendency for relatively long n-grams to work well, with the best results for n=7. Furthermore, in contrast to our intuition that the word level would suffer from OCR errors, we see better results for words than for n-grams. The overall best results are achieved by Cosine similarity on fastText embeddings which can be understood as an optimized combination of word and character n-gram information.

Next, we vary the number of clusters and retain the three best-performing similarity measures. (The analysis shown in Table 1 is robust across numbers of clusters). For the BYISSUE setting (see Table 2), we consider between 10 and 15 clusters. We find that Precision generally increases with increased number of clusters, while Recall decreases, as could be expected. The maximum F1 score of just above 68% is obtained for cluster sizes of 14 (fastText-based and 7-gram similarities) and 15 (word-based similarity). This corresponds closely to, and is a bit higher than, the average number of gold clusters in that dataset (viz., 12.6). Embedding-based similarity outperforms trigram-based similarity by about 2.8 points F1.

In the ALLISSUES setting, we expect to see around 53 articles and thus explore performance

Sim.	Cl.	B-Cubed		
		Prec.	Rec.	F1
Jaccard word	10	0.6290	0.6063	0.6139
	11	0.6511	0.5870	0.6148
	12	0.6880	0.5905	0.6328
	13	0.7053	0.5749	0.6296
	14	0.7213	**0.5659**	0.6315
	15	**0.7427**	0.5565	**0.6330**
Jaccard 7-gram	10	0.6162	**0.5790**	0.5927
	11	0.6519	0.5737	0.6060
	12	0.6774	0.5712	0.6158
	13	0.6938	0.5626	0.6177
	14	0.7063	0.5543	**0.6185**
	15	**0.7096**	0.5424	0.6120
Cosine fastText	10	0.6161	0.6276	0.6176
	11	0.6523	0.6342	0.6387
	12	0.6983	0.6316	0.6591
	13	0.7270	**0.6371**	0.6757
	14	**0.7504**	0.6309	**0.6810**
	15	0.7485	0.6095	0.6671

Table 2: Experiment 1: Article identification with gold standard segments, BYISSUE setting

between 50 and 55 clusters (see Table 3). The F1 scores are generally lower than for the BYISSUE setting, but still substantial. We find similar tendencies as before (Precision increasing and Recall decreasing with the number of clusters). However, there is more variance than in the BYISSUE setting, so the patterns are less clear. We achieve best performance for 7-gram-based similarity with 55 clusters, for the word-based similarity with 54 and for embedding-based similarity with 54 clusters. The best performing number of clusters is again close to, and a bit higher than, the true number of articles. Here, also the 7-gram Jaccard similarity performs better than using words and is essentially on par with the fastText embeddings. We interpret this finding as showing that long n-gram shared between segments (e.g. person names, place names, etc.) are a surprisingly good indicator of article identity, even in the face of noisy OCR output.

6.2 Experiment 2: Automatic boundaries

We first evaluate TextTiling, our automatic segmentation method (cf. Section 3) and find a low Precision (0.1168) but a comparatively high Recall (0.6602). This means that precise segmentation of the noisy, OCRed historical texts is challenging indeed: TextTiling over-segments the texts. This happens, for example, when parts of a page "look different" in a scan (e.g. due to folds) and OCR introduces systematically different errors. We still prefer over- to under-segmentation, since over-

Sim.	Cl.	B-Cubed		
		Prec.	Rec.	F1
Jaccard word	50	0.5581	0.4313	0.4865
	51	0.5618	0.4340	0.4896
	52	0.5645	0.4467	0.4986
	53	**0.5705**	**0.4493**	**0.5026**
	54	0.5622	0.4435	0.4957
	55	0.5608	0.4503	0.4995
Jaccard 7-gram	50	0.5930	0.4753	0.5274
	51	0.5843	0.4668	0.5189
	52	0.6045	0.4968	0.5451
	53	0.6116	0.4796	0.5376
	54	0.6059	0.4773	0.5339
	55	**0.6214**	**0.5010**	**0.5546**
Cosine fastText	50	0.5917	**0.5085**	0.5466
	51	0.5878	0.4876	0.5328
	52	0.5876	0.4746	0.5251
	53	0.5798	0.4751	0.5221
	54	**0.6246**	0.4927	**0.5506**
	55	0.6064	0.4839	0.5381

Table 3: Experiment 1: Article identification with gold standard segments, ALLISSUES setting

	Sim.	Cl.	B-Cubed		
			Prec.	Rec.	F1
BI	JC Word	15	0.4363	0.2125	0.2843
	JC 7-gram	14	0.4631	0.3313	0.3857
	Cos. fastText	14	**0.6168**	**0.3650**	**0.4563**
AI	JC Word	53	0.2442	0.0923	0.1339
	JC 7-gram	55	0.2726	0.1884	0.2228
	Cos. fastText	54	**0.4409**	**0.2105**	**0.2848**

Table 4: Experiment 2: Article identification with automatic segments (AI: ALLISSUES, BI: BYISSUE)

segmented articles stand a chance of being recombined in the clustering step.

Table 4 shows the results for article identification on automatically segmented text (we report only results for the previously best numbers of clusters). As can be expected given the segmentation results, performance drops substantially compared to Experiment 1. What is notable is the difference between the BYISSUE and the ALLISSUES settings: For BYISSUE, performance drops moderately from 0.68 to 0.46 F1, while for ALLISSUES we see a huge decrease from 0.55 to 0.28 F1. Similarity behaves consistently: fastText performs best for both settings, while word-based similarity yields the lowest scores.

6.3 Discussion

The results of our experiments show that processing historical newspaper is a challenging task, due to the high variance of the OCR quality. Sometimes,

Sim.	min. OCR quality		
	$\geq$-1.0	$\geq$0.0	$\geq$0.5
Jaccard Word	0.6315	0.6491	0.7133
Jaccard 7-gram	0.6185	0.6628	0.7252
Cosine fastText	0.6810	0.7008	0.7629
# of pages	82	74	55

Table 5: Article identification on pages filtered by OCR quality (Exp. 1, BYISSUE, B-Cubed F1, 14 clusters)

pages are hardly readable (cf. Figure 1); on other pages, the quality varies greatly among sections.

We further investigated the impact of OCR quality by annotating each page with an OCR quality indicator on a four-point Likert scale (-1: unusable, 0: bad, 1: medium, 2: good), averaging over two annotators. Then, we repeated the BYISSUE setting of Exp. 1 with 14 clusters, including only pages with a quality at or above different thesholds.

Table 5 shows the results. Even though performance might be expected to decrease for filtered datasets since the fixed number of clusters becomes less appropriate, it mostly remains similar (0.0) and improves using a threshold of 0.5.[6] This shows that OCR is indeed a leading source of problems.

7 Conclusion

This paper has introduced a new dataset for the text segmentation and identification of articles in historical newspapers with OCR-induced noise. We have shown results for two tasks: a) article segmentation and b) article clustering. Overall, results are promising for clustering based on gold standard segmentation, but degrade significantly when segmentation is performed automatically. This indicates manual segmentation, which involves much less effort than OCR postcorrection, is a worthy target when some manual annotation resources are available. Arguably, segmentation can also be improved further by the inclusion of visual features (Meier et al., 2017), which appears a promising direction for future research.

Acknowledgments

This study was supported by the DFG grant Oceanic Exchanges (KO 5362/2-1) and the CRETA center funded by the German Ministry for Education and Research (BMBF).

---

[6]We cannot apply any higher threshold filtering, as for some issues the number of clusters is higher than the number of sentences, i.e. possible segment boundaries.

References

Alexander A. Alemi and Paul Ginsparg. 2015. Text segmentation based on semantic word embeddings. In *Proceedings of the Conference on Knowledge Discovery and Data Mining*, Sydney, Australia.

Amit Bagga and Breck Baldwin. 1998. Entity-based cross-document coreferencing using the vector space model. In *Proceedings of COLING*, pages 79–85, Montreal, Canada.

Yves Bestgen. 2006. Improving text segmentation using latent semantic analysis: A reanalysis of Choi, Wiemer-Hastings, and Moore (2001). *Computational Linguistics*, 32(1):5–12.

Piotr Bojanowski, Edouard Grave, Armand Joulin, and Tomas Mikolov. 2017. Enriching word vectors with subword information. *Transactions of the Association for Computational Linguistics*, 5:135–146.

Freddy Y. Y. Choi. 2000. Advances in domain independent linear text segmentation. In *Proceedings of NAACL*, pages 26–33, Seattle, WA.

Jacob Cohen. 1960. A Coefficient of Agreement for Nominal Scales. *Educational and Psychological Measurement*, 20(1):37.

Wendy Duff, Barbara Craig, and Joan Cherry. 2004. Finding and using archival resources: A cross-canada survey of historians studying canadian history. *Archivaria*, 58(0):51–80.

Michel Galley, Kathleen McKeown, Eric Fosler-Lussier, and Hongyan Jing. 2003. Discourse segmentation of multi-party conversation. In *Proceedings of ACL*, pages 562–569, Sapporo, Japan.

Nikhil Garg, Londa Schiebinger, Dan Jurafsky, and James Zou. 2018. Word embeddings quantify 100 years of gender and ethnic stereotypes. *Proceedings of the National Academy of Sciences*, 115(16):E3635–E3644.

Marti A. Hearst. 1997. TextTiling: Segmenting Text into Multi-paragraph Subtopic Passages. *Computational Linguistics*, 23(1):33–64.

David Hebert, Thomas Palfray, Stephane Nicolas, Pierrick Tranouez, and Thierry Paquet. 2014. Automatic article extraction in old newspapers digitized collections. In *Proceedings of the First International Conference on Digital Access to Textual Cultural Heritage*, pages 3–8, Madrid, Spain.

Juliette Lonij and Frank Harbers. 2016. Genre classifier. KB Lab: The Hague. http://lab.kb.nl/tool/genre-classifier.

Elizabeth Lorang, Leen-Kiat Soh, Maanas Varma Datla, and Spencer Kulwicki. 2015. Developing an image-based classifier for detecting poetic content in historic newspaper collections. *D-Lib Magazine*, 21(7/8).

Michael Lund. 1993. *America's Continuing Story: An Introduction to Serial Fiction, 1850–1900*. Wayne State University Press.

B. Meier, T. Stadelmann, J. Stampfli, M. Arnold, and M. Cieliebak. 2017. Fully convolutional neural networks for newspaper article segmentation. In *Proceedings of the 14th IAPR International Conference on Document Analysis and Recognition*, pages 414–419.

Andrew Y Ng, Michael I Jordan, and Yair Weiss. 2002. On spectral clustering: Analysis and an algorithm. In *Proceedings of NIPS*, pages 849–856.

Martin Riedl and Chris Biemann. 2012. Text Segmentation with Topic Models. *Journal of Language Technology and Computational Linguistics*, 27(47-69):13–24.

Will Slauter. 2015. The rise of the newspaper. In Richard R. John and Jonathan Silberstein Loeb, editors, *Making News: The Political Economy of Journalism in Great Britain and the United States from the Glorious Revolution to the Internet*, pages 19–46. Oxford University Press.

David A. Smith, Ryan Cordell, and Abby Mullen. 2015. Computational Methods for Uncovering Reprinted Texts in Antebellum Newspapers. *American Literary History*, 27(3):E1–E15.

Efstathios Stamatatos. 2009. A survey of modern authorship attribution methods. *Journal of the American Society for Information Science and Technology*, 60(3).

Helen Tibbo. 2003. Primarily History in America: How U.S. historians search for primary materials at the dawn of the digital age. *The American Archivist*, 66(1):9–50.

Michael Tschuggnall, Efstathios Stamatatos, Ben Verhoeven, Walter Daelemans, Günther Specht, Benno Stein, and Martin Potthast. 2017. Overview of the author identification task at PAN-2017: Style breach detection and author clustering. In *Working Notes of CLEF 2017*, Dublin, Ireland.

The Scientization of Literary Study

Stefania Degaetano-Ortlieb
Language Science and Technology
Saarland University
Saarbrücken, Germany
s.degaetano@mx.uni-saarland.de

Andrew Piper
Languages, Literatures, and Cultures
McGill University
Montreal, Canada
andrew.piper@mcgill.ca

Abstract

Scholarly practices within the humanities have historically been perceived as distinct from the natural sciences. We look at literary studies, a discipline strongly anchored in the humanities, and hypothesize that over the past half-century literary studies has instead undergone a process of "scientization", adopting linguistic behavior similar to the sciences. We test this using methods based on information theory, comparing a corpus of literary studies articles (around 63,400) with a corpus of standard English and scientific English respectively. We show evidence for "scientization" effects in literary studies, though at a more muted level than scientific English, suggesting that literary studies occupies a middle ground with respect to standard English in the larger space of academic disciplines. More generally, our methodology can be applied to investigate the social positioning and development of language use across different domains (e.g. scientific disciplines, language varieties, registers).

1 Introduction

The study of literature has historically been seen as a scholarly practice that is distinct from the natural sciences (Wellmon, 2017; Rickman, 1976). This view became particularly pronounced in the twentieth century with the growth of scientific disciplines within universities and the expansion of government funding for such initiatives. Today, it remains a commonplace to argue that literary studies, as a subset of the humanities more generally, has a distinctive set of methods, concepts, and practices that produce a unique form of knowledge (Nussbaum, 1997; Kramnick, 2018).

Our aim in this paper is to test the opposing view to this consensus, namely, that literary studies has over the past half-century become more "scientific". By this we do not mean that literary studies has gradually come to share similar vo-cabulary or concepts to other scientific disciplines. To be "like science" in this sense does not mean the adoption of a distinctly scientific language. Rather, we define the process of *scientization* as a set of three interlocking linguistic practices, which we set out to test here: social differentiation, diachronic specialization, and phrasal standardization.

By social differentiation we mean the extent to which the language of a scholarly discipline distinguishes itself from standard linguistic practices within a given language or culture. The more distinctive a field is with respect to "common language use" the more socially differentiated that field is (Ure, 1982). As Degaetano-Ortlieb and Teich (2016) have shown, scientific language in English has gradually become increasingly divergent from standard representations of English over time. This is the first hypothesis of scientization: that literary studies should look increasingly different from standard English over time (H1).

Specialization on the other hand refers to a process of *self*-differentiation over time. Teich et al. (2016) and Degaetano-Ortlieb et al. (2019) have shown that as a scientific field develops, it will become increasingly specialized and expert-oriented. As a field specializes, it develops more technical and differentiated vocabulary (cf. Halliday (1988); Teich et al. (2016)), while retaining some past linguistic practices and frameworks. A growing aspect of its vocabulary will thus not be accounted for by its own past vocabulary. Past and present will become asymmetrically different from one another. Specialization thus captures the effect of directional linguistic change over time. To reflect increasing specialization, we hypothesize greater linguistic divergence between past and present than vice versa (H2).

Finally, we hypothesize that scientific language is partially defined by a growth of phrasal (i.e.

Proc. of the 3rd Joint SIGHUM Workshop on Computational Linguistics for Cultural Heritage, Social Sciences, Humanities and Literature, pp. 18–28
Minneapolis, MN, USA, June 7, 2019. ©2019 Association for Computational Linguistics

lexico-grammatical) standardization (H3). Less surprise at the local contextual level of linguistic phrases, i.e. more predictable word sequences, allows for more efficient communication – arguably important for the building of scientific knowledge (Harris, 2002; Halliday, 2006). For a discipline to become more scientific it should show evidence of greater standardization at the level of linguistic phrases.

Taken together, our model allows us to test the extent to which a particular field, in this case literary studies, indicates a process of linguistic scientization over time. As we will show, there is evidence that this has been the case, although with important caveats. While literary studies appears to remain more linguistically similar to standard English than scientific language, over time it has shown increased levels of all three dimensions of scientization we measure here: it has become more socially differentiated, diachronically specialized, and phrasally standardized. Our findings suggest that literary studies remains distinctive within the linguistic landscape of "science" in terms of its proximity to standard English, but has simultaneously undergone trends of scientization that point towards its allegiance to the larger project of scientific inquiry. Such conflicting points of view have important implications for any future meta-reflections on the place of literary studies within the university. We see this as a potential indicator of literary studies' bridge-like nature within the academic landscape, a hybrid undertaking that mediates between more fully specialized and differentiated disciplines and common public discourse.

2   Related work

Disciplinary self-knowledge has been integral to the study of literature for well over two-thousand years. As scholars have long demonstrated, the reproduction and reception of literary works was traditionally accompanied by prior critical voices, either in the form of marginal gloss or printed commentary (Reynolds and Wilson, 1991; Tribble, 1993). The "state of the field", as we might now refer to it, was part of the circulation of the field's objects of study. With the institutionalization of literary studies as an academic discipline in the twentieth century, there have been numerous meta-studies of different national and historical contexts of literary study (Kennedy, 1989; Fohrmann and Vosskamp, 1991; Graff, 2007).

More recently, a number of studies have argued for the distinctive nature of literary studies with respect to the social and natural sciences (Nussbaum, 1997; Lamont, 2009; Biber and Gray, 2016; Kramnick, 2018). This work draws on an older tradition that emerged at the start of the twentieth century in response to the era known as "big science" (Rickman, 1976; Wellmon, 2017). The study of creative writing was seen, then as now, as an important protection against the "rationalization" and "standardization" of scientific knowledge. While different hypotheses have been posited as to the unique contribution of literary study as a form of knowledge (whether it makes us more empathetic or critical minded for example), what is consistent throughout this work is the assumption that literary studies is distinct from the broader endeavor known as "science."

All of this work is importantly qualitative in nature. With one exception (Goldstone and Underwood, 2014), no studies have attempted to understand the field of literary studies from a quantitative perspective. In this respect we see our work as part of a growing body of research concerned with the data-driven study of academic disciplines, known as "metaknowledge" or the "science of science" (Evans and Foster, 2011; Fortunato et al., 2018). Researchers have examined the discursive evolution of scientific disciplines (Shi, 2004; Chavalarias and Cointet, 2013; Goldstone and Underwood, 2014), as well as the relationship between tradition and innovation within particular scientific fields (Foster et al., 2015) and the role that highly productive researchers play (Azoulay et al., 2014). Biber and Gray (2010, 2011, 2016) (a.o.) have studied the evolution of scientific writing towards increased linguistic complexity. Degaetano-Ortlieb and Teich (2018) have analyzed the development of scientific writing from the mid 17th to the 19th century towards an optimal code for scientific communication. Vilhena et al. (2014) have examined the linguistic relationships between disciplines and Teich et al. (2016) the linguistic development of interdisciplinary disciplines. Recent work has also studied the notion of paradigmaticness with respect to linguistic behavior within disciplines (Evans et al., 2016). Based on the idea of the productivity of scientific "paradigms" inherited from the work of Thomas Kuhn (Kuhn, 1962), Evans et al. (2016) observe distinctions between disciplines based on the extent of linguistic consensus and marginal innovation.

Our work fits within this line of research and extends it in novel ways. Similar to prior work, we use an information-theoretic notion of entropy and surprisal to model linguistic relationships (Hughes et al., 2012; Bochkarev et al., 2014; Fankhauser et al., 2014; Vilhena et al., 2014; Evans et al., 2016; Degaetano-Ortlieb, 2018; Degaetano-Ortlieb and Teich, 2018). The consideration of analyzing language change and the development of sublanguages from an information-theoretic perspective goes back to Harris (1991): in striving for successful communication, distinctive codes develop which facilitate communication – over time and within subgroups. However, where prior work has focused on relationships between disciplines or the evolution of individual disciplines with respect to notions of innovation or paradigmaticness, our interest is in developing a more general linguistic understanding of the process of scientization itself. Degaetano-Ortlieb and Teich (2016), e.g., have shown how scientific language and common language become increasingly distinct over time. In the same vain, we ask how disciplines evolve with respect to common language (extra-scientific meaning) and with respect to their own language in terms of specialization and standardization (intra-scientific meaning). Thus, adopting their methodology, we similarly add a further dimension to theories of scientific consensus-building, while also working on developing a theory of scientization more generally.

Finally, our work is important because all of the above mentioned quantitative work has focused on the natural and social sciences rather than the humanities. There is a paucity of large-scale understanding about the behavior of fields like literary studies. Given the commitment to a particular world-view as a means of disciplinary self-understanding and given the larger institutional importance of the field, it is vital that more empirical evidence is provided to justify, refute, or nuance beliefs about the field. We see our work and the data set we are introducing as initiating the means to do so.

3 Methodology

3.1 Data

Literary Research Article Corpus (LRA) The LRA corpus consists of 63,397 articles published between 1950 and 2010 drawn from 60 academic journals with approx. 285 million tokens. The data is provided by the JSTOR Data for Research platform which provides metadata and ngrams using their own methods of parsing and cleaning. Journals represent different dimensions of the discipline, including leading generalist journals (PMLA, New Literary History, Critical Inquiry, MLN), genre or period-specific journals (Studies in Romanticism, Studies in the Novel, Shakespeare Quarterly, Science Fiction Studies), language- or culture-specific journals (Yale French Studies, New German Critique, African American Review, Journal of Arabic Literature), as well as more theoretically oriented journals (boundary 2, Social Text, Transition).

Royal Society Corpus (RSC) The RSC corpus consists of journal publications of the Proceedings and Transactions of the Royal Society of London, the first and longest-running English periodical of scientific writing (Kermes et al., 2016). The full version of the RSC spans from 1665 to 1996 amounting at approx. 300 million tokens. Here, we only use texts from 1950 to 1996, containing approx. 170 million tokens, to match the LRA corpus. Metadata of the RSC contain text type (article, abstract), author, title, date of publication, and time periods (decades and fifty years). The corpus provides linguistic annotation at the level of tokens (with normalized and original forms), lemmas, and parts of speech using TreeTagger (Schmid, 1995). The current release of the RSC (version 4.0) is freely available as a vertical text format (vrt) on the CLARIN-D repository[1].

Corpus of Historical American English (COHA) The COHA corpus is the largest structured corpus of historical English spanning from the 1810s to the 2000s. It contains more than 400 million words of text in more than 100,000 individual texts, balanced by genre across decades. It covers the major genres of fiction, magazine, newspaper and non-fiction. A detailed description of each genre and genre size is available at https://corpus.byu.edu/coha/. Fiction

---

[1] https://fedora.clarin-d.uni-saarland.de/rsc

is the largest genre with 48-55% of the total in each decade, followed by magazine with around 23-30%, news with 11-15% and non-fiction with 11-13%. We use the COHA corpus to represent standard English.

3.2 Methods

Our methodology is based on two information-theoretic measures. First, to investigate how much LRAs diverge from standard English and scientific language and to investigate specialization processes (H1 and H2) we use *Kullback-Leibler Divergence* (KLD; cf. Kullback and Leibler (1951)). Second, for the analysis of diachronic trends of standardization (H3) we use *Surprisal* to calculate the amount of information linguistic units transmit in text.

3.3 Divergence

Kullback-Leibler Divergence is an asymmetric measure of divergence calculating the additional bits of information needed between two models A and B:

$$D(A||B) = \sum_i p(item_i|A) log_2 \frac{p(item_i|A)}{p(item_i|B)} \quad (1)$$

Here, $p(item_i|A)$ is the probability of the ith item (in our case a word) in corpus A and $p(item_i|B)$ of that item in corpus B. Thus, divergence D between A and B, $D(A||B)$, is the sum of the probabilities of all items in A by the log_2 probability of the item in A divided by the probability of the item in B. This allows us to measure the amount of additional bits needed to encode words distributed according to a corpus A by the words' distribution in corpus B. The higher the amounts of bits, the more the two corpora diverge according to the probability distributions of their words. Difference in vocabulary size is controlled for by using ngram language models with Jelinek-Mercer smoothing (lambda at 0.05; cf. Zhai and Lafferty (2004); Fankhauser et al. (2014)). In our case, we compare *language* models between the language of literary research articles (LRAs), standard English, and scientific language.

For the investigation of H1 (LRAs vs. standard English and scientific language), we build yearly models and compare each year model across LRAs, standard English and scientific language, determining the degree of divergence between the models. The models are based on a vocabulary of 3,000 top occurring words of each corpus (LRA, COHA, RSC), excluding punctuation, stop words, and words shorter than three characters. The vocabulary lists are manually evaluated to ensure omission of possible noise in the data. For H2 (specialization of LRAs over time), we build KLD models on decades to investigate the degree of divergence of LRAs over time. Comparison is done between each decade (e.g. 1950 vs. 1960, 1950 vs. 1970, etc.). The inherent asymmetry of KLD allows us to inspect changes from past to present by $D(2000||1950)$, i.e. how well can the present be modeled by the past, and from present to past by $D(1950||2000)$, i.e. how well can the past be modeled by the present.

3.4 Surprisal

Surprisal is a measure of informativity and can be thought of as the amount of information a word transmits in a message (Shannon, 1948). In online-comprehension, surprisal is used to estimate how probable a unit (e.g. a word) is in a particular context (see Equation 2).

$$S(unit) = -log_2 p(unit|context) \quad (2)$$

Surprisal has two fundamental properties: (1) linguistic units with low probability convey more information than those with high probability, and (2) not only the unit itself but crucially the context in which a unit occurs determines the information a unit conveys. The intuition behind this is that linguistic units that are highly predictable in a given context convey less information than those that are less predictable and thus surprising (see Hale (2001); Levy (2008) for psycholinguistic accounts and Crocker et al. (2016) for surprisal and linguistic encoding across levels of linguistic representation (e.g. phonetic, psycholinguistic, discourse, register)).

We use surprisal to observe possible phrasal standardization of literary research articles over time (H3). As the LRA corpus comes in an ngram version (uni- to trigrams), we use surprisal on trigrams calculating surprisal of the last word, w_i, in the trigram based on its preceding context consisting of two previous words, w_{i-1} and w_{i-2} (a trigram model, see Equation 3).

$$S(w_i) = -log_2 p(w_i|w_{i-1}w_{i-2}) \quad (3)$$

Training is done on the COHA corpus, confining the data to span the same time period as the

LRA corpus (i.e. using texts from 1950 onwards), converting the corpus to lower-case and excluding sentence markers. In addition, we exclude from the training data sentences with a sequence of @ signs, which are part of COHA due to copyright. In addition we confine our selection of trigrams per document by matching the last word in a trigram with a dictionary consisting of the 3,000 most often occurring words in LRA, COHA and RSC plus function words. To test our hypothesis of phrasal standardization over time in LRA, we compare surprisal values of documents across years and decades. Assuming an increased phrasal standardization, the proportion of low surprisal per document will increase over time.

4 Analysis

In the analysis, we test our three hypotheses of scientization reflected in the process of social differentiation (H1, Section 4.1), diachronic specialization (H2, Section 4.2), and phrasal standardization (H3, Section 4.3).

4.1 Social Differentiation

As a humanistic discipline literary studies is often claimed to be more unique than other scientific disciplines (especially those from the 'hard' sciences) and to have a lower degree of scientificness. We thus hypothesize that literary studies should (1) diverge less from standard English than scientific disciplines and (2) diverge less from standard English than from scientific disciplines. To test this, we use three corpora: Literary Research articles (LRAs), COHA as a standard American English corpus to be comparable with LRAs, and the Royal Society Corpus (RSC) as a diachronic corpus of science. As a measure of divergence we use Kullback-Leibler Divergence D (see Section 3.2) comparing years between LRA vs. COHA, RSC vs. COHA, and LRA vs. COHA, assuming the following:

(1) LRAs will diverge less from standard English than scientific language from standard English: $D(lra||coha) < D(rsc||coha)$

(2) LRAs will diverge less from standard English than LRAs from scientific language: $D(lra||coha) < D(lra||rsc)$

For our first assumption, Figure 1 shows KLD over time from the 1950s to the early 2000s on

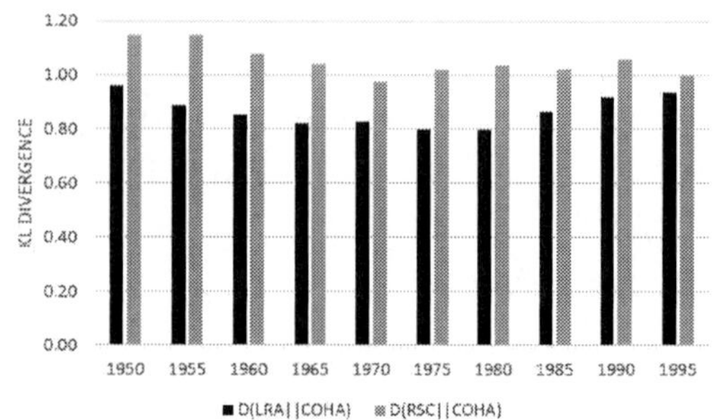

Figure 1: KLD over time for the comparisons of LRAs vs. COHA and RSC vs. COHA.

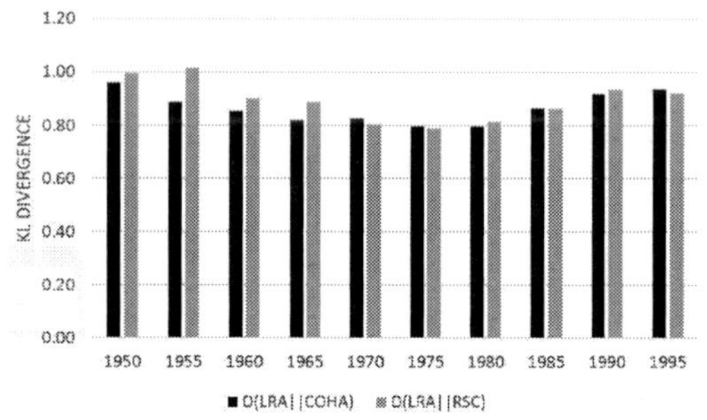

Figure 2: KLD over time for the comparisons of LRAs vs. COHA and LRAs vs. RSC.

a 5-year basis[2]. In general, LRAs diverge less from standard English than scientific language diverges from standard English, confirming our first assumption.

Based on Figure 2, our second assumption is only partially confirmed: from 1950 until the mid-1970s, LRAs are indeed more similar to standard English than they are to scientific language. However, the diachronic trend is a decreasing one. After 1965, LRAs tend to be equally distinct from standard English and scientific language, with an increasing divergence from both over time (from approx. 0.8 to 0.9 bits). By contrast, divergence between scientific language and standard English during that period remains relatively stable (around 1.05 bits). Thus, in the 1950s and 1960s, LRAs seem to have a lower degree of scientificness, being more similar to standard En-

---

[2]Note that COHA is genre-balanced by decades only. Thus, a yearly representation would be strongly biased by the change in genre distribution in COHA across years. We have chosen to use a 5-year scale, as the distribution across genres is relatively stable. An inspection of our word lists does not suggest that the differences we are seeing are due to differences in British and American spelling.

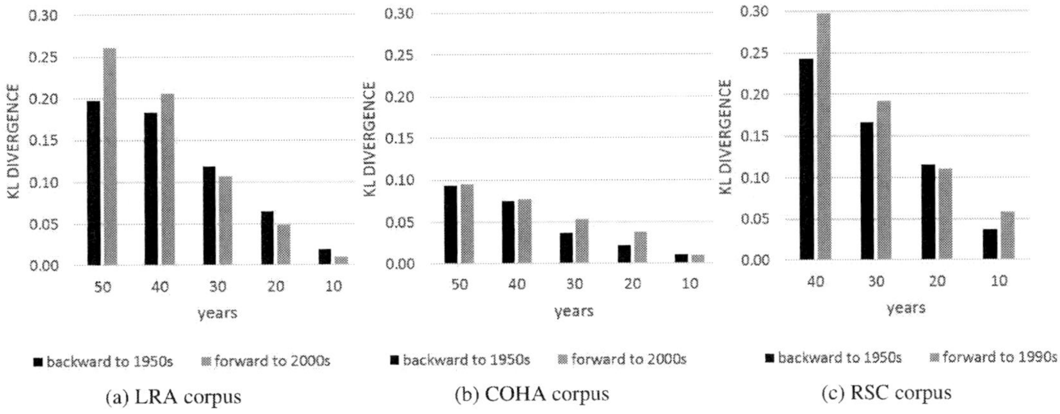

(a) LRA corpus   (b) COHA corpus   (c) RSC corpus

Figure 3: KLD over time for LRA, COHA, and RSC. (KLD models are built for the 1950s in comparison to the other decades (e.g., 10 years: $D(1950||1960)$, 20 years: $D(1950||1970)$, etc.). The same applies for the 2000s and 1990s.)

glish than scientific language. The 1970s seem to mark a transition point, where LRAs equally diverge from both standard English and scientific language. From the 1980s onwards, LRAs increasingly diverge from standard and scientific English possibly undergoing a process of specialization as their language use diverges both from scientific language and from common language.

4.2 Specialization of LRAs

We inspect a possible process of specialization by considering divergence between different time periods of the LRA corpus. The evolution of disciplines is inherently accompanied by periods of lexical expansion due to new discoveries, which are paralleled by processes of terminology formation as well as periods of lexical consolidation (cf. Degaetano-Ortlieb and Teich (2018)). Thus, as a discipline evolves, its vocabulary typically changes over time. In information-theoretic terms this would imply, first, that a language model of an earlier time period will match a more contemporary time period less well and vice versa. Second, we expect this process to be gradual, where more adjacent time periods will diverge less from each other than periods that are further apart. Finally, while vocabulary changes over time, we expect that it will keep elements from the past while developing new terminology. If a process of specialization is at work, more contemporary articles will be modeled less well by earlier time periods than vice versa because the present will enclose the vocabulary of the past in ways that the past cannot enclose the present. Past and present become asymmetrically different from one another.

Thus, for the LRA corpus, we hypothesize the following:

(1) LRAs of the 1950s will be better modeled by LRAs of the 2000s than vice versa, reflected in a lower divergence: $D(lra1950||lra2000)$ $< D(lra2000||lra1950)$

(2) The closer the time periods, the lower their divergence: $D(lra1950||lra1960)$ $< D(lra1950||lra1970)$

To test this, we build *forward* KLD models, i.e. models of the 2000s (or 1990s for the RSC) using past decades, e.g. $D(2000||1990)$, as well as *backward* models, i.e. models of the 1950s using future decades, e.g. $D(1950||1960)$. Figure 3a shows each model performance – the higher the KLD value the less well the models perform. As expected, the more adjacent the periods (e.g. only 10 years apart), the better the model in either direction, i.e. the forward model $D(1950||1960)$ performs quite well in modeling texts of 1950 when using 1960 texts (and vice versa). We also see our hypothesis about the assymetry in diachronic modeling confirmed, as the forward models show considerably higher divergence than the backward models for the longest time spans for both LRAs and the RSC (i.e. models 50 years apart).

A comparison to COHA (see Figure 3b) shows that the process of specialization (as defined here) does not adhere to standard English: KLD across comparisons is much lower than for LRAs, and the 50 year comparison $D(1950||2000)$ is almost equal to $D(2000||1950)$. In other words, we do not see the same directionality at work in general language use.

The growth in divergence over time and overall asymmetry between forward and backward models provide evidence to support our assumption of LRAs undergoing a process of specialization over time, similar to other disciplines (compare Figure 3a and 3c).

4.3 Standardization of Literary Research articles over time

At the level of linguistic phrases, we hypothesize a growth of phrasal standardization over time, i.e. a diachronic increase of standardized phrases in LRAs. While we have seen evidence above for the growing divergence from past linguistic practices in the field, our question here is whether there are higher levels of within-text standardization over time.

Surprisal is a well suited method for this kind of analysis, as it measures predictability of words in context. High predictability of words in phrases is reflected in low surprisal of these words and indicates standardized language use. To test this, we use a trigram version of the LRA corpus, approximating linguistic phrases by trigrams. We calculate surprisal of the last word in each trigram (see Section 3.4) to estimate predictability of possible phrases. In addition, we compare results to the RSC corpus to assess diachronic trends of standardization.

In Figure 4a, we see surprisal averaged by documents for the LRA and RSC corpora, showing significantly higher surprisal for LRAs (tested with a Wilcoxon rank sum test; p-value <2e-16). Inspecting the diachronic tendency of surprisal for LRAs, we can see how it significantly decreases over time, especially for the later time periods (see Figure 4b and Table 1). Thus, while LRAs use less standardized phrases than scientific language, over time surprisal of phrases in LRAs decreases, indicating an increase of standardized phrases.

	1950	1960	1970	1980	1990
1960	0.00019	-	-	-	-
1970	0.21622	0.00130	-	-	-
1980	0.04975	2.1e-12	3.0e-05	-	-
1990	1.9e-08	< 2e-16	< 2e-16	2.9e-07	-
2000	< 2e-16	< 2e-16	< 2e-16	< 2e-16	< 2e-16

Table 1: Pairwise comparisons of surprisal levels in LRAs by decade using Wilcoxon rank sum test and p-value adjustment with Benjamini-Hochberg method.

When inspecting the data more closely, we posit that a surprisal value <=0.5 bits appears to indi-

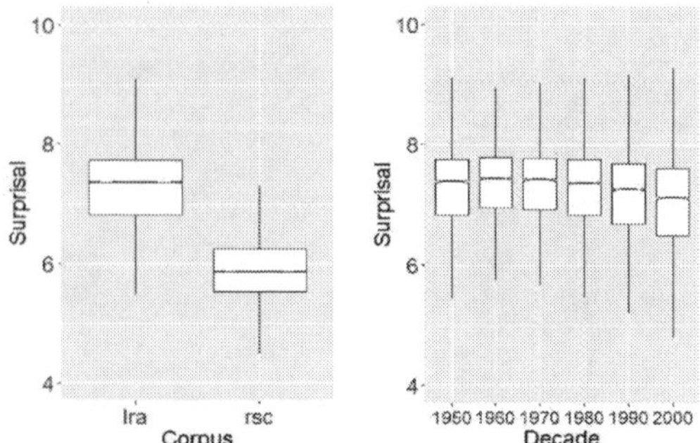

(a) LRA and RSC corpora   (b) LRA corpus over time

Figure 4: Surprisal for LRA and RSC.

phrase	surprisal
on behalf of	0.0116
be able to	0.0144
the nineteenth century	0.1710
in order to	0.2934
been forced to	0.4128
writings from the	1.2075
elaboration of the	2.0679
he complained of	3.1327
have suggested the	4.0291
his works of	5.0548
posits women as	6.9722
full of hope	7.7751
wrote two novels	7.8494
movement protesting on	8.0463
starving child like	9.3617
eighteenth century rhetoric	17.9100
high cultural romanticism	18.7972
a democratic poem	19.0587
a critical anti	19.0712
high cultural poetics	21.4387

Table 2: Examples of phrases from very low to high surprisal (LRA corpus).

cate standardized phrases in the LRA corpus (see first five examples in Table 2). These phrases transmit low informational content, indicated both by their surprisal value and their qualitative content. As we move up the surprisal scale, the information content transmitted appears to increase (compare *in order to* with *high cultural poetics*). This is in line with studies showing surprisal to be an indicator of processing effort, i.e. longer, low frequency words show higher surprisal, while shorter, high frequency words lower surprisal (cf. Hale (2001); Levy (2008)). In fact, phrases on the high surprisal end in Table 2 are lexical phrases (encompassing lower frequency words but high in information content), while phrases on the low surprisal end are grammatical phrases (encompassing high frequency words with lower information content). If we consider only phrases that fall below our 0.5 threshold, i.e. highly standardized phrases, we see how their percentage grows over time (Figure 5a), though modestly when compared to the science corpus (Figure 5b). In other words, the LRA corpus indicates a similar process of standardization as the scientific corpus, but it does so less strongly. It lends support to the scientization hypothesis, that the field engages in more standardized language now than in the past, but also the differentiation theory, that LRAs are still less "scientific" than science articles.

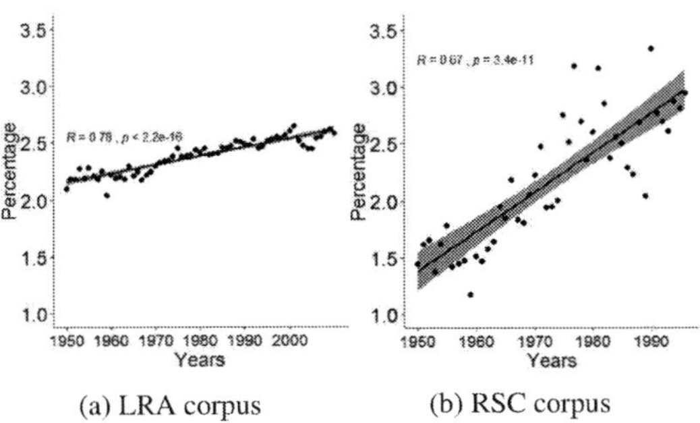

(a) LRA corpus   (b) RSC corpus

Figure 5: Percentage of standardized phrases (surprisal <=0.5 bits) over time.

5 Conclusion

We have investigated the evolution of literary studies with respect to two different kinds of language use: standard English on the one hand and scientific English on the other. In particular, we have tested three hypotheses with respect to a process of what we term scientization: social differentiation (H1, Section 4.1), diachronic specialization (H2, Section 4.2), and phrasal standardization (H3, Section 4.3). Methodologically, we used the information-theoretic measures of relative entropy (Kullback-Leibler Divergence) and surprisal. Kullback-Leibler Divergence is used to determine diverging trends between corpora/time periods. Surprisal is used to model the amount of information of words in context, providing us with a measure of phrasal standardization (the lower the surprisal, the more standardized a phrase is).

Doing so has indicated for us a complex portrait of the field, offering evidence to support two competing theories of disciplinary identity. On the one hand, we see evidence to support the idea that literary studies has indeed undergone a process of "scientization", which we define as the increased divergence from standard English, the increased divergence from past linguistic practices, and the increased use of standardized phrases. On the other hand, we see evidence to suggest that literary studies continues to occupy a middle-ground between science and common language. Literary research articles have remained consistently more similar to standard English than scientific articles, though the level of the difference of divergence has declined over time. Similarly, the divergence with past practices is considerably higher in LRAs than in standard English though somewhat lower than scientific articles. Language from the most recent decade is less well modeled by language from the past than the other way around, suggesting the emergence of field-specific vocabulary, even if not quite as strongly as in the RSC corpus. Finally, we see the uptick of standardized phrases, though once again with less overall strength than scientific articles.

These insights are important benchmarks for understanding the position of literary studies within the larger space of academic disciplines. They challenge the idea of literary studies' absolute distinctiveness from other disciplines and suggest that the field is gradually moving closer to the linguistic behavior of scientific domains. On the other hand, they indicate that this process is potentially not as distinctive for literary studies, as the field still maintains a closer approximation to common language than scientific fields. It suggests that one of the distinctive identities of literary studies might be its ability to mediate between scientific language practices on the one hand and common language practices on the other.

Our study could be expanded in various ways. Our collection of LRAs is limited to an Anglo-Saxon context and thus cannot account for disciplinary practices specific to other national contexts. Exploring further national frameworks within the discipline would reveal useful points of comparison. Second, as the title of our collection indicates, our results are only valid for articles, not monographs. While monographs play an important role in the field, articles are an equally central genre of scholarly discourse within literary studies. It would indeed be of interest to learn whether monographs behave differently with respect to the linguistic practices we uncover here. In terms of our language models used, one could test whether a broader vocabulary or the integration of function words and punctuation could lead to more insights on changing practices of grammatical consolidation (see e.g. Rubino et al. (2016); Degaetano-Ortlieb and Teich (2018)). And while we capture semantic context using trigrams, one could explore the effect of using word embeddings that capture broader contextual windows.

Finally, it is also important to point out that our definition of scientization does not encapsulate the full range of practices that belong to the linguistic or methodological behavior of academic disciplines. Citation practices and evidentiary norms are two obvious ways that disciplines communicate knowledge that are not captured by our models. It could be that these practices follow our trends or diverge in telling ways. Future research will have to decide. Similarly, our models cannot explain what is driving this process of scientization, which we see as the subject of future work. What mechanisms are at work that contribute to these movements toward scientization, such as editorial behavior of journals, administrative pressures of institutions, or demographic changes in the profession? Are different effects occurring at different points in time? While we cannot yet answer these questions they are essential for understanding the logic through which disciplines constitute themselves and produce new knowledge.

Acknowledgments

Funding for this project was provided by the Social Sciences and Humanities Research Council of Canada and by the German Research Foundation (Deutsche Forschungsgemeinschaft) under the grant SFB1102: Information Density and Linguistic Encoding (www.sfb1102.uni-saarland.de). We are also indebted to Stefan Fischer for support in corpus processing and Elke Teich for her comments on a previous version of this paper. Also, we thank the anonymous reviewers for their constructive and valuable comments.

References

Pierre Azoulay, Toby Stuart, and Yanbo Wang. 2014. Matthew: Effect or Fable? *Management Science*, 60(1):92–109.

Douglas Biber and Bethany Gray. 2010. Challenging Stereotypes about Academic Writing: Complexity, Elaboration, Explicitness. *Journal of English for Academic Purposes*, 9:2–20.

Douglas Biber and Bethany Gray. 2011. The Historical Shift of Scientific Academic Prose in English towards Less Explicit Styles of Expression: Writing without Verbs. In Vijay Bathia, Purificación Sánchez, and Pascual Pérez-Paredes, editors, *Researching Specialized Languages*, pages 11–24. John Benjamins, Amsterdam.

Douglas Biber and Bethany Gray. 2016. *Grammatical Complexity in Academic English: Linguistic Change in Writing*. Studies in English Language. Cambridge University Press, Cambridge, UK.

Vladimir Bochkarev, Valery D. Solovyev, and Soren Wichmann. 2014. Universals versus Historical Contingencies in Lexical Evolution. *Journal of The Royal Society Interface*, 11(101).

David Chavalarias and Jean-Philippe Cointet. 2013. Phylomemetic Patterns in Science Evolution - The Rise and Fall of Scientific Fields. *PloS one*, 8(2):e54847.

Matthew W. Crocker, Vera Demberg, and Elke Teich. 2016. Information Density and Linguistic Encoding (IDeaL). *KI - Künstliche Intelligenz*, 30(1):77–81.

Stefania Degaetano-Ortlieb. 2018. Stylistic Variation over 200 Years of Court Proceedings according to Gender and Social Class. In *Proceedings of the 2nd Workshop on Stylistic Variation at NAACL*, pages 1–10, New Orleans, USA. ACL.

Stefania Degaetano-Ortlieb, Hannah Kermes, Ashraf Khamis, and Elke Teich. 2019. An Information-Theoretic Approach to Modeling Diachronic Change in Scientific English. In Carla Suhr, Terttu Nevalainen, and Irma Taavitsainen, editors, *From Data to Evidence in English Language Research*, Language and Computers, pages 258–281. Brill, Leiden.

Stefania Degaetano-Ortlieb and Elke Teich. 2016. Information-based Modeling of Diachronic Linguistic Change: From Typicality to Productivity. In *Proceedings of the 10th LaTeCH Workshop*, pages 165–173, Berlin. ACL.

Stefania Degaetano-Ortlieb and Elke Teich. 2018. Using Relative Entropy for Detection and Analysis of Periods of Diachronic Linguistic Change. In *Proceedings of the 2nd Joint SIGHUM Workshop on Computational Linguistics for Cultural Heritage, Social Sciences, Humanities and Literature at COLING2018*, pages 22–33, Santa Fe, NM, USA. ACL.

Eliza D. Evans, Charles J. Gomez, and Daniel A. McFarland. 2016. Measuring Paradigmaticness of Disciplines Using Text. *Sociological Science*, 3(32):757–778.

James A. Evans and Jacob G. Foster. 2011. Metaknowledge. *Science*, 331(6018):721–725.

Peter Fankhauser, Jörg Knappen, and Elke Teich. 2014. Exploring and Visualizing Variation in Language Resources. In *Proceedings of the 9th LREC*, pages 4125–4128, Reykjavik. ELRA.

Jürgen Fohrmann and Wilhelm Vosskamp, editors. 1991. *Wissenschaft und Nation: Studien zur Entstehungsgeschichte der Deutschen Literaturwissenschaft*. Fink.

Santo Fortunato, Carl T. Bergstrom, Katy Börner, James A. Evans, Dirk Helbing, Staša Milojević, Alexander M. Petersen, Filippo Radicchi, Roberta Sinatra, Brian Uzzi, Alessandro Vespignani, Ludo Waltman, Dashun Wang, and Albert-László Barabási. 2018. Science of Science. *Science*, 359(6379).

Jacob G. Foster, Andrey Rzhetsky, and James A. Evans. 2015. Tradition and Innovation in Scientists Research Strategies. *American Sociological Review*, 80(5):875–908.

Andrew Goldstone and Ted Underwood. 2014. The Quiet Transformations of Literary Studies: What Thirteen Thousand Scholars Could Tell Us. *New Literary History*, 45(3):359–384.

Gerald Graff, editor. 2007. *Professing Literature: An Institutional History*, twentieth anniversary edition. University of Chicago Press, Chicago.

John Hale. 2001. A Probabilistic Earley Parser as a Psycholinguistic Model. In *Proceedings of the Second Meeting of the North American Chapter of the Association for Computational Linguistics on Language Technologies*, pages 1–8. Association for Computational Linguistics.

M.A.K. Halliday. 1988. On the Language of Physical Science. In Mohsen Ghadessy, editor, *Registers of Written English: Situational Factors and Linguistic Features*, pages 162–177. Pinter, London.

M.A.K. Halliday. 2006. *Language of Science*, volume 5. Bloomsbury Publishing, Continuum, London.

Zellig Harris. 1991. *A Theory of Language and Information. A Mathematical Approach*. Clarendon Pess, Oxford.

Zellig S. Harris. 2002. The Structure of Science Information. *Journal of Biomedical Informatics*, 35(4):215 – 221.

James M. Hughes, Nicholas J. Foti, David C. Krakauer, and Daniel N. Rockmore. 2012. Quantitative Patterns of Stylistic Influence in the Evolution of Literature. *Proceedings of the National Academy of Sciences*, 109(20):7682–7686.

George A. Kennedy, editor. 1989. *The Cambridge History of Literary Criticism*. Cambridge University Press, Cambridge.

Hannah Kermes, Stefania Degaetano-Ortlieb, Ashraf Khamis, Jörg Knappen, and Elke Teich. 2016. The Royal Society Corpus: From Uncharted Data to Corpus. In *Proceedings of the 10th LREC*, Portorož, Slovenia. ELRA.

Jonathan Kramnick. 2018. *Paper Minds: Literature and the Ecology of Consciousness*. University of Chicago Press, Chicago.

Thomas S Kuhn. 1962. *The Structure of Scientific Revolutions*, 3rd edition. University of Chicago Press, Chicago.

Solomon Kullback and Richard A. Leibler. 1951. On Information and Sufficiency. *The Annals of Mathematical Statistics*, 22(1):79–86.

Michèle Lamont, editor. 2009. *How Professors Think: Inside the Curious World of Academic Judgment*. Harvard University Press, Cambridge.

R. Levy. 2008. Expectation-based Syntactic Comprehension. *Cognition*, 106(3):1126–1177.

Martha C. Nussbaum, editor. 1997. *Cultivating Humanity: A Classical Defense of Reform in Liberal Education*. Harvard University Press, Cambridge.

Leighton Durham Reynolds and Nigel Guy Wilson. 1991. *Scribes and Scholars - A Guide to the Transmission of Greek and Latin Literature*. Oxford University Press, Oxford.

H.P. Rickman, editor. 1976. *W. Dilthey Selected Writings*. Cambridge University Press, Cambridge.

Raphael Rubino, Stefania Degaetano-Ortlieb, Elke Teich, and Joseph van Genabith. 2016. Modeling Diachronic Change in Scientific Writing with Information Density. In *Proceedings of the 26th International Conference on Computational Linguistics: Technical Papers*, pages 750–761, Osaka, Japan. ACL.

Helmut Schmid. 1995. Improvements in Part-of-Speech Tagging with an Application to German. In *Proceedings of the ACL SIGDAT-Workshop*, Kyoto, Japan.

Claude E. Shannon. 1948. A Mathematical Theory of Communication. *Bell System Technical Journal*, 27:379–423, 623–656.

Tian Shi. 2004. Ecological Economics as a Policy Science: Rhetoric or Commitment towards an Improved Decision-making Process on Sustainability. *Ecological Economics*, 48(1):23–36.

Elke Teich, Stefania Degaetano-Ortlieb, Peter Fankhauser, Hannah Kermes, and Ekaterina Lapshinova-Koltunski. 2016. The Linguistic Construal of Disciplinarity: A Data Mining Approach Using Register Features. *Journal of the Association for Information Science and Technology (JASIST)*, 67(7):1668–1678.

Evelyn B. Tribble, editor. 1993. *Margins and Marginality: The Printed Page in Early Modern England*. University Press of Virginia, Charlottesville.

Jean Ure. 1982. Introduction: Approaches to the Study of Register Range. *International Journal of the Sociology of Language*, 35:5–23.

Daril A. Vilhena, Jacob G. Foster, Martin Rosvall, Jevin D. West, James Evans, and Carl T. Bergstrom. 2014. Finding Cultural Holes: How Structure and Culture Diverge in Networks of Scholarly Communication. *Sociological Science*, 1:221.

Chad Wellmon. 2017. Loyal Workers and Distinguished Scholars: Big Humanities and the Ethics of Knowledge. *Modern Intellectual History*, pages 1–39.

Chengxiang Zhai and John Lafferty. 2004. A Study of Smoothing Methods for Language Models Applied to Information Retrieval. *ACM Transactions on Information Systems*, 22(2):179–214.

Are Fictional Voices Distinguishable?
Classifying Character Voices in Modern Drama

Krishnapriya Vishnubhotla
Department of Computer Science
University of Toronto
Toronto, Canada
vkpriya@cs.toronto.edu

Adam Hammond
Department of English
University of Toronto
Toronto, Canada
adam.hammond@utoronto.ca

Graeme Hirst
Department of Computer Science
University of Toronto
Toronto, Canada
gh@cs.toronto.edu

Abstract

According to the literary theory of Mikhail Bakhtin, a *dialogic* novel is one in which characters speak in their own distinct voices, rather than serving as mouthpieces for their authors. We use text classification to determine which authors best achieve dialogism, looking at a corpus of plays from the late nineteenth and early twentieth centuries. We find that the SAGE model of text generation, which highlights deviations from a background lexical distribution, is an effective method of weighting the words of characters' utterances. Our results show that it is indeed possible to distinguish characters by their speech in the plays of canonical writers such as George Bernard Shaw, whereas characters are clustered more closely in the works of lesser-known playwrights.

1 Introduction

The concept of *dialogism* has been a notable focus in recent computational literary scholarship (Brooke et al., 2017; Hammond and Brooke, 2016; Muzny et al., 2017). As theorized by Russian literary critic Mikhail Bakhtin (2013), a dialogic novel is one in which characters present "a plurality of independent and unmerged voices and consciousnesses, a genuine polyphony of fully valid voices". Bakhtin presents Dostoevsky as the preeminent dialogic author, arguing that his novels are "multi-accented and contradictory in [their] values", whereas the works of other novelists like Tolstoy are *monologic* or homogeneous in their style, with characters reflecting the prejudices as well as the distinctive mannerisms of their authors.

While previous computational studies of dialogism take this definition of dialogism for granted and seek to model it, here we take a step back to pose a series of fundamental questions: Can the voices of characters be distinguished in fictional texts? Which computational techniques are most effective in making these distinctions? Are certain authors better than others at creating characters with distinctive voices and do these authors tend to be more canonical? Focusing, for pragmatic purposes, on plays rather than novels, we argue here that character voices can, in the work of certain authors, be readily distinguished; that SAGE (Sparse Additive Generative) models (Eisenstein et al., 2011) are especially powerful in making these distinctions; and that canonical authors are, in our small sample, more successful in creating distinctive character voices than are less canonical authors.

2 Related Work

Computational approaches to the authorship attribution problem involve using certain textual features, called *style markers*, to build a representation of an author's texts, which is then passed to a classification algorithm. Stop-word frequencies, part-of-speech trigrams, and structural features such as sentence lengths have been shown to be good indicators of author identity (Stamatatos, 2009). The earliest work in authorship attribution focused on discovering the stylistic markers that would reveal the identity of the author or authors of disputed works (Mosteller and Wallace, 1963), and the bulk of contemporary work in authorship attribution continues in this vein (Rybicki, 2018). Our work draws on an alternative tradition that uses the techniques of authorship attribution to investigate what J. F. Burrows, in a study of the novels of Jane Austen, calls *idiolects*, the distinctive stylistic patterns of individual speakers within texts (Burrows, 1987). Whereas Burrows's approach focuses on very common words and relies on statistical methods whose results are not easily interpretable, our particular application requires us

Proc. of the 3rd Joint SIGHUM Workshop on Computational Linguistics for Cultural Heritage, Social Sciences, Humanities and Literature, pp. 29–34
Minneapolis, MN, USA, June 7, 2019. ©2019 Association for Computational Linguistics

to employ methods that are sensitive to rare and infrequent words, and whose results allow us to distinguish between stylistic and topical phenomena.

Recently, machine learning methods have been applied in computational stylometry for authorship attribution tasks, and also in the context of style transfer for texts. Bagnall (2015) uses a recurrent neural network (RNN) based model for the author identification task. Since neural architectures massively overfit the training set unless used with large datasets, the authors propose a shared recurrrent layer, with only the final softmax layer being author-specific. Shrestha et al. (2017) use convolutional neural networks (CNNs) over character n-grams for authorship attribution, which proves to be more interpretable than the former in identifying important features.

3   Corpus

Our corpus consists of plays published in the late 19th and early 20th centuries by George Bernard Shaw, Oscar Wilde, Cale Young Rice, Sydney Grundy, Somerset Maugham, Arthur Wing Pinero, and Hermann Sudermann (whose plays are translated from German) — giving a total of 63 plays. We would ideally have examined character dialogue in novels, Bakhtin's preferred genre, but the problem of sufficiently reliable quote attribution for novels remains unsolved. However, in plays, each utterance is explicitly labeled with the name of the character who speaks it. We use GutenTag (Brooke et al., 2015) to extract all plays from the specified authors, restricting the year of publication to 1880–1920 to roughly capture the literary period from which Bakhtin developed his theory of dialogism.

4   Methodology

Our primary method of measuring the distinguishability of character voices is classification. Our task is to build a classifier able to correctly discriminate between the speech of different characters. We perform experiments using several feature sets, in order to capture stylistic aspects that are syntactic as well as lexical. These include surface, syntactic, and generative topic-modeling induced features. Generative models that we used include latent Dirichlet allocation (Blei et al., 2003), naive Bayes, and SAGE models (Eisenstein et al., 2011). Accuracy of classification is measured using the F_1 score, which strikes a balance

between precision and recall. We experiment with both support vector machine (SVM) and logistic regression classifiers.

In addition, we experiment with vector representations of words as features. We use distributed word vectors trained on the Wikipedia corpus using the word2vec algorithm (Mikolov et al., 2013). Each dialogue is represented as a weighted average of the individual word vectors, where the weights are TF-IDF weights, or obtained from the SAGE algorithm.

We also look at representations obtained from lexicons that score words across a discrete set of stylistic dimensions. Brooke and Hirst (2013) pick three dimensions to rate words along, the opposing polarities of which give us six styles: colloquial vs. literary, concrete vs. abstract, and subjective vs. objective. We also use the NRC Emotion Intensity Lexicon (EmoLex) (Mohammad, 2018b) and the NRC Valence, Arousal, and Dominance Lexicon (VAD Lexicon) (Mohammad, 2018a). The former provides real-valued intensity scores for four basic emotions — anger, fear, sadness, and joy, and the latter for the three primary dimensions of word meaning — valence, arousal, and dominance. The scores along each dimension are normalized to give us a set of values ranging from 0 to 1. Principal component analysis (PCA) of these vectors gives us an insight into which authors are the most successful at creating characters whose style is highly mutually distinguishable.

We repeat these experiments for "artificial plays" constructed by sampling a random subset of characters either across plays (strategy 1) or across authors (strategy 2). Intuitively, we expect the character speech in these artificial plays to be more readily distinguishable than in actual plays, because the characters are likely to discuss a wider variety of topics and to come from a wider variety of classes, professional milieus, and dialect communities than a group of characters in any actual play (strategies 1 and 2), and because the characters are the creations of different authors, each with their own distinct stylistic fingerprints (strategy 2).

5   Classification Models

In this section, we describe the two main models of classification that we employed. All hyperparameters in both models are tuned using grid-search, along with 5-fold cross validation.

5.1 Lexical and Syntactic features

Our first feature set consists of lexical, syntactic and structural features. These include average sentence and word lengths, type-token ratio, and proportion of function words in each sentence. We also use n-gram frequencies of word and part-of-speech tags, where $n \in \{1, 2, 3\}$, and dependency triples of the form *(head-PoS, child-PoS, DepRel)* from the dependency parse of each sentence, where *child-PoS* and *head-PoS* are the parts-of-speech of the current word and its parent node, and *DepRel* is the dependency relation between them. All proper nouns in our sentences are masked, as they often serve as indicative clues as to who the speaker is or is not.

Because word and PoS n-grams are very sparse features, the resulting feature vector has a relatively high dimensionality. We therefore pass it through a feature selection pipeline before classification. Two main feature selection algorithms are used: variance threshold and k-best selection. The former removes all features with a zero variance across samples — i.e, features that have the same value at each datapoint. The k-best selection algorithm then picks the top-k features according to some correlation measure. Here, we use the chi-squared statistic, which gets rid of the features that are the most likely to be independent of class and therefore irrelevant for classification. We pass this feature vector through a support vector machine (SVM) classifier.

5.2 Sentence Vectors with SAGE

Since we are dealing with a dataset that can contain very few samples per class, we need a model that is sensitive to low-frequency word features. We use the Sparse Additive Generative (SAGE) model of text, proposed by Eisenstein et al. (2011), which models the word distribution of each class as a vector of log-frequency deviations from a background distribution. We take the background distribution to be the average of the word frequencies across all classes. An alternative to the naive Bayes and LDA-like models of text generation, the SAGE model enforces a sparse prior on its parameters, which biases it towards rare and infrequent terms in the text.

We use the SAGE model to derive weights for each sentence (i.e, each quote) in our dataset. Sentence vectors are obtained by averaging the vector representation of each word in the sentence with

Author	#Plays	Baseline	Avg F_1
Shaw	29	.153	.400
Wilde	6	.116	.376
Maugham	8	.137	.318
Grundy	4	.107	.283
Pinero	5	.090	.272
Sudermann	5	.084	.253
Rice	6	.151	.234
Weighted Avg.		.133	.342

Table 1: F_1 scores for classification of individual characters, by author, using lexical and syntactic features. Baseline is random classification with the class distribution of the training data. The final row reports the weighted average of the scores for each author, where the weights are proportional to the number of their plays in our dataset.

Author	Baseline	Avg F_1
Shaw	.148	.573
Wilde	.194	.376
Maugham	.182	.318
Grundy	.184	.283
Pinero	.140	.272
Sudermann	.119	.253
Rice	.186	.234
Average	.165	.329

Table 2: F_1 scores for classification, using lexical and syntactic features, of characters by each author in artificial plays generated by sampling characters from the all plays of that author. Baseline is computed in the same manner as in Table 1.

its corresponding SAGE weight. Classification is performed by passing these sentence vectors to a logistic regression classifier.

6 Results

We first present results for classification of individual characters with our lexical and syntactic features in Tables 1 and 2. We compare scores with a baseline that randomly generates predictions that respect the class distributions of the training data.

The classification scores are above the baseline for almost all the plays, though the absolute numbers themselves are not very high. Table 1 shows the average scores across all plays for each author, while Table 2 contains the average scores for the artificial plays. Shaw achieves the highest average score.

As expected, the scores for artificial plays are,

| | Average F_1 | |
Author	Original plays	Artificial plays
Wilde	.641	.669
Shaw	.635	.630
Maugham	.662	.645
Sudermann	.538	.574
Grundy	.517	.517
Pinero	.458	.543
Rice	.181	.208
Weighted Avg.	.561	.540

Table 3: F_1 scores for classification of characters in original artificial plays using out SAGE classification model.

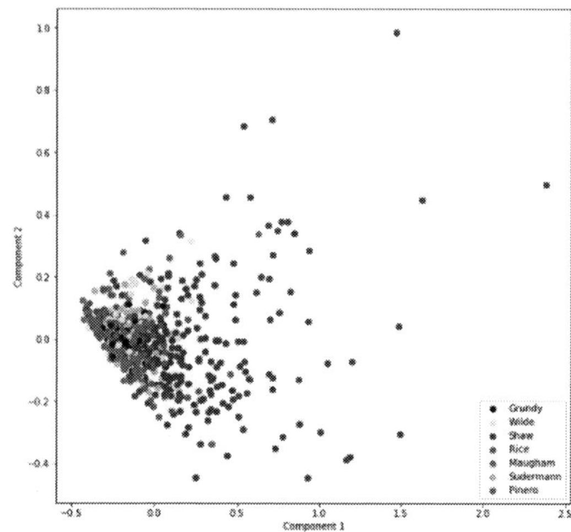

Figure 1: Plot of first two components of PCA on the lexical style vectors of each character of each author.

on average, higher than those of actual plays. We generate a maximum of 50 artificial plays for each author by sampling 7 characters from the complete set of characters, without repetition.

We achieve the best classification results, however, using the SAGE+word2vec classification algorithm described in Section 5.2. Table 3 shows the author-wise average F_1 scores for both original and artificial (strategy 1) plays. The average F_1 is higher still, at .605, for strategy 2 artificial plays (not presented in the table).

As an additional test, we performed PCA on vectors constructed using the style lexicons from Section 4. To construct our vectors, we replace our word2vec embeddings with a concatenated vector of the scores for each word along each of the 14 dimensions. Missing dimensions for words are assigned a score of zero. All the vectors are normalized along each dimension to account for variations in scale.

The results are shown in Figure 1, which plots the first two principal components. The two components combined account for 74.7% of the variance of the data. Each dot corresponds to a character in an actual play, and wider spacing between them indicates a wider range of styles and emotions. Even taking into account the fact that Shaw has significantly more plays, and thus more characters, than the other playwrights, he is nonetheless evidently the most successful, followed by Maugham, at creating characters with a wide range across all of the dimensions.

7 Discussion

Our work presents insights into a series of fundamental questions related to the phenomenon of literary dialogism and its tractability for computational analysis. The most fundamental is whether the voices of individual characters can be distinguished at all in literary texts. In a provocative argument in *Enumerations*, Andrew Piper uses computational methods to argue that "character-text" (the words used to describe characters) is — contrary to the intuitions of many literary scholars — relatively uniform within and across novels (Piper, 2018). Our work suggests that the same cannot be said of "dialogue-text" (the words that characters say). In a finding more in line with the intuitions of critics and the theories of Bakhtin, our experiment shows that the voices of characters can indeed be distinguished from one another, sometimes with quite high precision.

As to the question of whether certain authors are better able to distinguish their characters' voices than others, our results suggest that this is clearly the case. Although we approach the classification task from a variety of methodological perspectives, each of these reveals a continuum along which some playwrights are able to create distinctive character voices (e.g., Shaw) and some are not (e.g, Rice). That this continuum separates well-known playwrights like Shaw and Wilde from mostly forgotten playwrights like Pinero and Rice suggests that the ability to distinguish voices may be a property of more canonical — and, perhaps, more talented — writers.[1] A larger sample size would be necessary to draw such conclusions definitively, however, as would an investigation of the effect of genre on the distinctiveness of character speech — for instance, whether comedy, which tends to put characters of different classes (and class dialects) in conversation, produces higher distinctiveness scores.

Our experiments with different feature sets also provide insights into how these characters are distinguishable from one another. SAGE, as an alternative to TF-IDF and naive Bayes measures of vocabulary usage, proves to be a very good indicator of which words are most distinctive for a particular character. At the character level, looking at the top features from the SAGE algorithm provides insights into the easiest types of stylistic distinction one can make while creating characters. Servants and butlers are easily recognizable by their use of words such as *'sir'*, *'yes'*, and *'please'*, and achieve a high classification score despite having relatively fewer quotes. In Shaw's *Pygmalion*, the character of The Flower Girl is distinguished by her unique vocabulary of words like *'ow'*, *'ai'*, *'–'*, *' 'm'*, *'ah'*, *'oo'*, etc. These kinds of lexical, dialectal features seem to be the most popular way of creating unique character voices.

The semantic and syntactic information captured by word2vec vectors forms the other key component of our analysis. While these dense vectors are not directly interpretable, we did attempt an initial clustering experiment with the word embeddings, which resulted in some insightful clusters. Proper nouns were grouped into one, another had words associated with tragedy (*sad, dreadful, miserable, awful, horrible, terrible, unfortunate*), and yet another cluster had *duty, servants, rank, ideals*. These are indicative of some stylistic aspect of words being captured by the embeddings which, when combined with the SAGE weights, boosts our classification performance. However, we reiterate that quantifying this is a hard-to-solve problem. Our analysis with lexicon-based vectors more concretely illustrates some of the stylistic dimensions along which characters and authors differ.

An interesting observation we make is that the artificial plays do not achieve a significantly higher score when compared to the original ones, despite the intuition that they must deal with more disparate topics. The number of sources of variance in creating these plays makes it hard to interpret this; performing more controlled experiments in the future might provide a better explanation.

8 Conclusion

We propose new techniques for classifying character speech in the works of seven modern dramatists. We show that SAGE models achieve the highest classification scores. Our results suggest that, in many dramatic works, characters are distinguishable with relatively high precision; that certain playwrights are better able to create distinctive character voices; and that these playwrights tend to be more canonical. Given the small size and restricted domain of our dataset, we treat these results are preliminary. Further investigation with a wider range of authors and genres, including novels, would aid us in drawing more decisive conclusions.

Acknowledgements

This work was supported financially by the Natural Sciences and Engineering Research Council of Canada. We are grateful to the anonymous reviewers for their helpful comments.

References

Douglas Bagnall. 2015. Author identification using multi-headed recurrent neural networks. *arXiv preprint arXiv:1506.04891*.

Mikhail Bakhtin. 2013. *Problems of Dostoevsky's Poetics*. University of Minnesota Press.

David M Blei, Andrew Y Ng, and Michael I Jordan. 2003. Latent Dirichlet allocation. *Journal of Machine Learning Research*, 3(Jan):993–1022.

Julian Brooke, Adam Hammond, and Graeme Hirst. 2015. GutenTag: an NLP-driven tool for digital humanities research in the Project Gutenberg corpus. In *Proceedings of the Fourth Workshop on Computational Linguistics for Literature*, pages 42–47.

Julian Brooke, Adam Hammond, and Graeme Hirst. 2017. Using models of lexical style to quantify free indirect discourse in modernist fiction. *Digital Scholarship in the Humanities*, 32(2):234–250.

---

[1]Nonetheless, we acknowledge the alternative viewpoint expressed by one of the reviewers: "It could be that the characters from Rice are so rich and diverse that they cannot be classified and that Shaw's or Wilde's are so exaggerated or archetypal that even simple classification mechanisms can recognize them."

Julian Brooke and Graeme Hirst. 2013. A multidimensional Bayesian approach to lexical style. In *Proceedings of the 2013 Conference of the North American Chapter of the Association for Computational Linguistics: Human Language Technologies*, pages 673–679.

J. F. Burrows. 1987. *Computation into Criticism: A Study of Jane Austen's Novels and an Experiment in Method*. Oxford University Press.

Jacob Eisenstein, Amr Ahmed, and Eric P Xing. 2011. Sparse additive generative models of text. In *Proceedings of the 28th International Conference on International Conference on Machine Learning*, pages 1041–1048. Omnipress.

Adam Hammond and Julian Brooke. 2016. Project Dialogism: Toward a computational history of vocal diversity in English-language literature. In *Digital Humanities*, pages 543–544, Kraków.

Tomas Mikolov, Ilya Sutskever, Kai Chen, Greg S Corrado, and Jeff Dean. 2013. Distributed representations of words and phrases and their compositionality. In *Advances in Neural Information Processing Systems*, pages 3111–3119.

Saif Mohammad. 2018a. Obtaining reliable human ratings of valence, arousal, and dominance for 20,000 english words. In *Proceedings of the 56th Annual Meeting of the Association for Computational Linguistics (Volume 1: Long Papers)*, volume 1, pages 174–184.

Saif Mohammad. 2018b. Word affect intensities. In *Proceedings of the Eleventh International Conference on Language Resources and Evaluation (LREC-2018)*.

Frederick Mosteller and David L. Wallace. 1963. Inference in an authorship problem. *Journal of the American Statistical Association*, 58(302):275–309.

Grace Muzny, Mark Algee-Hewitt, and Dan Jurafsky. 2017. Dialogism in the novel: A computational model of the dialogic nature of narration and quotations. *Digital Scholarship in the Humanities*, 32(supplement 2):ii31–ii52.

Andrew Piper. 2018. *Enumerations: Data and Literary Study*. University of Chicago Press.

Jan Rybicki. 2018. Partners in life, partners in crime? In Arjuna Tuzzi and Michele A. Cortelazzo, editors, *Drawing Elena Ferrante's Profile*, pages 109–119. Padova University Press.

Prasha Shrestha, Sebastian Sierra, Fabio Gonzalez, Manuel Montes, Paolo Rosso, and Thamar Solorio. 2017. Convolutional neural networks for authorship attribution of short texts. In *Proceedings of the 15th Conference of the European Chapter of the Association for Computational Linguistics: Volume 2, Short Papers*, volume 2, pages 669–674.

Efstathios Stamatatos. 2009. A survey of modern authorship attribution methods. *Journal of the American Society for Information Science and Technology*, 60(3):538–556.

Automatic Alignment and Annotation Projection for Literary Texts

Uli Steinbach
Department of Computational Linguistics
Heidelberg University

Ines Rehbein
Leibniz ScienceCampus
IDS Mannheim/ Heidelberg University

{steinbach|rehbein}@cl.uni-heidelberg.de

Abstract

This paper presents a modular NLP pipeline for the creation of a parallel literature corpus, followed by annotation transfer from the source to the target language. The test case we use to evaluate our pipeline is the automatic transfer of quote and speaker mention annotations from English to German. We evaluate the different components of the pipeline and discuss challenges specific to literary texts. Our experiments show that after applying a reasonable amount of semi-automatic postprocessing we can obtain high-quality aligned and annotated resources for a new language.

1 Introduction

Recent years have seen an increasing interest in using computational and mixed method approaches for literary studies. A case in point is the analysis of literary characters using social network analysis (Elson et al., 2010; Rydberg-Cox, 2011; Agarwal et al., 2012; Kydros and Anastasiadis, 2014).

While the first networks have been created manually, follow-up studies have tried to automatically extract the information needed to fill the network with life. The manual construction of such networks can yield high quality analyses, however, the amount of time needed for manually extracting the information is huge. The second approach based on automatic information extraction is more adequate for large scale investigations of literary texts. However, due to the difficulty of the task the quality of the resulting network is often seriously hampered. In some studies, the extraction of character information is limited to explicit mentions in the text, and relations between characters in the network are often based on their co-occurence in a predefined text window, missing out on the more interesting but harder-to-get features encoded in the novel.

A more meaningful analysis requires the identification of character entities and their mentions in the text, as well as the attribution of quotes to their respective speakers. Unfortunately, this is not an easy task. Characters in novels are mostly referred to by anaphoric *mentions*, such as personal pronouns or nominal descriptors (e.g. "the old women" or "the hard-headed lawyer"), and these have to be traced back to the respective *entity* to whom they refer, i.e. the speaker.

For English, automatic approaches based on machine learning (Elson and McKeown, 2010; He et al., 2013) or rule-based systems (Muzny et al., 2017) have been developed for this task, and a limited amount of annotated resources already exists. For most other languages, however, such resources are not yet available. To make progress towards the fully automatic identification of speakers and quotes in literary texts, we need more training data. As the fully manual annotation of such resources is time-consuming and costly, we present a method for the automatic transfer of annotations from English to other languages where resources for speaker attribution and quote detection are sparse.

We test our approach for German, making use of publically available literary translations of English novels. We first create a parallel English-German literature corpus and then project existing annotations from English to German. The main contributions of our work are the following:

- We present a modular pipeline for creating parallel literary corpora and for annotation transfer.

- We evaluate the impact of semi-automatic postprocessing on the quality of the different components in our pipeline.

- We show how the choice of translation impacts the quality of the annotation transfer

35

Proc. of the 3rd Joint SIGHUM Workshop on Computational Linguistics for Cultural Heritage, Social Sciences, Humanities and Literature, pp. 35–45
Minneapolis, MN, USA, June 7, 2019. ©2019 Association for Computational Linguistics

and present a method for determining the best translation for this task.

2   Related work

Quote detection has been an active field of research, mostly for information extraction from the news domain (Pouliquen et al., 2007; Krestel et al., 2008; Pareti et al., 2013; Pareti, 2015; Scheible et al., 2016). Related work in the context of opinion mining has tried to identify the holders (speakers) and targets of opinions (Choi et al., 2005; Wiegand and Klakow, 2012; Johansson and Moschitti, 2013).

Elson and McKeown (2010) were among the first to propose a supervised machine learning model for quote attribution in literary text. He et al. (2013) extended their supervised approach by including contextual knowledge from unsupervised actor-topic models. Almeida et al. (2014) and Fertmann (2016) combined the task of speaker identification with coreference resolution. Grishina and Stede (2017) test the projection of coreference annotations, a task related to speaker attribution, using multiple source languages. Muzny et al. (2017) improved on previous work on quote and speaker attribution by providing a cleaned-up dataset, the QuoteLi3 corpus, which includes more annotations than the previous datasets. They also present a two-step deterministic sieve model for speaker attribution on the entity level and report a high precision for their approach[1]. This means that we can apply the rule-based sieve model to new text in order to generate more training data for the task at hand. The model, however, only works for English.

To be able to generate annotated data for languages other than English, we develop a pipeline for automatic annotation transfer. This enables us to exploit existing annotations created for English as well as the rule-based system of Muzny et al. (2017). In the paper, we test our approach by projecting the annotations from the English QuoteLi3 corpus to German parallel text. While German is not exactly a low-resourced language,[2] we would like to point out that (i) ML systems can always benefit from more training data, and (ii) that our

pipeline can be easily adapted to new languages.

In the next section, we present our approach to annotation transfer of quotes and speaker mentions based on an automatically created parallel corpus, with the aim of creating annotated resources for quote detection and speaker attribution for German literature.

3   Overview of the pipeline

Our pipeline makes use of well-known algorithms for sentence segmentation, sentence alignment and word alignment (figure 1). The entire pipeline is written in Python. Individual components are implemented as classes and integrated into the main class as sub-module imports. The modular architecture facilitates the integration of additional classes or class-methods inside the main class, the replacement of individual components as well as the integration of new languages and more sophisticated post-processing and transfer methods.

Sub-task specific outputs are flushed to file after each step in the pipeline. Thereby, the user is given the opportunity to modify the output at any stage of the process.

3.1   Sentence segmentation

Sentence segmentation is by no means a solved problem (see, e.g., Read et al. (2012) for a thorough evaluation of different segmentation tools). This is especially true when working with literary prose where embedded sentences inside of quotes pose a challenge for sentence boundary detection.

In our pipeline, we use the Stanford CoreNLP (Manning et al., 2014) which offers out-of-the-box tokenisation and sentence splitting. We selected CoreNLP because it offers support for many languages and is robust and easy to integrate. Once the input text is segmented into individual sentences, we need to align each source sentence to one or more sentences in the target text.

3.2   Sentence alignment

Sentence alignment is an active field of research in statistical machine translation (SMT). The task can be described as follows. Given a set of source language sentences and a set of target language sentences, assign corresponding sentences from both sets, where each sentence may be aligned with one sentence, more than one, or no sentence in the target text. It has been shown that one-to-one sentence alignments in literary texts

---

[1] When optimised for precision, the system obtains a score >95% on the development set from *Pride and Prejudice*.

[2] The DROC corpus (Krug et al., 2018) provides around 2000 manually annotated quotes and annotations for speakers and their mentions in 90 fragments from German literary prose.

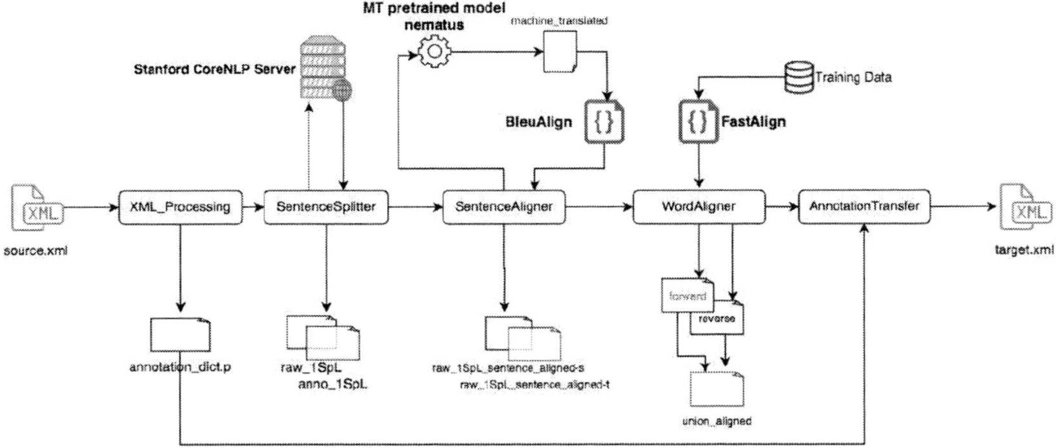

Figure 1: Overview of pipeline architecture and workflow

are less frequent than in other genres (Sennrich and Volk, 2010), and the alignments heavily depend on the lexical choices made by the translator. Even though Manning and Schütze (1999) suggest that, in general, around 90% of sentence alignments are 1:1 alignments, "sometimes translators break up or join sentences, yielding 1:2 or 2:1, and even 1:3 or 3:1 sentence alignments" (Manning and Schütze, 1999, p. 468). Sennrich and Volk (2010) manually align a set of 1000 sentences and report only 74% of 1:1 beads, showing that sentence alignments can vary considerably, depending on genre and text type.

While in early days sentence length - measured in tokens or characters - was used as an indicator for parallel text (Gale and Church, 1993a), more recent approaches often use length-based features in combination with lexical similarities for semi-supervised classifier training (Yu et al., 2012; Xu et al., 2015). Mújdricza-Maydt et al. (2013) model sentence alignment as a sequence labelling task and solve it using a CRF sequence classifier.

We use a different approach, proposed by Sennrich and Volk (2010), who first create an automatic translation of the source text, yielding aligned translations for each sentence in the original text. Then, they try to find matching sentences in the automatic translation of the source text and the human-translated target text based on sentence similarity according to the BLEU metric (Papineni et al., 2002).[3]

The alignment itself is based on the computed similarity scores and consists of a two-pass procedure. In the first step, the algorithm is looking for 1-to-1 alignments that maximize the BLEU score for the document, thereby respecting the monotonic order of the sentence pairs. Then, the sentences that remain unaligned are either forming 1:N alignments or are aligned based on a length-based algorithm. Sentences that cannot be aligned in the second pass are discarded.

While the majority of existing tools are not suitable for hard-to-align parallel texts such as literary prose (Sennrich and Volk, 2010, p.1), this approach showed good results on a corpus of historical texts, consisting of yearbooks of the Swiss Alpine Club from 1864-1982. We thus decided to integrate it in our pipeline.

Neural MT with Nematus For translating the source text into the target language, we use Nematus (Sennrich et al., 2017a,b), a neural encoder-decoder model with attention which is similar to Bahdanau et al. (2014).

An encoder (implemented as a bi-directional RNN) reads in word vectors (one vector for each word in a sentence) and generates an output vector of variable length from the sequence of hidden states. Subsequently, the decoder – another bi-directional RNN – learns which words in the source sentence are most relevant for generating a good translation. The model used in this work has been pre-trained with default parameters and configuration (subword segmentation, layer normalisation, a minibatch size of 80, a maximum sen-

---

[3]BLEU is a standard metric for MT evaluation, based on the overlap of word n-grams in the source and target texts.

tence length of 50 words, word embeddings with 500 dimensions and a hidden layer size of 1024).

Aligning MT and human translation The Bleualign algorithm is composed of two steps. In the first step, the algorithm tries to find a set of anchor points, using BLEU as a similarity score between the machine-translated source text and the human-translated target text. These anchor points are a set of 1:1 alignments considered reliable based on BLEU scores and sentence order.

In a second step, the sentences between these anchor points are either aligned using BLEU-based heuristics or the length-based algorithm of Gale and Church (1993b). The latter algorithm is applied to the target and translated source sentences and functions as a fallback for all gaps with a symmetrical size of unaligned sentences. Sentences that cannot be aligned are discarded.

We use default parameters for Bleualign (a maximum of 3 alternative BLEU-aligned sentences in the first run, a BLEU-scoring restriction on bigrams and second pass gap-filling by means of BLEU and the Gale and Church algorithm).

3.3 Word alignment

Once we have aligned the sentences in our parallel corpus, the next step is the alignment of words between the source and target sentences. We use fast_align (Dyer et al., 2013), a log-linear reparameterisation of IBM Model 2, the second of a set of well-known SMT alignment models developed by IBM in the late 1980s. Fast_align is unsupervised and thus applicable to any language for which training data is available. It outperforms the Giza++ implementation of the IBM Models 1-5 (Och and Ney, 2003) with regard to speed, translation quality (measured in BLEU score) and alignment error rate (Dyer et al., 2013). While the method has recently been outperformed by neural approaches (Legrand et al., 2016), its fast and efficient implementation and decent results make it well-suited for integration in our pipeline.

3.4 Annotation transfer

The final step in our pipeline is the transfer of annotations from the source to the target side. For the task at hand, we directly transfer the speaker and quote annotations based on the word alignments. We hypothesize that this simple and straightforward approach will be sufficient in our case where quotation marks are reliable anchor points for

	Emma	P & P	total
quotes	742	1,575	2,317
mentions	399	765	1,164
entities	49	32	81

Table 1: Annotations of quotes, speaker mentions and entities in the QuoteLi3 corpus (*Emma* and *Pride and Prejudice*).

word alignment. Speakers, on the other hand, are often referred to by proper names which, due to string similarity, will also show a high word alignment precision, and we also expect a higher-than-average precision for the alignment of referring noun phrases and personal pronouns.

In the next section, we test our approach and evaluate the individual components of our pipeline for annotation projection from English to German, based on the QuoteLi3 corpus.

4 Data

For English, the QuoteLi3 corpus (Muzny et al., 2017) provides manual annotations of speakers and quotes in three novels (*Emma* and *Pride and Prejudice* by Jane Austen and *The Steppe* by Anton Chekhov).[4] Since no publically available digital translation for the Chekhov novel was found, our evaluation will focus on the two Austen novels which include more than 2,300 annotations for quotes and more than 1,100 mentions for 81 speakers (table 1).

4.1 Impact of the literary translation

For many novels, not just one but a number of translations are available. We are thus confronted with the problem of having to choose one translation from a set of available texts, and it is not clear how to determine the most adequate translation for the task at hand.

Translation divergences are a known problem for MT (Dorr, 1994; Dorr et al., 2004). In parallel corpora of literary prose, however, divergences are even more prominent than in many other genres. A high-quality literary translation not only needs to transfer the semantic meaning of the source text into the target language but also has to consider stilistic devices such as metaphor, alliteration, hyperbole, oxymoron, simile and more that are difficult to translate. Therefore, the translator often has

---

[4]The corpus is available for download from `https://nlp.stanford.edu/muzny/quoteli.html`.

to diverge from the literal translation and resort to a freer phrasing that is more faithful to the underlying meaning or literary function of a certain text passage. This means that different translations of the same text can vary considerably, and the choice of translation for annotation projection might have a crucial impact on the quality of the outcome.

To investigate this issue, we use two different translations for the same novel, *Pride and Prejudice* (PP), in our experiments. The first one is by Karin von Schwab (PP_KS), the second is a translation by Helga Schulz (PP_HS). For *Emma*, a recent translation by Angelika Beck was chosen.

This allows us to evaluate how different translations of the same novel impact the quality of the output for different components in our pipeline.

4.2 Goldstandard

For evaluation, we created two goldstandards, including a total of 600 sentences (300 sentences for sentence alignment, another 300 sentences for word alignment). For each task, we selected 100 sentences from each of the translations (Emma, PP_HS, PP_KS). Sentence selection was not random but focussed on sentences including quotes and speaker mentions. This allowed us to reuse the goldstandard for evaluating the annotation transfer. As a result, sentence length in the goldstandard is slightly higher than the average sentence length in the corpus.[5]

4.3 Settings for evaluation

We compare two different settings in our experiments, (i) a *fully-automatic* setting and (ii) a *semi-automatic* setting. In the *fully-automatic* setting, the texts are extracted from the annotated XML files and directly fed into the pipeline, passing through sentence splitting, tokenisation, MT translation, sentence alignment, word alignment and annotation transfer without any intervention or correction by the user.

In the *semi-automatic* setting, the texts have been subject to a number of genre-dependent pre- and post-processing steps which are described below. These processing steps are adjusted to the text genre and translation specifics and probably need modification and further adaptation when transferred to other literary texts from potentially different domains.

Figure 2: Examples for missing merge in sentence alignment output.

P1: Sentence segmentation Before sentence segmentation, we automatically harmonised punctuation (e.g. " " " to ").

After segmentation, incorrectly split sentences were merged again, e.g. splits after short exclamations (*Oh! to be sure*) and after quotes (e.g. *"To be sure!" cried she playfully*). We merged the segmented parts with their preceding or subsequent sentence, based on regular expressions. We also harmonised punctuation (e.g. in the English version, commas are inside quotes while in the German translation, commas were put outside the quote: *"It is one thing," said she* vs. *"It is one thing", said she*). These task- and genre-specific processing steps could be done automatically, without manual effort.

P2: Sentence alignment In our experiments, we took empty lines in the output of the sentence aligner as a proxy for alignment errors and manually checked a total of 94 empty lines in the whole corpus[6]. This took – with support of a powerful editor and split screen functionality (Sublime) – less than one hour to complete. Most often, the missing merge was due to divergences in the translation - for example a varying use of punctuation (figure 2).

The impact of the *semi-automatic* pre- and post-processing steps on the quality of the different components in our pipeline are discussed below.

5 Evaluation

5.1 Sentence alignment

As the manual correction of the whole corpus is out of scope for this work, we report three different measures to assess the quality of the sentence alignment module:

1. Recall

2. Comparison against goldstandard

3. BLEU overlap with automatic translation

---

[5]The avg. sentence length in the goldstandard is 27.4 / 29.5 (Emma / PP), the avg. sentence length for the whole novel is 25.6 / 24.7 / 23.6 (Emma / PP_KS / PP_HS).

[6]Result are heavily dependent on sentence segmentation output, therefore we recommend to implement text- and genre-specific pre- and postprocessing steps for sentence segmentation optimisation.

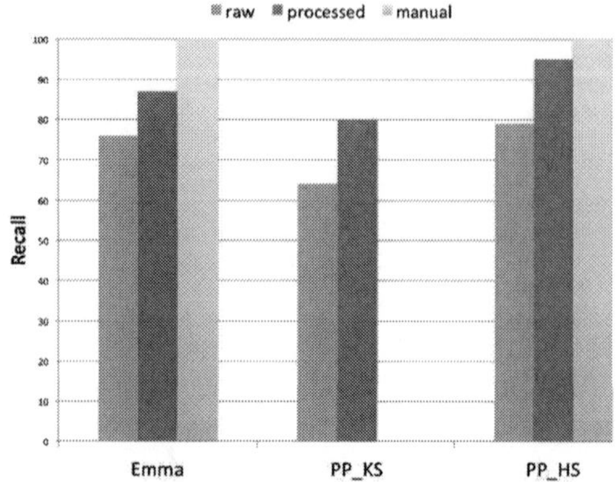

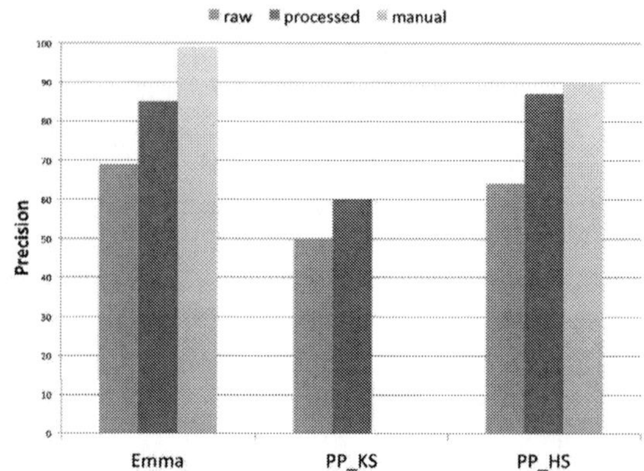

Figure 4: Recall (left) and precision (right) for sentence alignment for different settings (raw: no post-processing; processed: automatic pre-/post-processing; manual: resolution of null-aligned sentences) on the goldstandard.

Recall is computed as the total amount of source sentences in the corpus that have been aligned with (one or more) target sentences. Figure 3 shows that especially for the PP_KS translation, recall in the *fully-automatic* setting is low. However, preprocessing the sentence-segmented XML-input prior to sentence alignment (see P1) can increase recall from below 50% up to 90% and above. For the two other translations, preprocessing results in even higher recall (96% to 100%).

Our second evaluation reports precision and recall on the goldstandard (figure 4). Here we also evaluate the impact of the manual resolution of null-aligned sentences. Both precision and recall for the goldstandard testset increase after automatically pre/post-processing the data. Results show crucial improvements especially for the translation that is closer to the original text (PP_HS). This shows that the selection of the translation has a huge impact on the quality of annotation transfer for literary texts. We also showed that taking empty lines (null alignments) as an indica-

tor for alignment errors can reduce time requirements for manual correction considerably while yielding substantial improvements (precision and recall) for sentence alignment.

Our third evaluation measure reports the average BLEU (uni- to 4-gram) sentence similarity score between the machine-translated source sentences and their aligned target sentences from the human translations.[7] The automatic translation is expected to be much closer to the original novel than a professional human translation. We can thus take the similarity between the human translation and the *automatic* translation as a proxy for the closeness of the human translation to the *original* novel. We thus hypothesize that the translation of Pride and Prejudice that shows a higher average BLEU similarity to the automatically translated text will be more suitable for annotation projection than a translation with lower similarity scores.

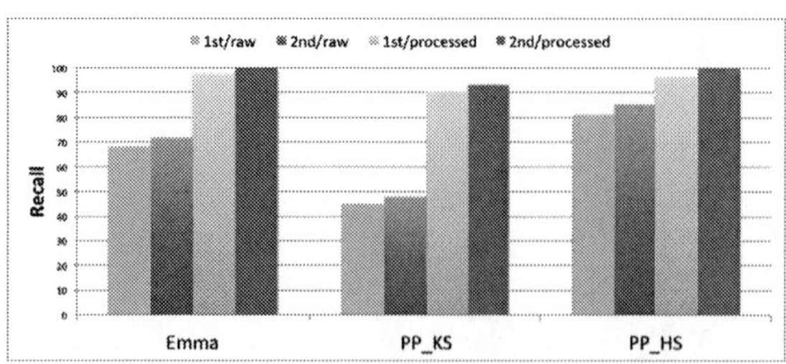

Figure 3: Recall for 1st and 2nd pass of sent. alignment for different settings on the whole corpus (raw: fully-automatic; processed: +automatic preprocessing (P1))

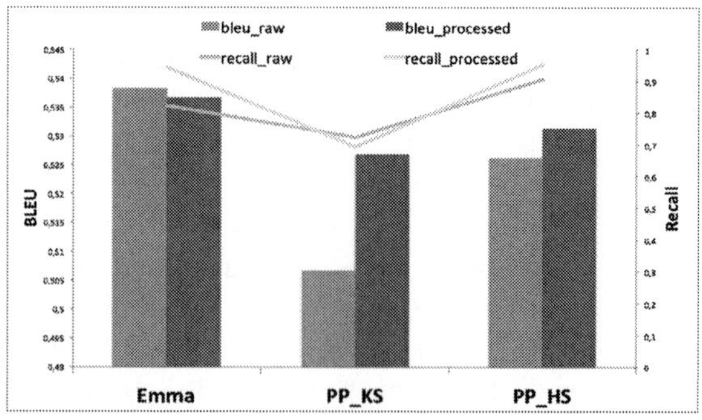

Figure 5: Avg. sentence BLEU score w.r.t source MT (w/wo processing/restricted to 1:1 alignments)

[7]The BLEU scores are calculated for those source sentences that are 1:1 aligned with a target sentence. Recall is thus relative to the amount of first-pass alignments.

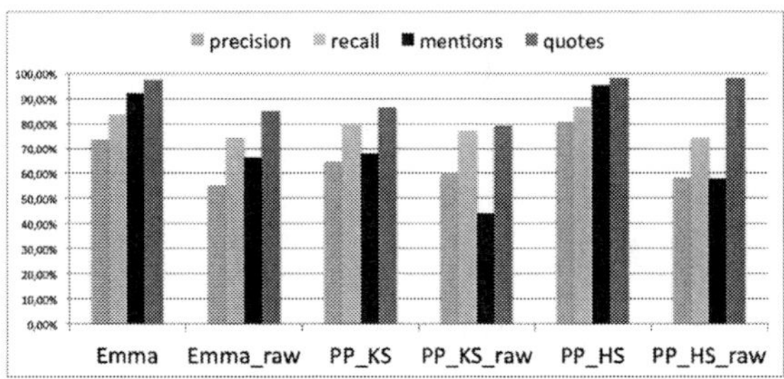

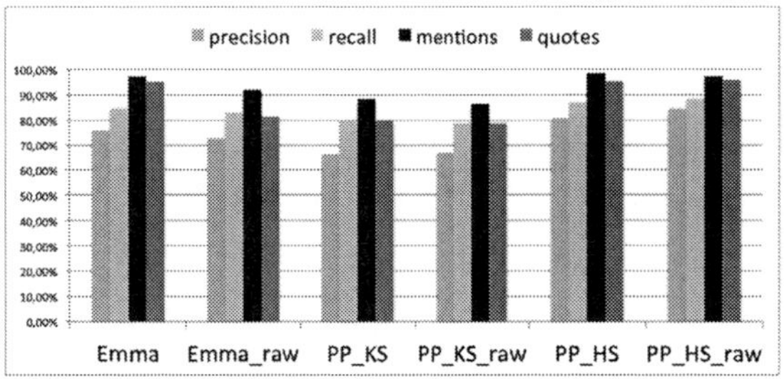

Figure 6: Word alignment evaluation (precision and recall) and precision for transfer of mentions/quotes (goldstandard: all sentences).

Figure 7: Word alignment evaluation (precision and recall) and precision for transfer of mentions/quotes (goldstandard: correctly aligned sentences only).

Figure 5 shows that BLEU similarity between PP_HS and the MT translation of the source text is much higher than for PP_KS. As expected, BLEU similarity corresponds to a higher recall for sentence alignment, showing that it is indeed a good measure for determining which translation (out of a set of candidate translations) should be chosen for high-quality annotation transfer.

For *Emma*, pre/post-processing did not further increase BLEU similarity, probably due to the already high similarity scores in the raw data. Surprising is the higher recall for PP_KS (raw) compared to the processed data. We can only suspect that due to the low similarity between source and target, alignment quality is low and thus recall on the raw data is unrealistically high and does not reflect the precision of the alignments.

5.2 Word alignment

Word alignment quality depends strongly on the quality of the sentence alignment output. Therefore, we report results for the *fully-automatic* and *semi-automatic* settings. We compare results for all sentences in the goldstandard (figure 6) with the ones we get when evaluating word alignments only on correctly aligned sentences (figure 7). In addition to precision and recall for word alignment (all words), we also report results for a task-based evaluation focussing on the projected annotations for speaker mentions and quotes.

Again, results are substantially higher for the *semi-automatic* setting, showing that our pre/post-processing can prevent error propagation from earlier components downstream. When looking only at those alignments that are relevant for annotation transfer of speaker mentions and quotes, we observe high precision in the nineties. This confirms our hypothesis that direct transfer based on

word alignments works well for our task.

As before, we observe significantly higher results for PP_HS, the translation that is closer to the original text than PP_KS. For the transfer of speaker mentions, this increases results from below 70% to around 95%, and for quotes we see an increase from around 87% (PP_KS) to over 98% (PP_HS). The high precision for quote alignments (especially for the *raw* texts) most probably is an artefact of the way quote alignments were evaluated. To count as a true positive, it suffices if the quotation marks are correctly word-aligned to a quotation mark in the source text. This can result in a false positive if the underlying sentences are misaligned, i.e. the quote is incorrectly aligned to a different quote of similar length. Therefore, we also evaluated word alignments on the smaller set of correctly aligned sentences in the goldstandard (figure 7), thus excluding false matches. Here we see a much smaller gap in precision between speaker mentions and quotes, and – naturally – a smaller gap between *fully-automatic* and *semi-automatic* which again emphasizes the importance of error correction in the first stages of the pipeline, especially for sentence alignment.

5.3 Error Analysis

Table 2 shows recall for annotation transfer on the whole dataset. While we observe only a small increase in recall between the *fully-automatic* and the *semi-automatic* setting, please keep in mind that the results do not consider the correctness of the transferred annotations and that recall for the whole dataset should be compared to precision and recall on the smaller goldstandard (figures 6, 7). Below, we present an analysis of the most frequent error types observed on the goldstandard.

Many errors are caused by translation diver-

			PP_KS (raw)	PP_KS (pr.)	PP_HS (raw)	PP_HS (pr.)	Emma (raw)	Emma (pr.)
Quotes found			92,6% (1551)	92,5% (1548)	99,0% (1657)	99,6% (1668)	93,2% (691)	98,8% (732)
of which	**1:1**		66,9% (1038)	69,4% (1074)	83,0% (1376)	87,5% (1459)	76,6% (529)	82,1% (601)
	1:N		23,7% (367)	23,6% (366)	10,4% (172)	9,3% (155)	14,9% (103)	13,5% (99)
	of which	Resolved	55,3% (203)	57,4% (210)	43,0% (74)	27,7% (43)	43,7% (45)	60,6% (60)
		Default	44,7% (164)	42,6% (156)	57,0% (98)	72,3% (112)	56,3% (58)	39,4% (39)
No Alignment			8,7% (146)	6,4% (108)	6,5% (109)	3,2% (54)	8,0% (59)	4,3% (32)
Mentions found			91,9% (751)	92,4% (755)	98,5% (805)	99,9% (816)	92,2% (367)	100 % (398)
of which	**1:1**		60,0% (451)	60,4% (456)	78,1% (629)	83,8% (684)	76,6% (281)	82,2% (327)
	1:N		22,8% (171)	22,6% (171)	13,0% (105)	10,7% (87)	14,7% (54)	15,8% (63)
	of which	resolved	31,0% (53)	31,0% (53)	34,3% (36)	36,8% (32)	50,0% (27)	52,4% (33)
		Default	69,0% (118)	69,0% (118)	65,7% (69)	63,2% (55)	50,0% (27)	47,6% (30)
No alignment			15,8% (129)	15,7% (128)	8,7% (71)	5,5% (45)	8,0% (32)	2,0% (8)

Table 2: Recall for annotation transfer for the whole corpus (raw: fully-automatic, pr.: semi-automatic setting).

gences (figure 8) where the sentence remains partly unaligned. In our example, the content of the English sentence was split into more than one sentence in the German translation. During sentence alignment, however, the German sentence was incorrectly aligned 1:1 to its English pendent. As a result, some of the content is missing, leading to poor word alignment. This type of error needs to be addressed during sentence alignment or in a post-precessing step before word alignment.

The high precision for annotation transfer can be partly explained by the high amount of 1:1 word alignments for speaker mentions and quotes, due to string equality between the word pairs in the source and target texts (e.g. proper names or pronouns for speaker mentions, see table 3).

n-gram	Emma	PP
unigram	254	528
bigram	126	229
trigram	15	7
4-gram	3	1

Table 3: N-gram statistics for mention words (raw frequencies) in the corpus.

A recurring pattern in our data is the incorrect co-alignment of target words to neighbouring tokens, resulting in 1:N word alignments (figure 9). These co-alignments pose a problem for our direct approach to annotation transfer but can be easily resolved using simple string-matching heuristics. As illustration, consider figure 9 where we can simply compare "Lydia" to both alignment candidates on the German side *{Lydia, wollte}* and so identify the correct projection site by string identity.

Unfortunately, this is not always an option. de Marneffe et al. (2009) show that the automatic resolution of multi-word alignments to the right target term is a hard problem and requires automatic recognition of multi-word expressions. For more complex projection tasks, we will thus need a more sophisticated alignment method, based on graph optimisation or machine learning. Previous work in the context of semantic role labelling has followed this approach, with promising results (Padó and Lapata, 2005, 2009; van der Plas et al., 2011; Kozhevnikov and Titov, 2013; Akbik et al., 2015; Akbik and Vollgraf, 2017; Aminian et al., 2017). We would like to explore this further in future work.

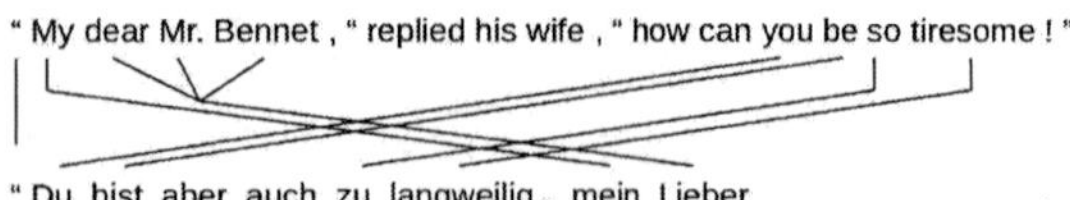

Figure 8: Transfer error caused by translation divergence (incorrect 1:1 sentence alignment).

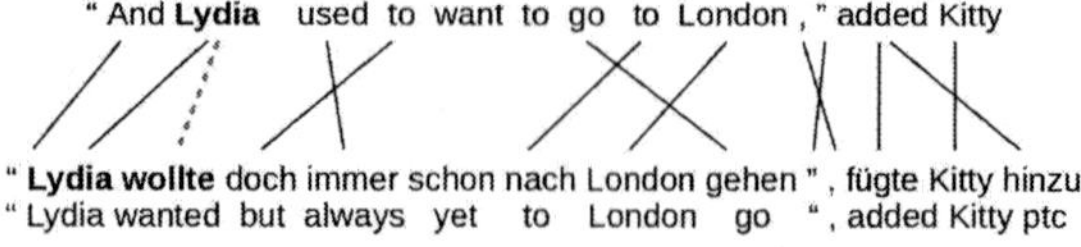

Figure 9: Transfer error caused by incorrect co-alignment.

6 Conclusions and future work

We have presented a modular NLP pipeline for annotation transfer in literary texts.[8] Our pipeline integrates freely available NLP tools into a modular toolkit that allows the user to run the whole pipeline in a fully automatic setting or to perform the different processing steps individually and apply post-processing to improve the quality of the output. The modularity of our toolkit also facilitates the adaptation of individual processing steps and the integration of new components as well as the adaptation to new languages.

Our pipeline can be used for annotation transfer and for the creation of large parallel corpora for computational literary studies, or to bootstrap additional in-domain training data to improve the precision of sentence and word alignment tools for literature.

We identified weak points and possible improvements that we would like to address in future work. One example is the integration of a module (or method) for automatic resolution of multi-word alignments after word alignment, or the resolution of null alignments after the sentence alignment step (for example by applying a translation-based sentence similarity measure). Another important issue for future work is to improve annotation projection by replacing the direct transfer based on word alignments with a more sophisticated method based on graph optimisation or ML.

Acknowledgments

This research has been partly conducted within the Leibniz Science Campus "Empirical Linguistics and Computational Modeling", funded by the Leibniz Association under grant no. SAS-2015-IDS-LWC and by the Ministry of Science, Research, and Art (MWK) of the state of Baden-Württemberg.

References

Apoorv Agarwal, Augusto Corvalan, Jacob Jensen, and Owen Rambow. 2012. Social network analysis of Alice in Wonderland. In *Workshop on Computational Linguistics for Literature*, CLfL 2012, pages 88–96.

Alan Akbik, Laura Chiticariu, Marina Danilevsky, Yunyao Li, Shivakumar Vaithyanathan, and Huaiyu Zhu. 2015. Generating high quality proposition banks for multilingual Semantic Role Labeling. In *The 53rd Annual Meeting of the Association for Computational Linguistics and the 7th International Joint Conference on Natural Language Processing of the Asian Federation of Natural Language Processing*, ACL 2015, pages 397–407.

Alan Akbik and Roland Vollgraf. 2017. The projector: An interactive annotation projection visualization tool. In *The 2017 Conference on Empirical Methods in Natural Language Processing*, EMNLP 2017, pages 43–48.

Mariana S. C. Almeida, Miguel B. Almeida, and André F. T. Martins. 2014. A joint model for quotation attribution and coreference resolution. In *Proceedings of the 14th Conference of the European Chapter of the Association for Computational Linguistics*, pages 39–48.

Maryam Aminian, Mohammad Sadegh Rasooli, and Mona T. Diab. 2017. Transferring semantic roles using translation and syntactic information. In *The 8th International Joint Conference on Natural Language Processing*, IJCNLP 2017, pages 13–19.

Dzmitry Bahdanau, Kyunghyun Cho, and Yoshua Bengio. 2014. Neural machine translation by jointly learning to align and translate. *CoRR*, abs/1409.0473.

Yejin Choi, Claire Cardie, Ellen Riloff, and Siddharth Patwardhan. 2005. Identifying sources of opinions with conditional random fields and extraction patterns. In *Human Language Technology Conference and Conference on Empirical Methods in Natural Language Processing*, HLT/EMNLP 2005, pages 355–362.

Bonnie Dorr, Necip Fazil Ayan, and Nizar Habash. 2004. Divergence unraveling for word alignment. *Natural Language Engineering*, 1(1):1–17.

Bonnie J. Dorr. 1994. Machine translation divergences: A formal description and proposed solution. *Computational Linguistics*, 20:597–633.

Chris Dyer, Victor Chahuneau, and Noah A. Smith. 2013. A simple, fast, and effective reparameterization of IBM model 2. In *The North American Chapter of the Association of Computational Linguistics*, NAACL 2013, pages 644–648.

David K. Elson, Nicholas Dames, and Kathleen R. McKeown. 2010. Extracting social networks from literary fiction. In *The 48th Annual Meeting of the Association for Computational Linguistics*, pages 138–147.

David K. Elson and Kathleen R. McKeown. 2010. Automatic attribution of quoted speech in literary narrative. In *The Twenty-Fourth AAAI Conference on Artificial Intelligence*, AAAI 2010.

[8]The software will be made available from `https://www.cl.uni-heidelberg.de/research/downloads/` (annot-transfer-lit).

Susanne Fertmann. 2016. Using speaker identification to improve coreference resolution in literary narratives. Master's thesis, Computational Linguistics.

William A. Gale and Kenneth Ward Church. 1993a. A program for aligning sentences in bilingual corpora. *Computational Linguistics*, 19(1):75–102.

William A. Gale and Kenneth Ward Church. 1993b. A program for aligning sentences in bilingual corpora. *Computational Linguistics*, 19(1):75–102.

Yulia Grishina and Manfred Stede. 2017. Multi-source projection of coreference chains: assessing strategies and testing opportunities. In *The 2nd Coreference Resolution Beyond OntoNotes Workshop*, CORBON-2017.

Hua He, Denilson Barbosa, and Grzegorz Kondrak. 2013. Identification of speakers in novels. In *The 51st Annual Meeting of the Association for Computational Linguistics*, ACL 2013, pages 1312–1320.

Richard Johansson and Alessandro Moschitti. 2013. Relational features in fine-grained opinion analysis. *Computational Linguistics*, 39(3):473–509.

Mikhail Kozhevnikov and Ivan Titov. 2013. Cross-lingual transfer of semantic role labeling models. In *The 51st Annual Meeting of the Association for Computational Linguistics*, ACL 2013, pages 1190–1200.

Ralf Krestel, Sabine Bergler, and René Witte. 2008. Minding the source: Automatic tagging of reported speech in newspaper articles. In *The International Conference on Language Resources and Evaluation*, LREC 2008.

Markus Krug, Frank Puppe, Isabella Reger, Lukas Weimer, Luisa Macharowsky, and Stephan Feldhaus. 2018. *Description of a Corpus of Character References in German Novels – DROC [Deutsches ROman Corpus]. DARIAH-DE Working Papers. Göttingen: DARIAH-DE.*

Dimitrios Kydros and Anastasios Anastasiadis. 2014. Social network analysis in literature. the case of The Great Eastern by A. Embirikos. In *5th European Congress of Modern Greek Studies*.

Joël Legrand, Michael Auli, and Ronan Collobert. 2016. Neural network-based word alignment through score aggregation. In *The First Conference on Machine Translation*, WMT 2016, pages 66–73.

Christopher D. Manning and Hinrich Schütze. 1999. *Foundations of Statistical Natural Language Processing.* Cambridge, MA, USA: MIT Press. Pp. 468.

Christopher D. Manning, Mihai Surdeanu, John Bauer, Jenny Rose Finkel, Steven Bethard, and David Mc-Closky. 2014. The Stanford CoreNLP Natural Language Processing Toolkit. In *The 52nd Annual Meeting of the Association for Computational Linguistics*, ACL 2014, pages 55–60.

Marie-Catherine de Marneffe, Sebastian Padó, and Christopher D. Manning. 2009. Multi-word expressions in textual inference: Much ado about nothing? In *The 2009 Workshop on Applied Textual Inference*, TextInfer 2009, pages 1–9.

Eva Mújdricza-Maydt, Huiqin Körkel-Qu, Stefan Riezler, and Sebastian Padó. 2013. High precision sentence alignment by bootstrapping from wood standard annotations. *Prague Bulletin of Mathematical Linguistics*, 99:5–16.

Grace Muzny, Angel X. Chang, Michael Fang, and Dan Jurafsky. 2017. A two-stage sieve approach for quote attribution. In *The 15th Conference of the European Chapter of the Association for Computational Linguistics*, EACL 2017, pages 460–470.

Franz Josef Och and Hermann Ney. 2003. A systematic comparison of various statistical alignment models. *Computational Linguistics*, 29(1):19–51.

Sebastian Padó and Mirella Lapata. 2005. Cross-lingual bootstrapping of semantic lexicons: The case of FrameNet. In *The National Conference on Artificial Intelligence*, pages 1087–1092.

Sebastian Padó and Mirella Lapata. 2009. Cross-lingual annotation projection for semantic roles. *Journal of Artificial Intelligence Research*, 36(1):307–340.

Kishore Papineni, Salim Roukos, Todd Ward, and Wei-Jing Zhu. 2002. BLEU: a method for automatic evaluation of machine translation. In *The 40th Annual Meeting of the Association for Computational Linguistics*, ACL-2002, pages 311–318.

Silvia Pareti. 2015. *Attribution: a computational approach.* Ph.D. thesis, University of Edinburgh, UK.

Silvia Pareti, Timothy O'Keefe, Ioannis Konstas, James R. Curran, and Irena Koprinska. 2013. Automatically detecting and attributing indirect quotations. In *The 2013 Conference on Empirical Methods in Natural Language Processing*, EMNLP 2013, pages 989–999.

Lonneke van der Plas, Paola Merlo, and James Henderson. 2011. Scaling up automatic cross-lingual semantic role annotation. In *The 49th Annual Meeting of the Association for Computational Linguistics: Human Language Technologies*, pages 299–304.

Bruno Pouliquen, Ralf Steinberger, and Clive Best. 2007. Automatic detection of quotations in multilingual news. In *The International Conference on Recent Advances in Natural Language Processing*, RANLP 2007, pages 487–492.

Jonathon Read, Rebecca Dridan, Stephan Oepen, and Lars Jørgen Solberg. 2012. Sentence boundary detection: A long solved problem? In *The 24th International Conference on Computational Linguistics*, COLING 2012, pages 985–994.

Jeff Rydberg-Cox. 2011. Social networks and the language of greek tragedy. *Journal of the Chicago Colloquium on Digital Humanities and Computer Science*, 1(3):1–11.

Christian Scheible, Roman Klinger, and Sebastian Padó. 2016. Model architectures for quotation detection. In *The 54th Annual Meeting of the Association for Computational Linguistics*, ACL 2016.

Rico Sennrich, Alexandra Birch, Anna Currey, Ulrich Germann, Barry Haddow, Kenneth Heafield, Antonio Valerio Miceli Barone, and Philip Williams. 2017a. The University of Edinburgh's neural MT systems for WMT17. In *The 2nd Conference on Machine Translation*, WMT 2017, pages 389–399.

Rico Sennrich, Orhan Firat, Kyunghyun Cho, Alexandra Birch, Barry Haddow, Julian Hitschler, Marcin Junczys-Dowmunt, Samuel Läubli, Antonio Valerio Miceli Barone, Jozef Mokry, and Maria Nadejde. 2017b. Nematus: a toolkit for neural machine translation. In *The 15th Conference of the European Chapter of the Association for Computational Linguistics (Software Demonstrations)*, EACL 2017, pages 65–68.

Rico Sennrich and Martin Volk. 2010. MT-based sentence alignment for OCR-generated parallel texts. In *The Ninth Conference of the Association for Machine Translation in the Americas*, AMTA 2010.

Michael Wiegand and Dietrich Klakow. 2012. Generalization methods for in-domain and cross-domain opinion holder extraction. In *The 13th Conference of the European Chapter of the Association for Computational Linguistics*, EACL 2012, pages 325–335.

Yong Xu, Max Aurélien, and Yvon Francois. 2015. Sentence alignment for literary texts – the state-of-the-art and beyond. *Linguistic Issues in Language Technology – LiLT*, 12(6).

Qian Yu, Max Aurélien, and Yvon Francois. 2012. Revisiting sentence alignment algorithms for alignment visualization and evaluation. In *The 5th Workshop on Building and Using Comparable Corpora*.

Inferring missing metadata from environmental policy texts

Steven Bethard, Egoitz Laparra, Sophia Wang, Yiyun Zhao
Ragheb Al-Ghezi, Aaron Lien, Laura López-Hoffman
University of Arizona
{bethard,laparra,rxnsp689,yiyunzhao,raghebalghezi,alien,lauralh}
@email.arizona.edu

Abstract

The National Environmental Policy Act (NEPA) provides a trove of data on how environmental policy decisions have been made in the United States over the last 50 years. Unfortunately, there is no central database for this information and it is too voluminous to assess manually. We describe our efforts to enable systematic research over US environmental policy by extracting and organizing metadata from the text of NEPA documents. Our contributions include collecting more than 40,000 NEPA-related documents, and evaluating rule-based baselines that establish the difficulty of three important tasks: identifying lead agencies, aligning document versions, and detecting reused text.

1 Introduction

Hurricanes inundating low-income neighborhoods. Air and noise pollution delaying learning in children. Raging wildfires displacing communities. These are *wicked problems* (Rittel and Webber, 1973) that span jurisdictions and disciplines; have multiple, complex causes; and undergo rapid change with high uncertainty. Solutions to such problems must integrate scientific information about causes, consequences, and uncertainties, with social and political information about public values, concerns, and needs.

In the United States, the National Environmental Policy Act (NEPA), passed by a near-unanimous US congress almost 50 years ago (91st Congress, 1970), is intended as a tool for such problems. NEPA is elegant in the simplicity of its vision: that science results in more informed decisions, and that a democratic process that engages the public results in better environmental and social outcomes. The heart of NEPA is the environmental impact statement (EIS), a detailed, scientific analysis of the expected impacts of federal actions (plans, projects, and activities) and an assessment of possible alternative actions. EISs are developed by the federal government with participation from the public in determining the scope and commenting on draft documents. Since 1970, some 37,000 EISs have analyzed the impacts of federal actions such as construction of transportation infrastructure; permit approvals for oil, gas, and mineral extraction; management of public lands; and proposed regulations.

Unfortunately, congress did not mandate the organized storage of the scientific data NEPA generates, nor the evaluation of its outcomes or of the public engagement processes it requires. There is no central database for this information and it is too voluminous to assess manually. As a result, scientists are able only to support decision-making about specific actions and to assess the outcomes only of specific projects. But systematic analysis across projects is stymied.

We describe a project that aims to enable such systematic research by using natural language processing (NLP) techniques to extract and organize metadata from the text of NEPA documents. Our main contributions are:

- Collecting a large set of environmental policy documents in need of NLP solutions.
- Implementing baseline NLP models for some of the high-priority text normalization tasks.
- Analyzing model performance and illustrating some of the remaining challenges.

2 Data collection

There is no single repository of NEPA documents, and each governmental department or agency chooses its own way to make the documents available to the public. We have thus begun a large-scale web-crawling effort to collect NEPA documents from across the many governmental websites. This means creating a custom scraping tool for each de-

Proc. of the 3rd Joint SIGHUM Workshop on Computational Linguistics for Cultural Heritage, Social Sciences, Humanities and Literature, pp. 46–51
Minneapolis, MN, USA, June 7, 2019. ©2019 Association for Computational Linguistics

Source of download	Documents
EPA	9238
DOI	13450
DOE	19484

Table 1: Documents collected so far from the different department or agency[1] websites.

		Document type	
		EIS	Other
	Draft	777	4305
Version type	Final	709	3055
	Other	3	40

Table 2: Breakdown of documents collected so far from the EPA. We could not recover version type or document type meta-data for 349 of the 9238 documents.

partment or agency, as none of the sites except for regulations.gov have any programmatic APIs. We have primarily focused on collecting EISs, but have also collected other related documents when they are available. Table 1 shows the progress of our collection efforts so far, and Table 2 shows a breakdown of just the epa.gov documents by whether the files are part of a draft or final version of an EIS.

Each EIS "document" downloaded from these sites is typically a zip archive many PDFs, with the different chapters and appendices of a each EIS broken out into separate PDFs. This is convenient for the distributing agency, but inconvenient for automated analysis. Since there is no standardized naming convention or organization, there is no simple way to automatically combine the various PDFs into a properly ordered single text for the entire EIS. Thus, in the analyses of the current paper, we often treat each PDF separately, but we acknowledge that future work will need a better solution to this PDF ordering and concatenation problem.

Most of the websites hosting these documents contain little or no metadata about them. Some critical metadata that is needed for all documents includes: Which governmental departments or agencies contributed to which documents? Which documents should be linked to each other (e.g., because one is a draft and one is a final version of the same EIS)? Which fine-grained locations (cities, mountains, rivers, etc.) are involved?

On 14 December 2018, NEPA.gov released a spreadsheet of additional metadata on 1161 EISs for which a a final EIS was published between Jan-

Agency	Count
USFS	276
BLM	128
FHWA	114
USACE	89
NPS	77

Table 3: Distribution of EISs for the top 5 agencies (out of 51 agencies and 1161 EISs in the data), according to the metadata released by NEPA on 14 Dec 2018.

uary 1, 2010, and December 31, 2017. This spreadsheet contains several useful things: a canonical title, the dates of all the versions of the EIS, and the lead department and agency for the EIS. Table 3 shows the number of EISs for each of the top agencies in this spreadsheet. Note that the spreadsheet does not link directly to any PDF documents, so work is required to match the metadata to the documents it is describing. Nonetheless, the spreadsheet provides an initial set of annotations that can enable NLP analysis of NEPA documents.

3   Challenge: Identifying lead agencies

A simple but critical piece of metadata needed for analyzing EISs is which governmental agency led the development of the EIS. US agencies are organized in a hierarchy, where, for example, the Forest Service (USFS) and the Animal and Plant Health Inspection Service (APHIS) are under the Department of Agriculture (USDA). Documents usually identify their lead agency in the first few pages, but how they do this varies widely from document to document. For instance, the leading agency may be identified by a logo, as text on the title page, on a later page with "leading agency" nearby, etc.

Note that the task of identifying lead agencies differs from the classic NLP task of named entity recognition in two important ways: not all organizations mentioned in a document are the lead agency (most organizations are not), and agency names must also be standardized (i.e., it is an *entity-linking* problem Shen et al., 2015).

3.1   Baseline model

To judge how sophisticated of an NLP system would be necessary for this task, we first applied a simple rule-based baseline. First, all phrases in the first 15 pages of the document that exactly match a department or agency name[1] were identified and sorted by their position in the document. Any agency in the sorted list that was followed by one of its children (according to the agency hierarchy) was discarded. The first name in the sorted, filtered list was then predicted as the lead agency. For an EIS "document" that consisted of multiple PDFs, we applied this rule-based model to each of the PDFs, and selected the most frequently predicted agency. If there was a tie, the rule-based model predicted no lead agency for this EIS.

We evaluated the performance of this baseline on 107 project folders (730 files), achieving an accuracy of 86%.

3.2 Remaining challenges

This baseline fails when the lead agency does not appear as the earliest agency in the majority of the PDFs representing the EIS "document". For example, in a document where *National Marine Fisheries Service* was specifically indicated as the leading agency, the model incorrectly predicted *National Oceanic and Atmospheric Administration* because it occurred earlier in the text where an National Oceanic and Atmospheric Administration Award was mentioned. As another example, the model correctly found the lead agency in the main PDF of one EIS, but supplementary documents of that EIS never mentioned the correct lead agency, and instead mentioned a few other agencies, so the final prediction after voting was incorrect.

In the future, we expect to achieve better performance on this task by training a machine learning classifier that considers the context of each candidate for useful trigger words like *lead* and *award*.

4 Challenge: Aligning document versions

Understanding an EIS means understanding the process of its creation, from draft EIS, through the public comment period, and on to the final EIS. Sometimes draft and final versions of an EIS are explicitly linked together on the governmental agency's website, but most of the time the documents are delivered separately, with no metadata explicitly linking them.

4.1 Baseline model

We applied a few simple rule-based baselines to establish how difficult of a task it would be to link

Matching model	Precision	Recall
TITLE	1.000	0.403
DATE+AGENCY+STATE	1.000	0.516
TITLE|DATE+AGENCY+STATE	1.000	0.674

Table 4: Performance of baseline models on matching draft and final versions of the same EIS in 1161 EISs in the 14 December 2018 metadata release.

draft and final versions of an EIS. The first baseline, TITLE, only matches a draft document with a final document when they have exactly the same title. The second baseline, DATE+AGENCY+STATE, uses the 14 December 2018 metadata release to establish how much additional metadata beyond the title would help. It takes a metadata entry, which gives a draft EIS date, a final EIS date, an agency, and a state, and finds all (draft, final) document pairs that are consistent with that entry. The final baseline, TITLE|DATE+AGENCY+STATE performs both of the above matching strategies.

If any of the above baselines would have matched more than two documents (one draft and one final), we marked such a prediction as incorrect. We applied this restriction because there should be only two versions of each document, draft and final, so finding more than two suggests that we were finding versions from more than one EIS.[2]

Table 4 shows the performance of these baselines on the 1161 EISs in the 14 December 2018 metadata release. Though all the baselines are highly precise, even the baseline that uses the manually curated metadata is unable to find a draft and final version of the EIS for more than 30% of the EISs in the metadata release.

4.2 Remaining challenges

The baselines fail when there is no exact match between the titles; when any of the information of date, state or agency is imprecise; or when multiple projects occur with the same date, state and leading agency. We found that unmatched titles may differ in only tiny ways (e.g., spelling errors) or in major ways (e.g., major reprhrasing). For example, in one project, the only difference was that the word *mccone* in the title was misspelled as *mccore*, whereas in another project, the title *entry control*

---

[1] The full hierarchy of department and agency acronyms is at https://www.loc.gov/rr/news/fedgov.html

[2] As we have further explored the data, it appears that there are occiasionally more than two versions of the same EIS (e.g., some have a *supplemental draft* version). We are thus in the process of manually annotating sets of similar titles allowing for more than two possible drafts.

reconfiguration area at wright-patterson air force base, ohio was changed to *base perimeter fence relocation in area a fairborn oh.* There are also agency/date/state metadata errors. For example, in one project, the agency is sometimes labeled as *NGB* but sometimes labeled as *DOD*.

It's also worth noting that the baselines that include dates are more oracles than baselines, since they assume that there is a metadata entry somewhere that gives draft and final dates of a single EIS. Such information is unavailable outside of the 1161 entries manually curated by NEPA.gov.

In the future, we expect to achieve better performance on this task by applying techniques that are more robust to word variations, such as measuring title similarity through cosines over word TF-IDF vectors, or more modern approaches like the Universal Sentence Encoder (Cer et al., 2018).

5 Challenge: Detecting reused text

An important research question about NEPA is the degree to which public comments result in changes to the proposed actions. One way of measuring such changes is to look at how much an EIS changes between its draft (pre-comments) version and its final (post-comments) version.

5.1 Baseline model

We apply the baseline from the PAN Plagiarism Detection shared task (Potthast et al., 2012), which partitions texts into 50-character chunks after ignoring non-alphanumeric characters and spaces. Then, it intersects the set of source chunks with the set of target chunks to determine the overlapping text between them. This baseline is representative of the other approaches to that task, which vary primarily on the size of chunks selected and under what conditions chunks were merged. We selected this baseline because it is more conservative, suggesting only very confident matches. We applied this model to 37 draft/final document pairs that we curated from 10 EIS "documents" (138 PDF files), where we, for example, manually confirmed that the draft file `SEP-HCP Draft EIS 10-10-2014` corresponded to the final file `SEP-HCP Final EIS 11-18-15 w app`.

For each draft/final pair, we calculated a DRAFT-REUSE score: the fraction of the text in the final version that was identified as being reused from the text in the draft version. Figure 1 plots the histogram of DRAFT-REUSE scores. The majority

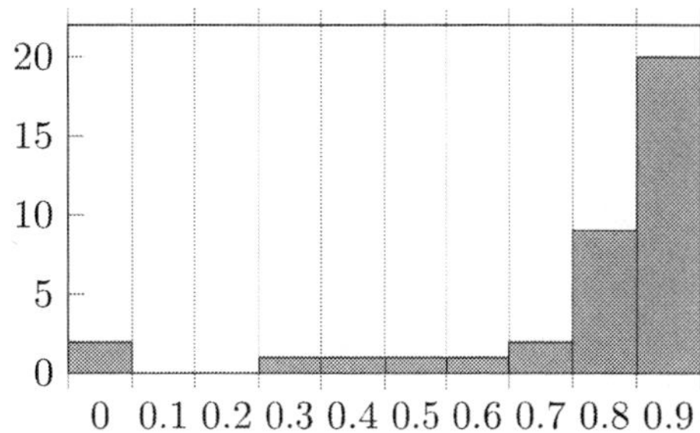

Figure 1: Distribution of EIS DRAFT-REUSE scores in a sample of 37 draft/final document pairs.

of final documents in our sample reused 90% or more of the text from their draft versions. That is, in most cases, less than 10% of the document changed as a result of the public comments.

5.2 Remaining challenges

The baseline model fails when text is reused with many small changes, and when there are failures in the PDF-to-text process. An example of many small changes is that the word *Draft* typically gets globally replaced with *Final*, so many near-copy-pastes are not detected since they mismatch at each point where *Draft* was previously in the text. An example of PDF-to-text failures is `ACP SHP FEIS Volume II part 3` and `ACP SHP DEIS Volume II part 3`, where the DRAFT-REUSE score was only 0.5 because the volumes are primarily diagrams and images, and even captions that should match do not because the PDF-to-text process produces many partial or weirdly segmented words when they are in captions.

In the future, we expect to achieve better performance on this task by incorporating some of the merging rules applied by the other systems in the PAN Plagiarism Detection shared task (Potthast et al., 2012). But we will first need to acquire at least a small set of examples where NEPA experts have annotated snippets of document reuse. This will allow us to fairly evaluate the performance of different models.

6 Related Work

There have been some previous projects that gathered, organized and extracted metadata from collections of political and social science documents, such as newswire sources (Sönmez et al., 2016) or historical archives (Zervanou et al., 2011). However, to the best of our knowledge, ours is the first project to consider the large number of environmental policy documents produced within the NEPA framework. Our project is also the first to look at extracting metadata fields specific to such documents, such as the lead federal agency. Though there is some relation between extracting lead agencies and extracting other organizational information like affiliations (Jonnalagadda and Topham, 2010) or science funding bodies (Kayal et al., 2017), the different role that lead agencies play in drafting environmental policy documents yields a different information extraction problem.

There is some prior work on automatically analyzing edits between document versions. Some have focused on classifying edits in Wikipedia articles (Bronner and Monz, 2012; Daxenberger and Gurevych, 2013), and Goyal et al. (2017) measured the importance of different kinds of changes between versions of news articles. The EIS documents we analyze have a very different semantics to their versioning. The NEPA process specifies that a public comment period must come between the draft and final EIS, and it is expected that the changes between versions will address issues raised during this period. Thus, our data yields a unique possibility of investigating how external comments influence document versions.

7 Discussion

We have presented our first steps toward extracting and organizing metadata from the texts of environmental policy documents produced under the National Environmental Policy Act (NEPA). We believe this data presents an interesting and challenging opportunity for the NLP community to support research on environmental policy. The current work has established baselines for three important tasks (identifying lead agencies, aligning document versions, and detecting reused text) and our analysis of the places where the baselines have failed should make an excellent starting point for the application of modern NLP techniques (e.g., deep learning models) to solve these challenges.

It is an explicit goal of our project to make avaialble for future research all documents we have collected and all metadata we have inferred. As all documents are generated and publicly released by the United States government, there are no copyright issues in providing access to such a collection. We are currently in the process of setting up a server and designing an application programming interface (API) to provide access to researchers and other interested parties. The server and API will be hosted at `http://nepaccess.org/`.

8 Acknowledgments

This material is based upon work supported by the National Science Foundation under Grant No. (1831551). Any opinions, findings, and conclusions or recommendations expressed in this material are those of the author(s) and do not necessarily reflect the views of the National Science Foundation.

References

Amit Bronner and Christof Monz. 2012. User edits classification using document revision histories. In *Proceedings of the 13th Conference of the European Chapter of the Association for Computational Linguistics*, pages 356–366. Association for Computational Linguistics.

Daniel Cer, Yinfei Yang, Sheng-yi Kong, Nan Hua, Nicole Limtiaco, Rhomni St. John, Noah Constant, Mario Guajardo-Cespedes, Steve Yuan, Chris Tar, Brian Strope, and Ray Kurzweil. 2018. Universal sentence encoder for english. In *Proceedings of the 2018 Conference on Empirical Methods in Natural Language Processing: System Demonstrations*, pages 169–174, Brussels, Belgium. Association for Computational Linguistics.

91st Congress. 1970. An act to establish a national policy for the environment; to authorize studies, surveys, and research relating to ecological systems, natural resources, and the quality of the human environment; and to establish a board of environmental quality advisers. Public Law 91-190. 83 Stat. 852.

Johannes Daxenberger and Iryna Gurevych. 2013. Automatically classifying edit categories in wikipedia revisions. In *Proceedings of the 2013 Conference on Empirical Methods in Natural Language Processing*, pages 578–589. Association for Computational Linguistics.

Tanya Goyal, Sachin Kelkar, Manas Agarwal, and Jeenu Grover. 2017. An empirical analysis of edit importance between document versions. In *Proceedings of the 2017 Conference on Empirical Methods in Natural Language Processing*, pages 2780–2784. Association for Computational Linguistics.

S. R. Jonnalagadda and P. Topham. 2010. NEMO: Extraction and normalization of organization names from PubMed affiliations. *J Biomed Discov Collab*, 5:50–75.

Subhradeep Kayal, Zubair Afzal, George Tsatsaronis, Sophia Katrenko, Pascal Coupet, Marius Doornenbal, and Michelle Gregory. 2017. Tagging funding agencies and grants in scientific articles using sequential learning models. In *BioNLP 2017*, pages 216–221. Association for Computational Linguistics.

Martin Potthast, Tim Gollub, Matthias Hagen, Jan Graßlegger, Johannes Kiesel, Maximilian Michel, Arnd Oberländer, Martin Tippmann, Alberto Barrón-Cedeõ, Parth Gupta, Paolo Rosso, and Benno Stein. 2012. Overview of the 4th international competition on plagiarism detection. In *CLEF2012 Working Notes*.

Horst W. J. Rittel and Melvin M. Webber. 1973. Dilemmas in a general theory of planning. *Policy Sciences*, 4(2):155–169.

W. Shen, J. Wang, and J. Han. 2015. Entity linking with a knowledge base: Issues, techniques, and solutions. *IEEE Transactions on Knowledge and Data Engineering*, 27(2):443–460.

Çağıl Sönmez, Arzucan Özgür, and Erdem Yörük. 2016. Towards building a political protest database to explain changes in the welfare state. In *Proceedings of the 10th SIGHUM Workshop on Language Technology for Cultural Heritage, Social Sciences, and Humanities*, pages 106–110. Association for Computational Linguistics.

Kalliopi Zervanou, Ioannis Korkontzelos, Antal van den Bosch, and Sophia Ananiadou. 2011. Enrichment and structuring of archival description metadata. In *Proceedings of the 5th ACL-HLT Workshop on Language Technology for Cultural Heritage, Social Sciences, and Humanities*, pages 44–53. Association for Computational Linguistics.

Stylometric Classification of Ancient Greek Literary Texts by Genre

Efthimios Tim Gianitsos
Department of Computer Science
University of Texas at Austin

Thomas J. Bolt
Department of Classics
University of Texas at Austin

Pramit Chaudhuri
Department of Classics
University of Texas at Austin

Joseph P. Dexter
Neukom Institute for Computational Science
Dartmouth College

Abstract

Classification of texts by genre is an important application of natural language processing to literary corpora but remains understudied for premodern and non-English traditions. We develop a stylometric feature set for ancient Greek that enables identification of texts as prose or verse. The set contains over 20 primarily syntactic features, which are calculated according to custom, language-specific heuristics. Using these features, we classify almost all surviving classical Greek literature as prose or verse with >97% accuracy and F1 score, and further classify a selection of the verse texts into the traditional genres of epic and drama.

1 Introduction

Classification of large corpora of documents into coherent groups is an important application of natural language processing. Research on document organization has led to a variety of successful methods for automatic genre classification (Stamatatos et al., 2000; Santini, 2007). Computational analysis of genre has most often involved material from a single source (e.g., a newspaper corpus, for which the goal is to distinguish between news articles and opinion pieces) or from standard, well-curated test corpora that contain primarily non-literary texts (e.g., the Brown corpus or equivalents in other languages) (Kessler et al., 1997; Petrenz and Webber, 2011; Amasyali and Diri, 2006).

Notions of genre are also of substantial importance to the study of literature. For instance, examination of the distinctive characteristics of various forms of poetry dates to classical Greece and Rome (for instance, by Aristotle and Quintilian) and remains an active area of humanistic research today (Frow, 2015). A number of computational analyses of literary genre have been reported, using both English and non-English corpora such as classical Malay poetry, German novels, and Arabic religious texts (Tizhoosh et al., 2008; Kumar and Minz, 2014; Jamal et al., 2012; Hettinger et al., 2015; Al-Yahya, 2018). However, computational prediction of even relatively coarse generic distinctions (such as between prose and poetry) remains unexplored for classical Greek literature.

Encompassing the epic poems of Homer, the tragedies of Aeschylus, Sophocles, and Euripides, the historical writings of Herodotus, and the philosophy of Plato and Aristotle, the surviving literature of ancient Greece is foundational for the Western literary tradition. Here we report a computational analysis of genre involving the whole of the classical Greek literary tradition. Using a custom set of language-specific stylometric features, we classify texts as prose or verse and, for the verse texts, as epic or drama with >97% accuracy. An important advantage of our approach is that all of the features can be computed without syntactic parsing, which remains in an early phase of development for ancient Greek. As such, our work illustrates how computational modeling of literary texts, where research has concentrated overwhelmingly on modern English literature (Elson et al., 2010; Elsner, 2012; Bamman et al., 2014; Chaturvedi et al., 2016; Wilkens, 2016), can be extended to premodern, non-Anglophone traditions.

2 Stylometric feature set for ancient Greek

The feature set is composed of 23 features covering four broad grammatical and syntactical categories. The majority of the features are function or non-content words, such as pronouns and syntactical markers; a minority concern rhetorical functions, such as questions and uses of superla-

Proc. of the 3rd Joint SIGHUM Workshop on Computational Linguistics for Cultural Heritage, Social Sciences, Humanities and Literature, pp. 52–60
Minneapolis, MN, USA, June 7, 2019. ©2019 Association for Computational Linguistics

	Feature
	Pronouns and non-content adjectives
1	ἄλλος
2	αὐτός
3	demonstrative pronouns
4	selected indefinite pronouns
5	personal pronouns
6	reflexive pronouns
	Conjunctions and particles
7	conjunctions
8	μέν
9	particles
	Subordinate clauses
10	circumstantial markers
11	conditional markers
12	ἵνα
13	ὅπως
14	sentences with relative pronouns
15	temporal and causal markers
16	ὥστε not preceded by ἤ
17	mean length of relative clauses
	Miscellaneous
18	interrogative sentences
19	superlatives
20	sentences with ὤ exclamations
21	ὡς
22	mean sentence length
23	variance of sentence length

Table 1: Full set of ancient Greek stylometric features.

Feature	Genre	Precision	Recall
4	verse	0.96	0.96
4	prose	0.97	1
10	verse	1	0.93
10	prose	1	1
14	verse	0.97	0.96
14	prose	1	1
19	verse	1	0.89
19	prose	1	1
20	verse	1	0.85
20	prose	1	1

Table 2: Error analysis of non-exact features. The features are numbered as in Table 1.

tive adjectives and adverbs. Function words are standard features in stylometric research on English (Stamatatos, 2009; Hughes et al., 2012) and have also been used in studies of ancient Greek literature (Gorman and Gorman, 2016). Our feature selection is not drawn from a prior source but has been devised based on three criteria: amenability to exact or approximate calculation without use of syntactic parsing, substantial applicability to the corpus, and diversity of function. The feature set is listed in Table 1. The first restriction is necessary because a general-purpose syntactic parser remains to be developed for classical Greek (notwithstanding promising early-stage research through the open-source Classical Language Toolkit and other projects). All features are per-character frequencies with the exception of a handful that are normalized by sentence (indicated in the table by "sentences with...").

Although some features overlap with those used in standard studies of English stylistics, such as pronouns, others are specific to ancient Greek. Attention to language-specific features enhances stylometric methods developed for the English language and not directly transferable to languages possessing a different structure (Rybicki and Eder, 2011; Kestemont, 2014). Greek particles, for example, are uninflected adverbs used for a wide range of logical and emotional expressions; in English their equivalent meaning is often expressed by a phrase or, in speech, tone. In order to avoid significant problems arising from dialectical variation, including a large increase in homonyms, we restrict features to the Attic dialect, in which the majority of classical Greek texts were composed. Many features are computed by counting all inflected forms of the appropriate word(s), which can be found in any standard ancient Greek textbook or grammar such as Smyth (1956). A detailed description of the methods for computing the features is given in Appendix A.

Calculation of five features relies on heuristics to disambiguate between words of similar morphology. (All other features can be calculated exactly.) To assess the effectiveness of these heuristics, we hand-annotate the five features in a representative sub-corpus containing three verse (Homer's *Odyssey* 6, Quintus of Smyrna's *Posthomerica* 12, and Euripides' *Cyclops*) and two prose (Lysias 7 and Plutarch's *Caius Gracchus*) texts. Table 2 lists the precision and recall of each feature on the aggregated verse and prose texts. In every instance, the precision is > 0.95 and the recall is > 0.85.

3 Experimental setup

3.1 Dataset

We use a corpus of ancient Greek text files, which was assembled by the Perseus Digital Library and further processed by Tesserae Project (Crane, 1996; Coffee et al., 2012). A full list of texts is provided in Appendix B. Each file typically contains either an entire work of literature (e.g., a play or a short philosophical treatise) or one book of a longer work (e.g., Book 1 of Homer's *Iliad*). 29 files are composites of multiple books included elsewhere in the Tesserae corpus and are omitted from our analysis, leaving 751 files. In total, this corpus contains essentially all surviving classical Greek literature and spans from the 8th century BCE to the 6th century CE.

For our first experiment, we hand-annotate the full set of texts as prose (610 files) or verse (141 files) according to standard conventions (Appendix B). For the second experiment, we hand-annotate the verse texts as epic (82 files) and drama (45 files), setting aside 14 files that contain poems of other genres (Appendix C).

3.2 Feature extraction

All text processing is done using Python 3.6.5. We first tokenize the files from the Tesserae corpus into either words or sentences using the Natural Language Toolkit (NLTK; v. 3.3.0) (Bird et al., 2009). For sentence tokenization, we use the PunktSentenceTokenizer class of NLTK Greek (Kiss and Strunk, 2006). After tokenization, the features are calculated either by tabulating instances of signal n-grams or (for length-based features) counting characters exclusive of whitespace, as described in Appendix A.

3.3 Supervised learning

All supervised learning is done using Python 3.6.5. For each experiment, we use the scikit-learn (v. 0.19.2) implementation of the random forest classifier. A full list of hyperparameters and other settings is given in Appendix D. For each binary classification experiment (prose vs. verse and epic vs. drama), we perform 400 trials of stratified 5-fold cross-validation; each trial has a unique combination of two random seeds, one used to initialize the classifier and the other to initialize the data splitter. Feature rankings are determined by the average Gini importance across the 400 trials.

	Accuracy (%)	Weighted F1 (%)
Fold 1	98.0	98.0
Fold 2	100	100
Fold 3	99.3	99.3
Fold 4	98.7	98.7
Fold 5	100	100
Mean	99.2	99.2
S.D.	1.9	1.9
Overall	98.9	98.9
S.D.	0.8	0.8

Table 3: Performance of prose vs. verse classifier for ancient Greek literary texts.

Feature	Gini	S.D.
αὐτός	0.209	0.074
conjunctions	0.159	0.062
demonstrative pronouns	0.121	0.057
reflexive pronouns	0.118	0.049
μέν	0.0623	0.029

Table 4: Feature rankings for prose vs. verse classifier.

4 Results

4.1 Prose vs. verse classification

Using the workflow described in Section 3.3, we classify each of the literary texts in the corpus as prose or verse. Table 3 lists the accuracy and weighted F1 score for a sample cross-validation trial, along with the mean for that trial and overall mean across the 400 trials. We find that the texts can be classified as prose or verse with extremely high accuracy using the set of 23 stylometric features and that, despite the small size of the corpus, classifier performance is robust to the choice of cross-validation partition. The five highest-ranked features are given in Table 4. Outside of these five, no other feature has a Gini importance of > 0.05. All five features predominate in prose rather than poetry, of which three are pronouns or pronominal adjectives. The sustained discussions commonly found in various prose genres may favor the use of pronouns to avoid extensive repetition of nouns and proper names. The high ranking of conjunctions is plausibly connected to the longer sentences characteristic of most prose (mean length 205 characters, compared to 166 characters for poetry).

	Accuracy (%)	**Weighted F1 (%)**
Fold 1	92.3	92.0
Fold 2	100	100
Fold 3	100	100
Fold 4	100	100
Fold 5	100	100
Mean	98.5	98.4
S.D.	3.4	3.6
Overall	99.8	99.8
S.D.	0.9	0.9

Table 5: Performance of epic vs. drama classifier for ancient Greek poetry.

Feature	**Gini**	**S.D.**
mean sentence length	0.186	0.12
demonstrative pronouns	0.155	0.095
interrogative sentences	0.127	0.12
ὡς	0.117	0.11
variance of sentence length	0.0952	0.075

Table 6: Feature rankings for epic vs. drama classifier.

4.2 Classification of poems as epic or drama

The genres of epic and drama are in certain respects quite distinct: they differ in length and poetic meter, and the vocabulary of Aristophanes' comic plays is unlike either epic or tragedy. In other aspects of form and content, however, they have much in common, including passages of direct speech, high register diction, and mythological subject matter. The playwright Aeschylus is even reported to have described his tragedies as "slices from the great banquets of Homer" (Athenaeus, *Deipnosophistae* 8.347E). The similarities between epic and drama thus present an intuitively greater challenge for classification.

Table 5 summarizes the results of the epic vs. drama experiment, for which we achieve performance comparable to that of the prose vs. verse experiment. Table 6 lists the top features, which reflect several important differences between the genres. The most important feature - sentence length - highlights the relatively shorter sentences of drama compared to epic, which can be explained at least in part by the rapid exchanges between speakers that occur throughout both tragedy and comedy. Although sentence length is a feature that can be affected by modern editorial practice, the difference between drama and epic on this score is sufficiently large that it cannot be explained by variations in editorial practice alone ($<$ 80 characters/sentence on average across dramatic texts, $>$ 150 characters/sentence for epic). The importance of demonstrative pronouns, ranked second, plausibly captures a different side of drama - the habit of characters referring, often indexically, to persons or objects in the plot (e.g., ἐκεῖνος οὗτός εἰμι, ekeinos houtos eimi, "I am that very man," Euripides, *Cyclops* 105, which uses two

demonstrative pronouns in succession). Another typical characteristic of dramatic plot and dialogue accounts for the third highly-ranked feature - interrogative sentences - since both tragedies and comedies often show characters in a state of uncertainty or ignorance, or making inquiries of other characters. Although many of the features in the full set are correlated (e.g., sentence length and various markers of subordinate clauses), none of the top 5 plausibly are, suggesting that the analysis identifies a diverse set of stylistic markers for epic and drama.

4.3 Misclassifications

For epic vs. drama, no text is misclassified in more than 12% of the trials. For prose vs. verse, only five texts are misclassified in $>50\%$ of the trials (Demades, *On the Twelve Years*; Dionysius of Halicarnassus, *De Antiquis Oratoribus Reliquiae* 2; Plato, *Epistle* 1; Aristotle, *Virtues and Vices*; Sophocles, *Ichneutae*). Most of the common misclassifications result from highly fragmentary or short texts. Almost half the speech of Demades, for example, contains short or incomplete sentences. The misclassified text of Dionysius of Halicarnassus amounts to only a few unconnected sentences; Sophocles' *Ichneutae* (the only verse text misclassified in over half the trials) is also fragmentary. The third most frequently misclassified text, Plato's *First Epistle*, in fact highlights the classifier's effectiveness, as it contains several verse quotations, which (given the short length of the text) plausibly account for the error.

5 Conclusion

In this paper, we demonstrate that ancient Greek literature can be classified by genre using a straightforward supervised learning approach and stylometric features calculated without syntactic parsing. Our work suggests a number of natural follow-up analyses, especially extension of the experiments to encompass the full range of traditional prose genres (such as historiography, philosophy, and oratory) and application of the feature set to other questions in classical literary criticism. In addition, we hope that our heuristic approach will motivate and inform analogous work on other premodern traditions for which natural language processing research remains at an early stage.

Acknowledgments

This work was conducted under the auspices of the Quantitative Criticism Lab (www.qcrit.org), an interdisciplinary group co-directed by P.C. and J.P.D. and supported by a National Endowment for the Humanities Digital Humanities Start-Up Grant (grant number HD-10 248410-16) and an American Council of Learned Societies (ACLS) Digital Extension Grant. T.J.B. was supported by an Engaged Scholar Initiative Fellowship from the Andrew W. Mellon Foundation, P.C. by an ACLS Digital Innovation Fellowship and a Mellon New Directions Fellowship, and J.P.D. by a Neukom Fellowship.

References

Maha Al-Yahya. 2018. Stylometric analysis of classical Arabic texts for genre detection. *The Electronic Library*, 36:842–855.

M. Fatih Amasyali and Banu Diri. 2006. Automatic Turkish text categorization in terms of author, genre and gender. In Christian Kop, Günther Fliedl, Heinrich C. Mayr, and Elisabeth Mtais, editors, *Natural Language Processing and Information Systems*, pages 221–226. Springer-Verlag, Berlin.

David Bamman, Ted Underwood, and Noah A. Smith. 2014. A Bayesian mixed effects model of literary character. In *Proceedings of the 53nd Annual Meeting of the Association for Computational Linguistics*, pages 370–379.

Steven Bird, Ewan Klein, and Edward Loper. 2009. *Natural Language Processing with Python*. O'Reilly Media.

Snigdha Chaturvedi, Hal Daumé III, Shashank Srivastava, and Chris Dyer. 2016. Modeling evolving relationships between characters in literary novels. In *Proceedings of the Thirtieth AAAI Conference on Artificial Intelligence*, pages 2704–2710.

Neil Coffee, J.-P. Koenig, Shakthi Poornima, Roelant Ossewaarde, Christopher Forstall, and Sarah Jacobson. 2012. Intertextuality in the digital age. *Transactions of the American Philological Association*, 142:383–422.

Gregory Crane. 1996. Building a digital library: The Perseus Project as a case study in the humanities. In *Proceedings of the First ACM International Conference on Digital Libraries*, pages 3–10.

Micha Elsner. 2012. Character-based kernels for novelistic plot structure. In *Proceedings of the 13th Conference of the European Chapter of the Association for Computational Linguistics*, pages 634–644.

David K. Elson, Nicholas Dames, and Kathleen R. McKeown. 2010. Extracting social networks from literary fiction. In *Proceedings of the 48th Annual Meeting of the Association for Copmutational Linguistics*, pages 138–147.

John Frow. 2015. *Genre*. Routledge, London and New York.

Vanessa B. Gorman and Robert J. Gorman. 2016. Approaching questions of text reuse in ancient greek using computational syntactic stylometry. *Open Linguistics*, 2:500–510.

Lena Hettinger, Martin Becker, Isabella Reger, Fotis Jannidis, and Andreas Hotho. 2015. Genre classification on German novels. In *2015 26th International Workshop on Database and Expert Systems Applications*, pages 138–147.

James M. Hughes, Nicholas J. Fotia, David C. Krakauer, and Daniel N. Rockmore. 2012. Quantitative patterns of stylistic influence in the evolution of literature. *Proceedings of the National Academy of Sciences USA*, 109:7682–7686.

Noraini Jamal, Masnizah Mohd, and Shahrul Azman Noah. 2012. Poetry classification using support vector machines. *Journal of Computer Science*, 8:1411–1416.

Brett Kessler, Geoffrey Numberg, and Hinrich Schütze. 1997. Automatic detection of text genre. In *Proceedings of the 35th Annual Meeting of the Association for Computational Linguistics and Eighth Conference of the European Chapter of the Association for Computational Linguistics*, pages 32–38.

Mike Kestemont. 2014. Function words in authorship attribution. From black magic to theory? In *Proceedings of the 3rd Workshop on Computational Linguistics for Literature @ EACL 2014*, pages 59–66.

Tibor Kiss and Jan Strunk. 2006. Unsupervised multilingual sentence boundary detection. *Computational Linguistics*, 32:485–525.

Vipin Kumar and Sonajharia Minz. 2014. Poem classification using machine learning approach. In *Proceedings of the Second International Conference on Soft Computing for Problem Solving*, pages 675–682.

Philipp Petrenz and Bonnie Webber. 2011. Stable classification of text genres. *Computational Linguistics*, 37:385–393.

Jan Rybicki and Maciej Eder. 2011. Deeper Delta across genres and languages: Do we really need the most frequent words? *Literary and Linguistic Computing*, 26(3):315–321.

Marina Santini. 2007. Automatic genre identification: Towards a flexible classification scheme. In *Proceedings of the 1st BCS IRSG Conference on Future Directions in Information Access*, page 1.

Herbert Weir Smyth. 1956. *Greek Grammar. Revised by Gordon M. Messing*. Harvard University Press.

Efstathios Stamatatos. 2009. A survey of modern authorship attribution methods. *Journal of the American Society For Information Science and Technology*, 60:538–556.

Efstathios Stamatatos, Nikos Fakotakis, and George Kokkinakis. 2000. Automatic text categorization in terms of genre and author. *Computational Linguistics*, 26:471–495.

Hamid Tizhoosh, Farhang Sahba, and Rozita Dara. 2008. Poetic features for poem recognition: A comparative study. *Journal of Pattern Recognition Research*, 3:24–39.

Matthew Wilkens. 2016. Genre, computation, and the varieties of twentieth-century U.S. fiction. *Journal of Cultural Analytics*.

A Details of stylometric features for ancient Greek

A.1 Pronouns and non-content adjectives

- ἄλλος (allos, "other") is computed by counting all inflected forms of ἄλλος, -η, -ο.

- αὐτός (autos, "self" or "him/her/it") is computed by counting all inflected forms of αὐτός, -ή, -ό.

- Demonstrative pronouns are computed by counting all inflected forms of the three Greek demonstrative pronouns οὗτος, αὕτη, τοῦτο (houtos, haute, touto, "this"), ὅδε, ἥδε, τόδε (hode, hede, tode, "this"), and ἐκεῖνος, ἐκείνη, ἐκεῖνο (ekeinos, ekeine, ekeino, "that").

- Selected indefinite pronouns are computed by counting all inflected forms of τις, τις, τι (tis, tis, ti, "any") in non-interrogative sentences. Interrogative sentences are excluded because the Greek interrogative pronoun (τίς) is often identical in form to the indefinite pronoun.

- Personal pronouns are computed by counting all inflected forms of the pronouns ἐγώ (ego, "I") and σύ (su, "you").

- Reflexive pronouns are computed by counting all inflected forms of ἐμαυτοῦ (emautou, "he himself").

A.2 Conjunctions and particles

- Conjunctions are computed by counting all instances of the common conjunctions τε, τ' (te or t, "and"), καί, καὶ (kai, "and"), ἀλλά, ἀλλὰ (alla, "but"), καίτοι (kaitoi, "and indeed"), οὐδέ, οὐδὲ, οὐδ' (oude or oud, "and not"), μηδέ, μηδὲ, μηδ' (mede or med, "and not"), οὔτε, οὔτ' (oute or out, "and not"), μήτε, μήτ' (mete or met, "and not"), and ἤ, ἤ (e, "or").

- μέν (men, "indeed") is computed by counting all instances of μέν and μὲν.

- Particles are computed by counting all instances of ἄν, ἂν (an, a particle used to express uncertainty or possibility), ἄρα (ara, "then"), γέ, γ' (ge or g, "at least"), δ', δέ, δὲ (d or de, "but"), δή, δὴ (de, "indeed"), ἕως (heos, "until"), κ', κε, κέ, κὲ, κέν, κὲν, κεν (k, ke, ken, a particle used to express uncertainty or possibility), μά (ma, used in oaths and affirmations, "by"), μέν, μὲν (men, "indeed"), μέντοι (mentoi, "however"), μὴν, μήν (men, "truly"), μῶν (mon, "surely not"), νύ, νὺ, νυ (nu, "now"), οὖν (oun, "so"), περ (per, an intensifying particle, "very"), πω (po, "yet"), and τοι (toi, "let me tell you").

A.3 Subordinate clauses

- Circumstantial markers are computed by counting all instances of ἔπειτα, ἔπειτ' (epeita or epeit, "then"), ὅμως (homos, "all the same"), ὁμῶς (homos, "equally"), καίπερ (kaiper, "although"), and ἄτε, ἄτ' (hate or hat, "seeing that").

- Conditional markers are computed by counting all instances of εἰ, εἴ, εἰ, ἐάν, and ἐὰν (ei, ei, ei, ean, ean, all translated "if").

- ἵνα (hina, an adverb of place often translated "where" or a conjunction indicating purpose often translated "in order that") is computed by counting all instances of ἵνα and ἵν' (hin).

- ὅπως (hopos, an adverb of manner often translated "how" or a conjunction indicating purpose often translated "in order that") is computed by counting all instances of ὅπως.

- Fraction of sentences with a relative clause is determined by counting sentences that have one or more of the inflected forms of the Greek relative pronouns ὅς, ἥ, ὅ (hos, he, ho, "who" or "which").

- Temporal and causal markers are computed by counting all instances of μέχρι (mekri, "until"), ἕως (heos, "until"), πρίν (prin, "before"), ἐπεί (epei, "when"), ἐπειδή (epeide, "after" or "since"), ἐπειδάν (epeiden, "whenever"), ὅτε (hote, "when"), and ὅταν (hotan, "whenever").

- ὥστε (hoste, a conjunction used to indicate a result, "so as to") not preceded by ἥ is calculated by counting all instances of ὥστε not immediately preceded by ἥ. This limitation is imposed to exclude instances in which ὥστε is part of a comparative phrase.

- The mean length of relative clauses is determined by counting the number of characters between each relative pronoun and the next punctuation mark.

A.4   Miscellaneous

- Interrogative sentences are computed by counting all instances of ";" (the Greek question mark).

- Regular superlatives adjectives are computed by counting all instances of -τατος, -τάτου, -τάτῳ, -τατον, -τατοι, -τάτων, -τάτοις, -τάτους, -τάτη, -τάτης, -τάτῃ, -τάτην, -τάταις, -τάτας, -τατα, -τατά, and τατε at word end. One inflected form, -ταται, is excluded so as to avoid confusion with the Homeric third person singular middle/passive indicative verb ending -αται. This method does not detect certain irregular superlatives, such as ἄριστος (aristos, "best") or πρῶτος (protos, "first"), which would be significantly harder to disambiguate from non-superlative forms.

- Sentences with ὦ exclamations is determined by identifying sentences that have at least one instance of ὦ (o, "O"), a Greek exclamation.

- ὡς (hos, an adverb of manner often translated "how" or a conjunction often translated as "that," "so that," or "since," among several other possibilities) is computed by counting all instances of ὡς.

- Mean and variance of sentence length is determined by counting the number of characters in each tokenized sentence (see Section 3.2 of main paper).

B   List of ancient Greek literary texts

Verse texts: Aeschylus, *Agamemnon, Eumenides, Libation Bearers, Persians, Prometheus Bound, Seven Against Thebes,* and *Suppliant Women;* Apollonius, *Argonautica;* Aristophanes, *Acharnians, Birds, Clouds, Ecclesiazusae, Frogs, Knights, Lysistrata, Peace, Plutus, Thesmophoriazusae,* and *Wasps;* Bacchylides, *Dithyrambs* and *Epinicians;* Bion of Phlossa, *Epitaphius, Epithalamium,* and *Fragmenta;* Callimachus, *Epigrams* and *Hymns;* Colluthus, *Rape of Helen;* Euripides, *Alcestis, Andromache, Bacchae, Cyclops, Electra, Hecuba, Helen, Heracleidae, Heracles, Hippolytus, Ion, Iphigenia at Aulis, Iphigenia in Tauris, Medea, Orestes, Phoenissae, Rhesus, Suppliants,* and *Trojan Women;* Homer, *Iliad* and *Odyssey;* Lucian, *Podraga;* Lycophron, *Alexandra;* Nonnus of Panopolis, *Dionysiaca;* Oppian, *Halieutica;* Oppian of Apamea, *Cynegetica;* Pindar, *Isthmeans, Nemeans, Olympians,* and *Pythians;* Quintus Smyrnaeus, *Fall of Troy;* Sophocles, *Ajax, Antigone, Electra, Ichneutae, Oedipus at Colonus, Oedipus Tyrannus, Philoctetes,* and *Trachiniae;* Theocritus, *Epigrams;* Tryphiodorus, *The Taking of Ilios.*

Prose texts: Achilles Tatius, *Leucippe et Clitophon;* Aelian, *De Natura Animalium, Epistulae Rusticae,* and Varia Historia; Aelius Aristides, *Ars Rhetorica* and *Orationes;* Aeschines, *Against Ctesiphon, Against Timarchus,* and *On the Embassy;* Andocides, *Against Alcibiades, On His Return, On the Mysteries,* and *On the Peace;* Antiphon, *Against the Stepmother for Poisoning, First Tetralogy, Second Tetralogy, Third Tetralogy, On the Murder of Herodes,* and *On the Choreutes;* Apollodorus, *Epitome* and *Library;* Appian, *Civil Wars;* Aretaeus, *Curatione Acutorum Morbum* and *Signorum Acutorum Morbum;* Aristotle, *Constitution, Economics, Eudemian Ethics, Metaphysics, Nicomachean Ethics, Poetics, Politics, Rhetoric,* and *Virtues and Vices;* Athenaeus, *Deipnosophists;* Barnabas, *Barnabae Epistulae;* Basil of Caesarea, *De Legendis* and *Epistulae;* Callistratus, *Statuarum Descriptiones;* Chariton, *De*

Chaerea; Clement, *Exhortation*, *Protrepticus*, and *Quis Dis Salvetur*; Demades, *On the Twelve Years*; Demetrius, *Elocutione*; Demosthenes, *Against Androtion*, *Against Apatourius*, *Against Aphobus*, *Against Aristocrates*, *Against Aristogiton*, *Against Boeotus*, *Against Callicles*, *Against Callippus*, *Against Conon*, *Against Dionysodorus*, *Against Eubulides*, *Against Evergus and Mnesibulus*, *Against Lacritus*, *Against Leochares*, *Against Leptines*, *Against Macartatus*, *Against Midias*, *Against Nausimachus and Xenopeithes*, *Against Neaera*, *Against Nicostratus*, *Against Olympiodorus*, *Against Onetor*, *Against Pantaenetus*, *Against Phaenippus*, *Against Phormio*, *Against Polycles*, *Against Spudias*, *Against Stephanus*, *Against Theocrines*, *Against Timocrates*, *Against Timotheus*, *Against Zenothemis*, *Erotic Essay*, *Exordia*, *For Phormio*, *For the Megalopitans*, *Funeral Speech*, *Letters*, *Olynthiac*, *On Organization*, *On the Accession of Alexander*, *On the Chersonese*, *On the Crown*, *On the False Embassy*, *On the Halonnesus*, *On the Liberty of the Rhodians*, *On the Navy*, *On the Peace*, *On the Trierarchic Crown*, *Philip*, *Philippic*, and *Reply to Philip*; Dinarchus, *Against Aristogiton*, *Against Demosthenes*, and *Against Philocles*; Dionysius of Halicarnassus, *Ad Ammaeum*, *Antiquitates Romanae*, *De Antiquis Oratoribus*, *De Compositione Verborum*, *De Demosthene*, *De Dinarcho*, *De Isaeo*, *De Isocrate*, *De Lysia*, *De Thucydide*, *De Thucydidis Idiomatibus*, *Epistula ad Pompeium*, and *Libri Secundi de Antiquis Oratoribus Reliquiae*; Epictetus, *Discourses*, *Enchiridion*, and *Fragments*; Euclid, *Elements*; Eusebius of Caesarea, *Historia Ecclesiastica*; Flavius Josephus, *Antiquitates Judaicae*, *Contra Apionem*, *De Bello Judaico*, and *Vita*; Galen, *Natural Faculties*; Herodotus, *Histories*; Hippocrates, *De Aere Aquis et Locis*, *De Alimento*, *De Morbis Popularibus*, *De Prisca Medicamina*, and *Jusjurandum*; Hyperides, *Against Athenogenes*, *Against Demosthenes*, *Against Philippides*, *Funeral Oration*, *In Defense of Euxenippus*, and *In Defense of Lycophron*; Isaeus, *Speeches*; Isocrates, *Letters* and *Speeches*; Lucian, *Abdicatus*, *Adversus Indoctum et Libros Multos Ementem*, *Alexander*, *Anacharsis*, *Apologia*, *Bacchus*, *Bis Accusatus Sive Tribunalia*, *Calumniae Non Temere Credundum*, *Cataplus*, *Contemplantes*, *De Astrologia*, *De Domo*, *De Luctu*, *De Mercede*, *De Morte Peregrini*, *De Parasito Sive Artem Esse Parsiticam*, *De Sacrificiis*, *De Salta-*
tione, *De Syria Dea*, *Dearum Iudicium*, *Demonax*, *Deorum Consilium*, *Dialogi Deorum*, *Dialogi Marini*, *Dialogi Meretricii*, *Dialogi Mortuorum*, *Dipsades*, *Electrum*, *Eunuchus*, *Fugitivi*, *Gallus*, *Harmonides*, *Hercules*, *Hermotimus*, *Herodotus*, *Hesiod*, *Hippias*, *Icaromenippus*, *Imagines*, *Iudicium Vocalium*, *Iuppiter Confuatus*, *Iuppiter Tragoedus*, *Lexiphanes*, *Macrobii*, *Muscae Encomium*, *Navigium*, *Necyomantia*, *Nigrinus*, *Patriae Encomium*, *Phalaris*, *Philopseudes*, *Piscator*, *Pro Imaginibus*, *Pro Lapsu Inter Salutandum*, *Prometheus*, *Prometheus Es In Verbis*, *Pseudologista*, *Quomodo Historia Conscribenda Sit*, *Rhetorum Praeceptor*, *Saturnalia*, *Scytha*, *Soleocista*, *Somnium*, *Symposium*, *Timon*, *Toaxris vel Amicitia*, *Tyrannicida*, *Verae Historiae*, *Vitarum Auctio*, and *Zeuxis*; Lycurgus, *Against Leocrates*; Lysias, *Speeches*; Marcus Aurelius, *M. Antoninus Imperator Ad Se Ipsum*; Pausanias, *Description of Greece*; Philostratus the Athenian, *De Gymnastica*, *Epistulae et Dialexeis*, *Heroicus*, *Vita Apollonii*, and *Vitae Sophistarum*; Philostratus the Lemnian, *Imagines*; Plato, *Alcibiades*, *Apologia*, *Charmides*, *Cleitophon*, *Cratylus*, *Critias*, *Crito*, *Epinomis*, *Epistles*, *Erastai*, *Euthydemus*, *Euthyphro*, *Gorgias*, *Hipparchus*, *Hippias Maior*, *Hippias Minor*, *Ion*, *Laches*, *Leges*, *Lovers*, *Lysis*, *Menexenus*, *Meno*, *Minos*, *Parmenides*, *Phaedo*, *Phaedrus*, *Philebus*, *Protagoras*, *Respublica*, *Sophista*, *Statesman*, *Symposium*, *Theaetetus*, *Theages*, and *Timaeus*; Plutarch, *Ad Principem Ineruditum*, *Adversus Colotem*, *Aemilius Paulus*, *Agesilaus*, *Agis*, *Alcibiades*, *Alexander*, *Amatoriae Narrationes*, *Amatorius*, *An Recte Dictum Sit Latenter Esse Vivendum*, *An Seni Respublica Gerenda Sit*, *An Virtus Doceri Possit An Vitiositas Ad Infelicitatem Sufficia*, *Animine An Corporis Affectiones Sint Piores*, *Antony*, *Apophthegmata Laconica*, *Aquane An Ignis Sit Utilior*, *Aratus*, *Aristides*, *Artaxerxes*, *Bruta Animalia Ratione Uti*, *Brutus*, *Caesar*, *Caius Gracchus*, *Caius Marcius Coriolanus*, *Caius Marius*, *Camillus*, *Cato Minor*, *Cicero*, *Cimon*, *Cleomenes*, *Comparationis Aristophanes et Menandri Compendium*, *Comparison of Aegisalius and Pompey*, *Comparison of Agis Cleomenes and Gracchi*, *Comparison of Alcibiades and Coriolanus*, *Comparison of Aristides and Cato*, *Comparison of Demetrius and Antony*, *Comparison of Demosthenes with Cicero*, *Comparison of Dion and Brutus*, *Comparison of Lucullus and Cimon*, *Comparison of*

Lycurgus and Numa, Comparison of Lysander and Sulla, Comparison of Nicias and Crassus, Comparison of Pelopidas and Marcellus, Comparison of Pericles and Fabius Maximus, Comparison of Philopoemen and Titus, Comparison of Sertorius and Eumenes, Comparison of Solon and Publicola, Comparison of Theseus and Romulus, Comparison of Timoleon and Aemilius, Conjugalia Praecepta, Consolatio ad Apollonium, Consolatio ad Uxorem, Crassus, De Alexandri Magni Fortuna aut Virtute, De Amicorum Multitudine, De Amore Prolis, De Animae Procreatione in Timaeo, De Capienda Ex Inimicis Utilitate, De Cohibenda Ira, De Communibus Notitiis Adversus Stoicos, De Cupiditate Divitiarum, De Curiositate, De Defectu Oraculorum, De E Delphos, De Esu Carnium, De Exilio, De Faciae Quae in Orbe Lunae Apparet, De Fato, De Fortuna, De Fortuna Romanorum, De Fraterno Amore, De Garrulitate, De Genio Socratis, De Gloria Atheniensium, De Herodoti Malignitate, De Invidia et Odio, De Iside et Osiride, De Liberis Educandis, De Primo Frigido, De Pythiae Oraculis, De Recta Ratione Audiendi, De Se Ipsum Citra Invidiam Laudando, De Sera Numinis Vindicta, De Sollertia Animalium, De Stoicorum Repugnantis, De Superstitione, De Tranquillitate Animi, Demetrius, Epitome Argumenti Stoicos, Epitome Libri de Animae Procreatione, Fabius Maximus, Galba, Instituta Laconica, Lacaenarum Apophthegmata, Lucullus, Lycurgus, Marcellus, Marcus Cato, Maxime Cum Principibus Philosopho Esse Diserendum, Mulierum Virtutes, Nicias, Non Posse Suaviter Vivi Secundum Epicurum, Numa, Otho, Parallela Minora, Pelopidas, Pericles, Philopoemen, Phocion, Platonicae Quaestiones, Pompey, Praecepta Gerendae Reipublicae, Publicola, Pyrrhus, Quaestiones Convivales, Quaestiones Graecae, Quaestiones Naturales, Quaestiones Romanae, Quomodo Adolescens Poetas Audire Debeat, Quomodo Adulator ab Amico Internoscatur, Quomodo Quis Suos in Virtute Sentiat Profectus, Regum et Imperatorum Apophthegmata, Romulus, Septem Sapientium Convivium, Sertorius, Solon, Sulla, Themistocles, Theseus, Tiberius Gracchus, Timoleon, Titus Flamininus, and *Vitae Decem Oratorum*; Polybius, *Histories*; Pseudo-Plutarch, *De Musica* and *Placita Philosophorum*; Strabo, *Geography*; Thucydides, *Peloponnesian War*; Xenophon, *Anabasis*.

C Genre labels for verse texts

Epic: Apollonius, *Argonautica*; Colluthus, *Rape of Helen*; Homer, *Iliad* and *Odyssey*; Nonnus of Panopolis, *Dionysiaca*; Oppian, *Halieutica*; Oppian of Apamea, *Cynegetica*; Quintus Smyrnaeus, *Fall of Troy*; Tryphiodorus, *The Taking of Ilios*.

Drama: Aeschylus, *Agamemnon, Eumenides, Libation Bearers, Persians, Prometheus Bound, Seven Against Thebes,* and *Suppliant Women*; Aristophanes, *Acharnians, Birds, Clouds, Ecclesiazusae, Frogs, Knights, Lysistrata, Peace, Plutus, Thesmophoriazusae,* and *Wasps*; Euripides, *Alcestis, Andromache, Bacchae, Cyclops, Electra, Hecuba, Helen, Heracleidae, Heracles, Hippolytus, Ion, Iphigenia at Aulis, Iphigenia in Tauris, Medea, Orestes, Phoenissae, Rhesus, Suppliants,* and *Trojan Women*; Sophocles, *Ajax, Antigone, Electra, Ichneutae, Oedipus at Colonus, Oedipus Tyrannus, Philoctetes,* and *Trachiniae*.

Other: Bacchylides, *Dithyrambs* and *Epinicians*; Bion of Phlossa, *Epitaphius, Epithalamium,* and *Fragmenta*; Callimachus, *Epigrams* and *Hymns*; Lucian, *Podraga*; Lycophron, *Alexandra*; Pindar, *Isthmeans, Nemeans, Olympians,* and *Pythians*; Theocritus, *Epigrams*.

D Parameters for random forest models

For all experiments, the parameters for the scikit-learn random forest classifier are set to 'bootstrap': True, 'class_weight': None, 'criterion': 'gini', 'max_depth': None, 'max_features': 'auto', 'max_leaf_nodes': None, 'min_impurity_decrease': 0.0, 'min_impurity_split': None, 'min_samples_leaf': 1, 'min_samples_split': 2, 'min_weight_fraction_leaf': 0.0, 'n_estimators': 10, 'n_jobs': 1, 'oob_score': False, 'random_state': 0, 'verbose': 0, 'warm_start': False.

A framework for streamlined statistical prediction using topic models

Vanessa Glenny[1,2]   Jonathan Tuke[1,2]   Nigel Bean[1,2]   Lewis Mitchell[1,2,3]

[1]ARC Centre of Excellence for Mathematical and Statistical Frontiers (ACEMS)
[2]School of Mathematical Sciences, The University of Adelaide, SA 5005, Australia
[3]Data to Decisions CRC Stream Lead
lewis.mitchell@adelaide.edu.au

Abstract

In the Humanities and Social Sciences, there is increasing interest in approaches to information extraction, prediction, intelligent linkage, and dimension reduction applicable to large text corpora. With approaches in these fields being grounded in traditional statistical techniques, the need arises for frameworks whereby advanced NLP techniques such as topic modelling may be incorporated within classical methodologies. This paper provides a classical, supervised, statistical learning framework for prediction from text, using topic models as a data reduction method and the topics themselves as predictors, alongside typical statistical tools for predictive modelling. We apply this framework in a Social Sciences context (applied animal behaviour) as well as a Humanities context (narrative analysis) as examples of this framework. The results show that topic regression models perform comparably to their much less efficient equivalents that use individual words as predictors.

1   Introduction

For the past 20 years, topic models have been used as a means of dimension reduction on text data, in order to ascertain underlying themes, or 'topics', from documents. These probabilistic models have frequently been applied to machine learning problems, such as web spam filtering (Li et al., 2013), database sorting (Krestel et al., 2009) and trend detection (Lau et al., 2012).

This paper develops a methodology for incorporating topic models into traditional statistical regression frameworks, such as those used in the Social Sciences and Humanities, to make predictions. Statistical regression is a supervised method, however it should be noted the majority of topic models are themselves unsupervised.

When using text data for prediction, we are often confronted with the problem of condensing the data into a manageable form, which still retains the necessary information contained in the text. Methods such as using individual words as predictors, or n-grams, while conceptually quite simple, have a tendency to be extremely computationally expensive (with tens of thousands of predictors in a model). Except on extremely large corpora, this inevitably leads to overfitting. As such, methods that allow text to be summarised by a handful of (semantically meaningful) predictors, like topic models, gives a means to use large amounts of text data more effectively within a supervised predictive context.

This paper outlines a statistical framework for predictive topic modelling in a regression context. First, we discuss the implementation of a relatively simple (and widely used) topic model, latent Dirichlet allocation (LDA) (Blei et al., 2003), as a preprocessing step in a regression model. We then compare this model to an equivalent topic model that incorporates supervised learning, supervised LDA (sLDA) (Blei and McAuliffe, 2008).

Using topic models in a predictive framework necessitates estimating topic proportions for new documents, however retraining the LDA model to find these is computationally expensive. Hence we derive an efficient likelihood-based method for estimating topic proportions for previously unseen documents, without the need to retrain.

Given these two models hold the 'bag of words' assumption (*i.e.*, they assume independence between words in a document), we also investigate the effect of introducing language structure to the model through the hidden Markov topic model (HMTM) (Andrews and Vigliocco, 2010). The implementation of these three topic models as a dimension reduction step for a regression model provides a framework for the implementation of

61

Proc. of the 3rd Joint SIGHUM Workshop on Computational Linguistics for Cultural Heritage, Social Sciences, Humanities and Literature, pp. 61–70
Minneapolis, MN, USA, June 7, 2019. ©2019 Association for Computational Linguistics

further topic models, dependent on the needs of the corpus and response in question.

1.1 Definitions

The following definitions are used when considering topic models.

Vocabulary (V): a set of v unique elements (generally words) from which our text is composed.

Topic (ϕ): a probability distribution over the vocabulary. That is, for word i in the vocabulary, a probability $p_i \in [0, 1]$ is assigned of that word appearing, given the topic, with $\sum_{i=1}^{v} p_i = 1$. In general, there are a fixed number k of topics, $\phi = \{\phi_1, ..., \phi_k\}$.

Document $(\mathbf{w})$: a collection of n_j units (or words) from the vocabulary. Depending on the topic model, the order of these words within the document may or may not matter.

Corpus $(\mathbf{D})$: a collection of m documents over which the topic model is applied. That is, $\mathbf{D} = \{\mathbf{w}_1, ..., \mathbf{w}_m\}$, each with length n_j, $j = 1, 2, ..., m$.

Topic proportion (θ_j): a distribution of topics over the document j. A corpus will then have an $m \times k$ matrix $\boldsymbol{\theta}$, where each row $j = 1, 2, ..., m$ corresponds to the distribution of topics over document j.

2 LDA regression model

Latent Dirichlet allocation (LDA) (Blei et al., 2003), due to its simplicity and effectiveness, continues to be the basis for many topic models today. When considering topic regression, we take LDA as our 'baseline' model; *i.e.*, we measure all subsequent models against the performance of the LDA regression model.

LDA is an unsupervised process that assumes both topics and topic proportions are drawn from Dirichlet distributions. One reason for its simplicity is that it makes the 'bag of words' assumption. LDA assumes the process outlined in Algorithm 1 when generating documents.

Here, α (length k) and β (length v) are hyperparameters of the distributions of the θ_j and ϕ_l respectively.

When topic modelling, we are generally interested in inferring topic proportions $\boldsymbol{\theta} = \{\theta_1, ..., \theta_m\}$ and topics ϕ themselves, given the

---

for $l = 1, 2, ..., k$ **do**
   generate the k topics $\phi_l \sim \mathrm{Dir}(\beta)$;
end
for $j = 1, 2, ..., m$ **do**
   let $n_j \sim \mathrm{Poisson}(\xi)$, the length of document j;
   choose the topic proportions $\theta_j \sim \mathrm{Dir}(\alpha)$;
   for $i = 1, 2, ..., n_j$ **do**
      choose the topic assignment $z_{ji} \sim \mathrm{Multi}(\theta_j)$;
      choose a word $w_{ji} \sim \mathrm{Multi}(\phi_{z_{ji}})$;
   end
   create the document $w_j = \{w_{ji}\}_{i=1,2,...,n_j}$;
end

Algorithm 1: LDA generative process.

corpus $\mathbf{D}$. That is, we wish to find

$$P(\boldsymbol{\theta}, \boldsymbol{\phi} | \mathbf{D}, \alpha, \beta) = \frac{P(\boldsymbol{\theta}, \boldsymbol{\phi}, \mathbf{D} | \alpha, \beta)}{P(\mathbf{D} | \alpha, \beta)}.$$

The denominator, $P(\mathbf{D} | \alpha, \beta)$, the probability of the corpus, is understandably generally intractable to compute. For the purposes of this paper, we use collapsed Gibbs sampling as outlined in Griffiths and Steyvers (2004), as an approximate method for finding the LDA model given the corpus.

2.1 Regression model and number of topics

Given an LDA model on a corpus with some corresponding response variable, we use the topic proportions generated as predictors in a regression model. More specifically, we use the topic proportions $\boldsymbol{\theta}$ as the predictors, as the amount of a document belonging to each topic may be indicative of its response.

When applying LDA as a preprocessing step to a regression model, we must also bear in mind the number of topics k we choose for the LDA model. While this number is assumed to be fixed in advance, there are various measures for determining the number that best 'fits' the corpus, such as perplexity (Blei et al., 2003) and the log likelihood measure outlined in Griffiths and Steyvers (2004).

However, given we are inferring this topic model with a specific purpose in mind, it would be prudent to include this information into the decision making process. For that reason, we choose the 'best' number of topics k to be the number

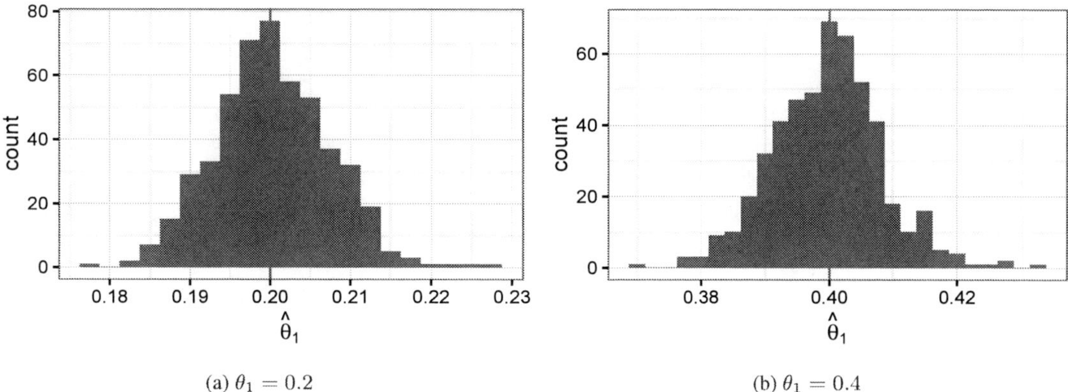

(a) $\theta_1 = 0.2$ (b) $\theta_1 = 0.4$

Figure 1: Histograms of the maximum likelihood estimates of θ_1 for corpora of two topics, given relative true values of 0.2 and 0.4.

that reduces the cross validation prediction error (CVPE) (Geisser, 1975) of the corresponding LDA regression model, found from K-fold cross validation of the model on the corpus. The CVPE is here defined to be

$$\mathrm{CVPE}_K = \sum_{i=1}^{K} \frac{m_i}{m} \mathrm{MSE}_i,$$

where K is the number of folds, m_i is the number of documents in the ith fold, and m the total number of documents in the corpus. The mean square error for the ith fold, denoted by MSE_i, is defined as

$$\mathrm{MSE}_i = \sum_{j \in C_i} \frac{1}{m_i} \left(y_j - \hat{y}_j\right)^2,$$

where $\hat{y}_j$ is the model estimate of response y_j for all documents in the set C_i, the ith fold. It follows that the better a model performs, the smaller the MSE and thus the CVPE.

While we choose the best number of topics based on the information in the regression model, it should be noted that LDA is still unsupervised, and that the topics have not been generated with the response in mind.

2.2 Introducing new documents

When it comes to prediction, we generally have a corpus for which we find our regression model, and use this model to predict the response of new documents that are not in the original corpus. Because our regression model requires us to know θ_j, the topic proportion, for any new document j, we have two options. Either the topic model can be

retrained with the new document added to the corpus, and the regression model retrained with the new topics on the old documents, or the topic proportions can be found based on the existing topic model.

For both efficiency's sake (*i.e.*, to avoid retraining the model for every prediction), and for the sake of true prediction, the second option is preferable. Particularly in cross validation, it is necessary to have a completely distinct traning and test set of data. In retraining a topic model with new documents, we do not have a clear distinction between the two sets.

Blei et al. (2003) outline a procedure for estimating the topic proportions of a held-out document, however this procedure follows a posterior approach that requires variationally inferring the posterior parameters, which are then used to approximate the expected number of words belonging to each topic, as an estimate for θ_j.

We propose here a likelihood-based approach to estimation of topic proportions of new documents, by treating the problem as a case of maximum likelihood estimation. That is, we want to find $\hat{\theta}_j$, the estimate of θ_j that maximises the likelihood of document j occurring, given our existing topic model. Therefore, we aim to maximise

$$\begin{aligned} L(\theta_j) &= f(\mathbf{w}_j | \theta_j) \\ &= f(w_{j1}, ..., w_{jn_j} | \theta_j), \end{aligned}$$

where $w_{j1}, ..., w_{jn_j}$ are the words in document j. As LDA is a 'bag of words' model, we are able to

63

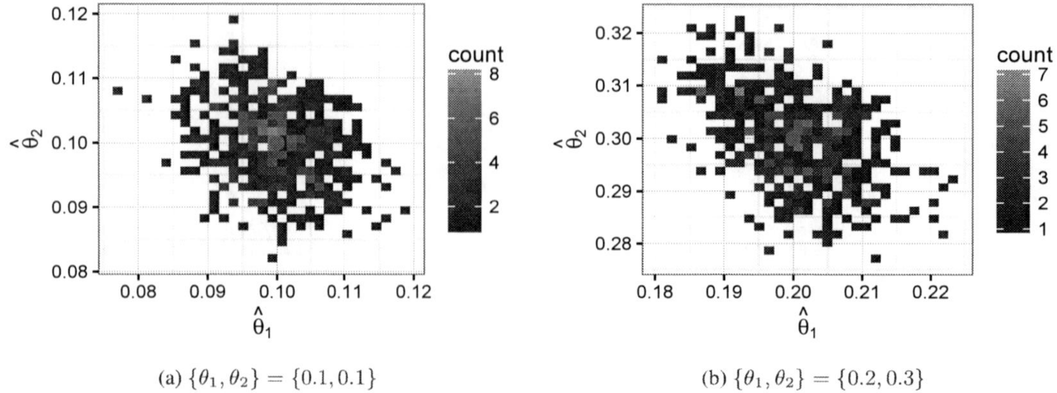

(a) $\{\theta_1, \theta_2\} = \{0.1, 0.1\}$ (b) $\{\theta_1, \theta_2\} = \{0.2, 0.3\}$

Figure 2: Histograms of the maximum likelihood estimates of $\{\theta_1, \theta_2\}$ for corpora of three topics, given relative true values of $\{0.1, 0.1\}$ and $\{0.2, 0.3\}$.

express this as

$$L(\theta_j) = \prod_{i=1}^{n_j} f(w_{ji}|\theta_j).$$

The law of total probability gives

$$L(\theta_j) = \prod_{i=1}^{n_j} \sum_{l=1}^{k} f(w_{ji}|z_{ji} = l, \theta_j) f(z_{ji} = l|\theta_j),$$

where z_{ji} is the topic assignment for the ith word in document j. However, as the choice of word w_{ji} is independent of the topic proportions θ_j given its topic assignment z_{ji}, we can write

$$L(\theta_j) = \prod_{i=1}^{n_j} \sum_{l=1}^{k} f(w_{ji}|z_{ji} = l) f(z_{ji} = l|\theta_j).$$

The likelihood is now expressed as the products of the topic proportions and the topics themselves.

$$L(\theta_j) = \prod_{i=1}^{n_j} \sum_{l=1}^{k} \phi_{l,w_{ji}} \theta_{jl}.$$

If we express the document as a set of word counts $\mathbf{N} = \{N_1, ..., N_v\}$, where N_i is the number of times the ith word of the vocabulary appears in document j, then we can write the log likelihood of θ_j as

$$l(\theta_j) = \mathbf{N} \cdot \log\left(\theta_j \phi\right).$$

In order to deal with words that appear in a new document, and not the original corpus, we assign a probability of 0 to any such word of appearing in any of the k topics; this is equivalent to removing those words from the document.

To demonstrate the effectiveness of this method for estimation, we generate documents for which we know the topics and topic proportions. Suppose there exists a corpus comprising of two topics, with a vocabulary of 500 words. Given an assumed LDA model, we generate 500 documents with lengths between 5,000 and 10,000 words.

Given our newly generated documents, and known topics ϕ, we are able to test the validity of the MLE process outlined above by finding the estimates $\hat{\theta}_j$ for each document j and comparing them to known topic proportions θ_j. Figure 1 shows the results of the MLE method for finding topic proportion estimates for documents with certain true values of θ_j. From these figures, there is a tight clustering around the true value θ_j, and thus it is reasonable to assume that the MLE process for estimating the topic proportions of a new document given previously existing topics is sound. This process also holds for greater numbers of topics, as evidenced in Figure 2, which estimates topic proportions for a three-topic document.

3   sLDA regression model

LDA is an unsupervised process, which does not take into account the response variable we are predicting when inferring topics. Several supervised methods have been developed to incorporate this knowledge, generally for the purpose of finding 'better' topics for the corpus in question. Notably, supervised LDA (sLDA) (Blei and McAuliffe, 2008) builds on the LDA model by assuming that some response y_j is generated alongside each document $j = 1, 2, ..., m$ in the cor-

64

pus, based on the topics prevalent in the document. When inferring the sLDA model, we are therefore inclined to find topics that best suit the response and therefore the prediction problem at hand.

Unlike LDA, we treat the topics ϕ as unknown constants rather than random variables. That is, we are interested in maximising

$$P\left(\boldsymbol{\theta}, \mathbf{z} | \mathbf{D}, \mathbf{y}, \phi, \alpha, \eta, \sigma^2\right),$$

where η and σ^2 are parameters of the normally distributed response variable, $y_j \sim N(\eta^T \bar{z}_j, \sigma^2)$, where $\bar{z}_j = (1/n_j) \sum_{i=1}^{n_j} z_{ji}$.

As with LDA, this probability is computationally intractable, and thus we require an approximation method for model inference. For the purposes of this paper, we use a variational expectation-maximisation (EM) algorithm, as outlined in Blei and McAuliffe (2008).

When it comes to choosing the model with the most appropriate number of topics for the regression problem at hand, we use the same method as outlined for the LDA regression model in Section 2.1.

The method behind sLDA is specifically developed for prediction. As such, we are able to compute the expected response y_j from the document $\mathbf{w}_j$ and the model $\{\alpha, \phi, \eta, \sigma^2\}$. For a generalised linear model (as we use in this paper), this is approximated by

$$E\left[Y_j | \mathbf{w}_j, \alpha, \phi, \eta, \sigma^2\right] \approx E_q\left[\mu\left(\eta^T \bar{\mathbf{z}}_j\right)\right],$$

where $\mu\left(\eta^T \mathbf{z}_j\right) = E\left[Y_j | \zeta = \eta^T \bar{\mathbf{z}}_j\right]$ and ζ is the natural parameter of the distribution from which the response is taken. Again, further detail on this method is found in Blei and McAuliffe (2008).

4 HMTM regression model

Topic modelling is designed as a method of dimension reduction, and as such we often deal with large corpora that cannot otherwise be analysed computationally. Given the complexity of human language, we therefore have to choose what information about our corpus is used to develop the topic model. The previous two models, LDA and sLDA, have relied on the 'bag of words' assumption in order to maintain computational efficiency. While for some corpora, the loss of all information relating to language and document structure may not have a particularly large effect on the predictive capability of the topic model, this may not hold for all prediction problems.

One simple way of introducing structure into the model is through a hidden Markov model (HMM) structure (Baum and Eagon, 1967; Baum et al., 1970); in fact, there already exist multiple topic models which do so. We look here at the hidden Markov topic model (HMTM) (Andrews and Vigliocco, 2010), which assumes that the topic assignment of a word in a document is dependent on the topic assignment of the word before it. That is, the topic assignments function as the latent states of the HMM, with words in the document being the observations. The HMTM assumes the generative process outlined in Algorithm 2 for documents in a corpus.

---

for $l = 1, 2, ..., k$ **do**
    generate topics $\phi_l \sim \mathrm{Dir}(\beta)$;
end
for $j = 1, 2, ...m$ **do**
    generate starting probabilities
      $\boldsymbol{\pi}_j \sim \mathrm{Dir}(\alpha)$;
    for $l = 1, 2, ..., k$ **do**
      generate the lth row of the transition
      matrix, $\boldsymbol{\Theta}_j$, $\Theta_{jl} \sim \mathrm{Dir}(\gamma_l)$;
    end
    choose the topic assignment for the first
    word $z_{j1} \sim \mathrm{Multi}(\boldsymbol{\pi}_j)$;
    select a word from the vocabulary
    $w_{j1} \sim \mathrm{Multi}(\phi_{z_{j1}})$;
    for $i = 2, 3, ..., n_j$ **do**
      choose the topic assignment z_{ji} based
      on transition matrix $\boldsymbol{\Theta}_j$;
      select a word from the vocabulary
      $w_{ji} \sim \mathrm{Multi}(\phi_{z_{ji}})$;
    end
    create the document $\mathbf{w}_j = \{w_{ji}\}_{i=1,...,n_j}$;
end

Algorithm 2: HMTM generative process.

Here, α, β and $\boldsymbol{\gamma} = \{\gamma_1, ..., \gamma_k\}$ are Dirichlet priors of the starting probabilities, topics and transition probabilities respectively.

When it comes to prediction, we are able to use the transition matrices for each document $\boldsymbol{\Theta}_j$ as predictors, but to keep consistency with the previous models we take the equilibrium distributions of the matrices as the topic proportions θ_j. That is, we find θ_j such that

$$\theta_j \boldsymbol{\Theta}_j = \theta_j, \quad \text{and} \quad \theta_j \mathbf{e} = 1.$$

This also fits with the concept of topic models as a form of dimension reduction, allowing $k - 1$

variables, as opposed to $k(k-1)$ when using the transition matrix Θ_j. As models are often fit using hundreds of topics (Blei, 2012; Griffiths and Steyvers, 2004), this makes models faster to compute. We choose the number of topics k here with the same method outlined in Section 2.1.

4.1 Introducing new documents

Like with the LDA regression model, we require a method for estimating the topic proportion θ_j of any new documents from which we are predicting a response, that does not involve retraining the entire model. To do so, we rely on techniques used for HMMs; specifically, we use a modified Baum-Welch algorithm.

The Baum-Welch algorithm is used as an approximate method to find an HMM $\Omega = \{\Theta, \phi, \pi\}$, given some observed sequence (in this case, a document). However, the key difference here is that our emission probabilities (or topics) ϕ are common across all documents in our corpus, and thus when introducing any new documents for prediction we assume that we already know them. Given the Baum-Welch algorithm calculates forward and backward probabilities based on an assumed model, and updates estimates iteratively, we may simply take our assumed ϕ found from the initial HMTM as the truth and refrain from updating the emission probabilities.

We are generally dealing with very small probabilities in topic modelling - ϕ generally has tens of thousands of columns (the length of the vocabulary) over which probabilities must sum to one. While in theory this does not change how we would approach parameter estimation, computationally these probabilities are frequently recognised as zero. To make the process more numerically stable, we implement the adapted Baum-Welch algorithm demonstrated and justified in Shen (2008).

While we are ultimately interested in finding topic proportions θ_j for prediction, the Baum-Welch algorithm finds the transition matrix Θ_j for some document. We are able to deal with this in the same way as finding the original HMTM regression model, by taking θ_j to be the equilibrium probabilities of Θ_j.

5 Testing the topic regression models

To demonstrate the use of topic models in a regression framework, we apply them to a prob-lem involving online advertisements. Specifically, we have a corpus containing 4,151 advertisements taken from the trading website, Gumtree[1], pertaining to the sale of cats in Australia, and hand-labelled by an expert. Of these advertisements, 2,187 correspond to relinquished cats and 1,964 to non-relinquished. We train a model to predict 'relinquished status' from the text of an advertisement, using a topic regression model. A cat is considered to be relinquished if it is being given up by its owner after a period of time, as opposed to cats that are sold, either by breeders or former owners.

In order to improve efficiency and model quality, we first clean our text data. Details on the cleaning steps can be found in Appendix A.1.

5.1 Word count model

Before investigating regression models that use topic proportions as predictors, it is worth developing a 'gold standard' model, *i.e.*, a model whose predictive capability we aim to match with our topic regression models. Because the problem here involves a relatively small corpus (advertisements with a median word count of 35), we are able to compare our topic regression models to a model that uses individual words as its predictors.

In a much larger corpus, this kind of prediction would be cumbersome to compute - hence our reliance on topic models and other dimension reduction techniques.

Because we are predicting a categorical, binary variable, we use logistic regression. Rather than using all words in the corpus (as this would drastically overfit the model), we use a step-up algorithm based on the Akaike information criterion (AIC) (Akaike, 1974) to choose the most significant words for the model, without overfitting.

Instead of applying the step-up process to the entire vocabulary (of exactly 13,000 words), we apply it to the 214 most common words (*i.e.*, words that appear in at least 2.5% of the documents in the corpus). The chosen model uses 97 predictors, with coefficients appearing consistent with what you would expect from the problem: for example, the word *kitten* is indicative of non-relinquished advertisements, while *cat* is the opposite, which is expected as younger cats are less likely to be relinquished.

To assess the predictive capability of this and other models, we require some method by which

---

[1] www.gumtree.com.au

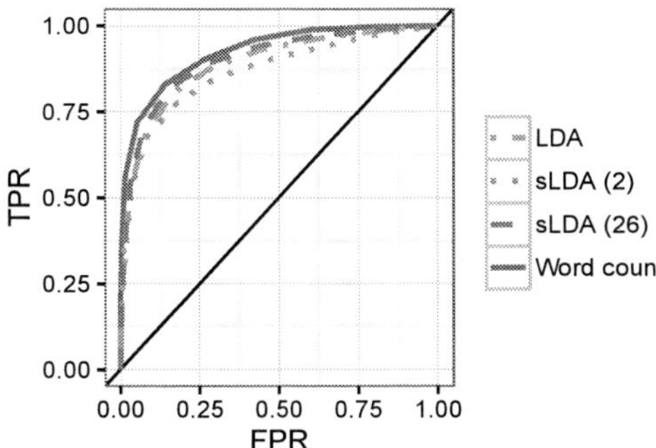

Figure 3: Threshold-averaged ROC curves of the word count model, LDA regression model, and sLDA regression models with two and 26 topics respectively.

we can compare the models. For that purpose, we use receiver operating characteristic (ROC) curves as a visual representation of predictive effectiveness. ROC curves compare the true positive rate (TPR) and false positive rate (FPR) of a model's predictions at different threshold levels. The area under the curve (AUC) (between 0 and 1) is a numerical measure, where the higher the AUC is, the better the model performs.

We cross-validate our model by first randomly splitting the corpus into a training set (95% of the corpus) and test set (5% of the corpus). We then fit the model to the training set, and use it to predict the response of the documents in the test set. We repeat this process 100 times. The threshold-averaged ROC curve (Fawcett, 2006) is found from these predictions, and shown in Figure 3. Table 1 shows the AUC for each model considered.

Model	AUC	95% CI
Word count	0.9264	$(0.9234, 0.9294)$
LDA	0.8913	$(0.8871, 0.8955)$
sLDA (2 topics)	0.8588	$(0.8534, 0.8642)$
sLDA (26 topics)	0.9030	$(0.8988, 0.9073)$

Table 1: TArea under the curve (AUC) for the models used on the Gumtree dataset, with their 95% confidence intervals.

5.2 Topic regression models

Using the method outlined in Section 2.1, we choose the LDA regression model with 26 topics as the 'best' for this problem. Inspection of the top words included in these 26 topics shows individual topics associated with different breeds (e.g.,

'persian', 'manx') as well as urgency of selling (e.g., 'urgent', 'asap'), suggesting that the model is not overfit to the data. We generate a threshold-averaged ROC curve using the same cross validation method as earlier, yielding an area under the curve (AUC) of 0.8913. The curve can be seen in Figure 3. While not as high as the AUC for the word count model, the LDA regression model is significantly more efficient, taking only 3% of the time to calculate.

We can compare this result to that of an sLDA regression model. The model chosen for this problem has two topics, giving a threshold-averaged ROC curve under cross validation with an AUC of 0.8588. It is surprising that the LDA regression model should outperform sLDA, as sLDA incorporates the response variable when finding the most appropriate topics. However, this can be attributed to the number of topics in the model: the sLDA regression model with 26 topics outperforms the LDA model, with an AUC of 0.9030.

The word count model still outperforms the sLDA model, however once again the topic regression model is significantly more efficient, taking only 0.6% of the time to calculate. Further details on the models and their calculation can be found in Appendix A.2.

6 Incorporating language structure

When evaluating the usefulness of incorporating document structure into a topic model for regression, we require a corpus and problem that we would expect would be heavily influenced by this structure. To understand the predictive capability of the HMTM regression model over that of the more simplistic LDA, we therefore consider predicting the storylines of the 2003 film *Love Actually*[2], known for its interwoven yet still quite distinct storylines. We therefore ask if we are able to predict to which storyline a scene belongs, based on the dialogue in that scene.

The film consists of 79 scenes, each pertaining to one of 10 storylines. The scenes were hand-classified by storyline, and their dialogue forms the documents of our corpus. We once again clean our data; more detail can be found in Appendix A.1.

---

[2]www.imdb.com/title/tt0314331/

6.1 Word count model

As with the Gumtree dataset, we first construct a word count model against which we can measure the performance of our topic regression models. Once again, this can be done because we are working with a small corpus; otherwise, we would generally consider this approach to be computationally too heavy.

As we have a categorical, non-binary response variable (storyline) with 10 levels, we use a multinomial logistic regression model. We again use a step-up process with AIC as the measure to determine which words in our vocabulary to use as predictors in our model. As our vocabulary consists of only 1,607 unique words, we consider all of them in our step-up process. After applying this process, the model with three predictors, *minister*, *night* and *around*, is chosen.

We are no longer able to easily apply ROC curves as a measure of performance to this problem, as we are dealing with a non-binary response. We instead use a Brier score (Brier and Allen, 1951), a measure for comparing the predictive performance of models with categorical responses. The Brier score is

$$\text{BS} = \frac{1}{m} \sum_{j=1}^{m} \sum_{i=1}^{s} (\hat{y}_{ji} - o_{ji})^2,$$

where $\hat{y}_{ji}$ is the probability of document j belonging to storyline i, and $o_{ji} = 1$ if document j belongs to storyline i, and 0 otherwise, for document $j = 1, 2, ..., m$ and storyline $i = 1, 2, ..., s$. Each term in the sum goes to zero the closer the model gets to perfect prediction, and as such our aim is to minimise the Brier score in choosing a model.

For each document in the corpus, we find the probabilities of each outcome by using the remaining 78 documents (or training dataset) as the corpus in a multinomial logistic regression model with the same three predictors as found above. Due to the fact that the training dataset here is smaller than the Gumtree dataset, we perform leave-one-out cross validation on each document in the corpus (rather than using a 95/5 split). We then predict the outcome based on the words found in the left-out document (or test dataset), and repeat for all 79 scenes. However, due to the short length of some scenes, and the fact that unique words must be thrown out, we restrict the testing to 57 of the 79 scenes: the remaining scenes do not

generate a numerically stable approximation for θ_j for the HMTM regression model.

The Brier score calculated using this method for the step-up word count model is 0.8255.

6.2 Topic regression models

For the LDA regression model for this problem, we determine the 'best' number of topics k to be 16. As with the word count model, we use the Brier score to evaluate the performance of this model compared to others in the chapter. We again use the leave-one-out cross validation approach to predict the probabilities of a scene belonging to each storyline.

The Brier score found for the LDA regression model is 1.6351. While this is higher and therefore worse than the Brier score for the word count model above, this is not unexpected and we are more interested in seeing how the LDA model fares against other topic models.

We compare these results to the HMTM regression model, as outlined in Section 4. We choose the model with 12 topics, according to the CVPE. The Brier score calculated from 57 scenes for the HMTM regression model is 1.5749. While still not up to the standard of the word count model at 0.8255, this appears to be a slight improvement on the LDA model, meaning that dropping the 'bag of words' assumption may in fact improve the predictive performance of the model. However, it should be kept in mind that the LDA model is better at handling short documents. It would be worth applying these models to corpora with longer documents in future, to see how they compare. Further details on the computation of these models can be found in Appendix A.2.

One of the motivating ideas behind having topic dependencies between consecutive words, as in the HMTM model, is that some documents will have a predisposition to stay in the same topic for a long sequence, such as a sentence or a paragraph. This argument particularly applies to narrative-driven corpora such as the *Love Actually* corpus. To that end, we may adapt the HMTM described above so that the model favours long sequences of the same topic, by adjusting the Dirichlet priors of the transition probabilities, $\gamma = \{\gamma_1, ..., \gamma_k\}$, to favour on-diagonal elements. By specifying these priors to be

$$\gamma_{ls} = \begin{cases} 0.99 + 0.01/k & \text{if} \quad l = s \\ 0.01/k & \text{elsewhere,} \end{cases}$$

for $l = 1, 2, ..., k$, we choose the persistent HMTM regression model with three topics. This results in a Brier score of 0.9124, which is a massive improvement on the original HMTM regression model and makes it very competitive with the word count model. Table 2 summarises these results.

Model	Accuracy	Brier score
Word count	26.58	0.8255
LDA	12.66	1.6351
HMTM	14.04	1.5749
Persistent HMTM	15.58	0.9124

Table 2: Table of the percentage of hard classifications of storylines for each left-out scene in the corpus that are correct, alongside the Brier score, for each model.

7 Discussion and further research

This paper outlines and implements a streamlined, statistical framework for prediction using topic models as a data processing step in a regression model. In doing so, we investigate how various topic model features affect how well the topic regression model makes predictions.

While this methodology has been applied to three specific topic models, the use of any particular topic model depends heavily on the kind of corpus and problem at hand. For that reason, it may be worth applying this methodology to incorporate different topic models in future, depending on the needs of the problem at hand.

In particular, we investigate here the influence of both supervised methods, and the incorporation of document structure. A logical next step would be to propose a model that incorporates these two qualities, in order to see if this improves predictive capability on corpora with necessary language structure.

References

Hirotugu Akaike. 1974. A new look at the statistical model identification. *IEEE Transactions on Automatic Control*, 19(6):716–723.

Mark Andrews and Gabriella Vigliocco. 2010. The hidden Markov topic model: A probabilistic model of semantic representation. *Topics in Cognitive Science*, 2(1):101–113.

Leonard E Baum and J A Eagon. 1967. An inequality with applications to statistical estimation for probabilistic functions of Markov processes and to a model for ecology. *Bulletin of the American Mathematical Society*, 73(3):360–363.

Leonard E Baum, Ted Petrie, George Soules, and Norman Weiss. 1970. A maximization technique occurring in the statistical analysis of probabilistic functions of Markov chains. *The Annals of Mathematical Statistics*, 41(1):164–171.

David M Blei. 2012. Probabilistic topic models. *Communications of the ACM*, 55(4):77–84.

David M Blei and Jon D McAuliffe. 2008. Supervised topic models. In *Advances in Neural Information Processing Systems*, pages 121–128.

David M Blei, Andrew Y Ng, and Michael I Jordan. 2003. Latent Dirichlet allocation. *Journal of Machine Learning Research*, 3:993–1022.

Glenn W Brier and Roger A Allen. 1951. Verification of weather forecasts. In *Compendium of Meteorology*, pages 841–848. Springer.

Tom Fawcett. 2006. An introduction to ROC analysis. *Pattern Recognition Letters*, 27(8):861–874.

Seymour Geisser. 1975. The predictive sample reuse method with applications. *Journal of the American Statistical Association*, 70(350):320–328.

Thomas L Griffiths and Mark Steyvers. 2004. Finding scientific topics. *Proceedings of the National Academy of Sciences*, 101(suppl 1):5228–5235.

Ralf Krestel, Peter Fankhauser, and Wolfgang Nejdl. 2009. Latent Dirichlet allocation for tag recommendation. In *Proceedings of the Third ACM Conference on Recommender Systems*, pages 61–68. ACM.

Jey Han Lau, Nigel Collier, and Timothy Baldwin. 2012. On-line trend analysis with topic models:\# twitter trends detection topic model online. *Proceedings of COLING 2012*, pages 1519–1534.

Jiwei Li, Claire Cardie, and Sujian Li. 2013. TopicSpam: A topic-model based approach for spam detection. In *51st Annual Meeting of the Association for Computational Linguistics: Proceedings of the Conference*, volume 2, pages 217–221.

Martin Porter. 2001. Snowball: A language for stemming algorithms. Available at *http://snowballstem.org*. Last checked 13 December 2017.

Dawei Shen. 2008. Some mathematics for HMM. *Massachusetts Institute of Technology*.

A Appendix

A.1 Text cleaning

The following steps were taken to clean the Gumtree corpus:

- removal of punctuation and numbers,

- conversion to lower case,

- removal of stop words (*i.e.*, common words such as *the* and *for* that contribute little lexically), and

- removal of grammatical information from words (*i.e.*, stemming).

When stemming words in this paper, we use the stemming algorithm developed by Porter for the Snowball stemmer project (Porter, 2001). Similarly, when removing stop words, we use the (English language) list compiled, again, in the Snowball stemmer project.

In cleaning the *Love Actually* corpus, we perform the first three steps outlined here. However, unlike with the Gumtree dataset, we do not stem words, as grammatical information is more pertinent when incorporating language structure.

A.2 Topic model inference

For each topic model, we choose the best number of topics from models generated with between two and 40 topics.

For the LDA models found in this paper, we use the *LDA* function from the R package **topicmodels**, with the following parameters:

- `burnin = 1000`,

- `iterations = 1000`, and

- `keep = 50`.

The sLDA model in this paper was found using the `slda.em` function from the R package **lda**, with the following parameters:

- `alpha = 1.0`,

- `eta = 0.1`,

- `variance = 0.25`,

- `num.e.iterations = 10`, and

- `num.m.iterations = 4`.

We use the Python code from Andrews and Vigliocco (2010) for the generation of our HMTM.

Revisiting NMT for Normalization of Early English Letters

Mika Hämäläinen, Tanja Säily, Jack Rueter, Jörg Tiedemann and Eetu Mäkelä
Department of Digital Humanities
University of Helsinki
`firstname.lastname@helsinki.fi`

Abstract

This paper studies the use of NMT (neural machine translation) as a normalization method for an early English letter corpus. The corpus has previously been normalized so that only less frequent deviant forms are left out without normalization. This paper discusses different methods for improving the normalization of these deviant forms by using different approaches. Adding features to the training data is found to be unhelpful, but using a lexicographical resource to filter the top candidates produced by the NMT model together with lemmatization improves results.

1 Introduction

Natural language processing of historical data is not a trivial task. A great deal of NLP tools and resources work out of the box with modern data, whereas they can be of little use with historical data. Lack of a written standard in the early days, and the fact that the language has changed over the centuries require addressing in order to achieve higher-level NLP tasks.

The end goal of our project is to identify neologisms and study their spread in the CEEC (Corpora of Early English Correspondence) (Nevalainen et al., 1998–2006), a letter corpus consisting of texts starting from the 15th century ranging all the way to the 19th century. In order to achieve a higher recall in neologisms, the corpus needs to be normalized to present-day spelling.

A regular-expression based study of neologisms (Säily et al., In press) in the same corpus suggested the use of the Oxford English Dictionary (OED, n.d.) as a viable way of detecting neologism candidates. Words occurring in the corpus before the earliest attestation in the OED would thus be considered potential neologism candidates. However, in order to achieve this, the words in the corpus need to be mappable to the OED, in other words,

normalized to their modern spelling. As we are dealing with historical data, the fact that a neologism exists in the OED is a way of ensuring that the new word has become established in the language.

A previous study in automatic normalization of the CEEC comparing different methods (Hämäläinen et al., 2018) suggested NMT (neural machine translation) as the single most effective method. This discovery is the motivation for us to continue this work and focus only on the NMT approach, expanding on what was proposed in the earlier work by using different training and post-processing methods.

In this paper, we will present different NMT models and evaluate their effectiveness in normalizing the CEEC. As a result of the previous study, all the easily normalizable historical forms have been filtered out and we will focus solely on the historical spellings that are difficult to normalize with existing methods.

2 Related Work

Using character level machine translation for normalization of historical text is not a new idea. Research in this vein has existed already before the dawn of neural machine translation (NMT), during the era of statistical machine translation (SMT).

Pettersson et al. (2013) present an SMT approach for normalizing historical text as part of a pipeline where NLP tools for the modern variant of the language are then used to do tagging and parsing. The normalization is conducted on a character level. They do alignment of the parallel data on both word and character level.

SMT has also been used in normalization of contemporary dialectal language to the standardized normative form (Samardzic et al., 2015). They test normalization with word-by-word trans-

Proc. of the 3rd Joint SIGHUM Workshop on Computational Linguistics for Cultural Heritage, Social Sciences, Humanities and Literature, pp. 71–75
Minneapolis, MN, USA, June 7, 2019. ©2019 Association for Computational Linguistics

lation and character level SMT. The character level SMT improves the normalization of unseen and ambiguous words.

Korchagina (2017) proposes an NMT based normalization for medieval German. It is supposedly one of the first attempts to use NMT for historical normalization. The study reports NMT outperforming the existing rule-based and SMT methods.

A recent study by Tang et al. (2018) compared different NMT models for historical text normalization in five different languages. They report that NMT outperforms SMT in four of the five languages. In terms of performance, vanilla RNNs are comparable to LSTMs and GRUs, and also the difference between attention and no attention is small.

3   The Corpus

We use the CEEC as our corpus. It consists of written letters from the 15th all the way to the 19th century. The letters have been digitized by hand by editors who have wanted to maintain the linguistic form as close to the original as possible. This means that while our data is free of OCR errors, words are spelled in their historical forms.

The corpus has been annotated with social metadata. This means that for each author in the corpus we can get various kinds of social information such as the rank and gender of the author, time of birth and death and so on. The corpus also records additional information on a per letter basis, such as the year the letter was written, the relationship between the sender and the recipient, and so on.

4   The NMT Approach

We use OpenNMT[1] (Klein et al., 2017) to train the NMT models discussed in this paper. The models are trained on a character level. This means that the model is supplied with parallel lists of historical spellings and their modern counterparts, where the words have been split into individual characters separated by white spaces.

The training is done for pairs of words, i.e. the normalization is to be conducted without a context. The NMT model would then treat individual characters as though they were words in a sentence and "translate" them into the corresponding modernized spelling.

[1] Version 0.2.1 of opennmt-py

4.1   The Parallel Data

We use different sources of historical-modern English parallel data. These include the normalized words from the CEEC, the historical forms provided in the OED and the historical lemmas in the Middle English Dictionary (MED, n.d.) that have been linked to the OED lemmas with modern spelling. This parallel data of 183505 words is the same as compiled and used in Hämäläinen et al. (2018).

For testing the accuracy of the models we prepare by hand gold standards by taking sets of 100 words of the previously non-normalized words in the CEEC. The accuracy is tested as an exact match to the gold standard. We prepare one generic test set and four century specific test sets of the 15th, 16th, 17th and 18th century words. Each of these five gold-annotated test sets consists of 100 words normalized by a linguist knowledgeable in historical English. The reason why we choose to prepare our own gold standard is that we are interested in the applicability of our approach in the study of the CEEC corpus as a step in our neologism identification pipeline.

4.2   Different NMT models

The previous work (Hämäläinen et al., 2018) on the normalization of the CEEC corpus used the default settings of OpenNMT. This means that the encoder is a simple recurrent neural network (RNN), there are two layers both in the encoder and the decoder and the attention model is the general global attention presented by Luong et al. (2015).

In this section we train the model with different parameters to see their effect on the accuracy of the model. The accuracy is evaluated and reported over a concatenated test set of all the five different gold standards.

At first, we change one parameter at a time and compare the results to the default settings. We try two different encoder types, bi-directional recurrent neural networks (BRNNs) and mean, which is an encoder applying mean pooling. BRNN uses two independent encoders to encode the sequence reversed and without reversal. The default RNN, in contrast, only encodes the sequence normally without reversing it.

In addition to the default attention model, we also try out the MLP (multi-layer perceptron) model proposed by Bahdanau et al. (2014). We change the number of layers used by the encoder and decoder and run the training with four and six layers for both encoding and decoding.

	default	mlp	mean	brnn	4 layers	6 layers
acc.	35.6%	36.6%	13%	39.8%	37.2%	36.6%

Table 1: Accuracy of each method

Table 1 shows the accuracy of the model trained with the different parameters. BRNNs seem to produce the best results, while the MLP attention model and additional layers can be beneficial over the default attention and number of layers. Next, we will try out different combinations with the BRNN encoder to see whether we can increase the overall accuracy.

	brnn	brnn +mlp	brnn +4 layers	brnn+mlp +4 layers
acc.	39.8%	36%	35.8%	38.2%

Table 2: Accuracy of BRNN models

We can see in Table 2 that the BRNN with the default attention and the default number of layers works better than the other combinations. This means that for our future models, we will pick the BRNN encoder with default settings.

4.3 Additional Information

The previous study (Hämäläinen et al., 2018) showed that using information about the centuries of the historical forms in training the NMT and SMT models was not beneficial. However, there might still be other additional information that could potentially boost the performance of the NMT model. In this part, we show the results of models trained with different additional data.

In addition to the century, the CEEC comes with social metadata on both the letters and the authors. We use the sender ID, sender rank, relationship code and recipient rank as additional information for the model. The sender ID is used to uniquely identify different senders in the CEEC, the ranks indicate the person's social status at the time of the letter (such as nobility or upper gentry) and the relationship code indicates whether the sender and recipient were friends, had a formal relationship and so on.

The social information is included in the parallel data in such a way that for each historical form,

	15th	16th	17th	18th	generic
eSpeak IPA with graphemes	22%	25%	31%	14%	20%
Only eSpeak IPA	43%	35%	52%	20%	36%
Metaphone	22%	23%	25%	12%	23%
Bigram	16%	9%	11%	3%	9%
No feature	45%	35%	48%	25%	42%

Table 3: Results with additional information

the social metadata is added if the form has appeared in the CEEC. If the form has not appeared in the CEEC, generic placeholders are added instead of real values. The metadata is appended as a list separated by white spaces to the beginning of each historical form.

When reading the historical letters, what is helpful for a human reader in understanding the historical forms is reading them out loud. Because of this discovery, we add pronunciation information to the parallel data. We add an estimation of pronunciation to the beginning of each historical form as an individual token. This estimation is done by the Metaphone algorithm (Philips, 1990). Metaphone produces an approximation of the pronunciation of a word, not an exact phonetic representation, which could be useful for the NMT model.

In addition to the Metaphone approximation, we use eSpeak NG[2] to produce an IPA transcription of the historical forms. For the transcription, we use British English as the language variant, as the letters in our corpus are mainly from different parts of England. We use the transcription to train two different models, one where the transcription is appended character by character to the beginning of the historical form, and another where we substitute the transcription for the historical form.

The final alteration in the training data we try in this section is that instead of providing more information, we try to train the model with character bigrams rather than the unigrams used in all the other models.

The results for the different approaches discussed in this section are shown in Table 3. As we can see, only the eSpeak produced IPA, when it no longer includes the original written form, comes close to using the character unigrams from the parallel data. Training with just the IPA transcription outperforms the character approach only in the 17th century.

---

[2]https://github.com/espeak-ng/espeak-ng/

4.4 Picking Normalization Candidate

Looking at the results of the NMT model, we can see that more often than not, when the normalization is not correct, the resulting word form is not a word of the English language. Therefore, it makes sense to explore whether the model can reach a correct normalization if instead of considering the best normalization candidate produced by the NMT model, we look at multiple top candidates.

During the translation step, we make the NMT model output 10 best candidates. We go through these candidates starting from the best one and compare them against the OED. If the produced modern form exists in the OED or exists in the OED after lemmatization with Spacy (Honnibal and Montani, 2017)[3], we pick the form as the final normalization. In other words, we use a dictionary to pick the best normalization candidate that exists in the English language.

	15th	16th	17th	18th	generic
OED +Lemma	49%	42%	51%	19%	43%
Lemma	45%	35%	48%	25%	42%

Table 4: Results with picking the best candidate with OED

Table 4 shows the results when we pick the first candidate that is found in the OED and when we only use the top candidate for the BRNN model. We can see improvement on all the test sets except for the 18th century.

	15th	16th	17th	18th	generic
OED +Lemma	69%	78%	71%	50%	61%
Lemma	61%	67%	63%	45%	53%

Table 5: Results with OED and lemmatization

If we lemmatize both the input of the NMT model and the correct modernized form in the gold standard with Spacy before the evaluation, we can assess the overall accuracy of OED mapping with the normalization strategies. The results shown in Table 5 indicate a performance boost in the mapping task, however this type of normalization does not match the actual inflectional forms. Nevertheless, in our case, lemmatization is possible as we

are ultimately interested in mapping words to the OED rather than their exact form in a sentence.

5 Conclusions

Improving the NMT model for normalization is a difficult task. A different sequence-to-sequence model can improve the results to a degree, but the gains are not big. Adding more features, no matter how useful they might sound intuitively, does not add any performance boost. At least that is the case for the corpus used in this study, as the great deal of social variety and the time-span of multiple centuries represented in the CEEC are reflected in the non-standard spelling.

Using a lexicographical resource and a good lemmatizer, as simplistic as they are, are a good way to improve the normalization results. However, as getting even more performance gains for the NMT model seems tricky, probably the best direction for the future is to improve on the method for picking the contextually most suitable normalization out of the results of multiple different normalization methods as originally explored in Hämäläinen et al. (2018). Thus, the small improvement of this paper can be brought back to the original setting as one of the normalization methods.

References

Dzmitry Bahdanau, Kyunghyun Cho, and Yoshua Bengio. 2014. Neural machine translation by jointly learning to align and translate. *arXiv preprint arXiv:1409.0473*.

Matthew Honnibal and Ines Montani. 2017. spaCy 2: Natural Language Understanding with Bloom Embeddings, Convolutional Neural Networks and Incremental Parsing. *To appear.*

Mika Hämäläinen, Tanja Säily, Jack Rueter, Jörg Tiedemann, and Eetu Mäkelä. 2018. Normalizing early English letters to Present-day English spelling. In *Proceedings of the 2nd Joint SIGHUM Workshop on Computational Linguistics for Cultural Heritage, Social Sciences, Humanities and Literature*, pages 87–96.

Guillaume Klein, Yoon Kim, Yuntian Deng, Jean Senellart, and Alexander M. Rush. 2017. Open-NMT: Open-Source Toolkit for Neural Machine Translation. In *Proc. ACL.*

Natalia Korchagina. 2017. Normalizing medieval german texts: from rules to deep learning. In *Proceedings of the NoDaLiDa 2017 Workshop on Processing Historical Language*, pages 12–17.

---

[3]With model en_core_web_md

Minh-Thang Luong, Hieu Pham, and Christopher D Manning. 2015. Effective approaches to attention-based neural machine translation. *arXiv preprint arXiv:1508.04025*.

MED. n.d. Middle English Dictionary. University of Michigan. Https://quod.lib.umich.edu/m/med/.

Terttu Nevalainen, Helena Raumolin-Brunberg, Jukka Keränen, Minna Nevala, Arja Nurmi, Minna Palander-Collin, Samuli Kaislaniemi, Mikko Laitinen, Tanja Säily, and Anni Sairio. 1998–2006. CEEC, Corpora of Early English Correspondence. Department of Modern Languages, University of Helsinki. Http://www.helsinki.fi/varieng/CoRD/corpora/CEEC/.

OED. n.d. OED Online. Oxford University Press. Http://www.oed.com/.

Eva Pettersson, Beáta Megyesi, and Jörg Tiedemann. 2013. An SMT approach to automatic annotation of historical text. In *Proceedings of the workshop on computational historical linguistics at NODAL-IDA 2013; May 22-24; 2013; Oslo; Norway. NEALT Proceedings Series 18*, 087, pages 54–69. Linköping University Electronic Press.

Lawrence Philips. 1990. Hanging on the Metaphone. *Computer Language*, 7(12).

Tanja Samardzic, Yves Scherrer, and Elvira Glaser. 2015. Normalising orthographic and dialectal variants for the automatic processing of swiss german. In *Proceedings of the 7th Language and Technology Conference*.

Tanja Säily, Eetu Mäkelä, and Mika Hämäläinen. In press. Explorations into the social contexts of neologism use in early English correspondence. *Pragmatics & Cognition*.

Gongbo Tang, Fabienne Cap, Eva Pettersson, and Joakim Nivre. 2018. An evaluation of neural machine translation models on historical spelling normalization. In *Proceedings of the 27th International Conference on Computational Linguistics*, pages 1320–1331.

Graph convolutional networks for exploring authorship hypotheses

Tom Lippincott
Johns Hopkins University / Baltimore, MD
`tom@cs.jhu.edu`

Abstract

This work considers a task from traditional literary criticism: annotating a structured, composite document with information about its sources. We take the Documentary Hypothesis, a prominent theory regarding the composition of the first five books of the Hebrew bible, extract stylistic features designed to avoid bias or overfitting, and train several classification models. Our main result is that the recently-introduced graph convolutional network architecture outperforms structurally-uninformed models. We also find that including information about the granularity of text spans is a crucial ingredient when employing hidden layers, in contrast to simple logistic regression. We perform error analysis at several levels, noting how some characteristic limitations of the models and simple features lead to misclassifications, and conclude with an overview of future work.

1 Background

In this paper, we consider the Documentary Hypothesis (DH),which proposes a specific combination of sources underlying the existing form of the first five books of the Hebrew Bible known as the *Torah* (Friedman, 1987).[1] Table 1 lists the eight sources in the DH and short description. We use "sources" in a more general sense than in straightforward author attribution literature: the labels may resolve to original material from particular authors, but could also be insertions from contemporary sources, redaction by a new liturgical community, translation of another document, and so forth.

Related areas such as authorship attribution and plagiarism detection, that rely on characterizing

Name	Time period and location
Elohist	9th to 7th century, Israel
Jehovist	9th to 7th century, Judah
Priestly	6th and 5th centuries
1Deuteronomist	7th century (pre-exilic)
2Deuteronomist	6th century (post-exilic)
Redactor	Post-exilic
nDeuteronomist	Single large span in Deuteronomy
Other	Assorted (poems, repetitions)

Table 1: Standard sources for the Documentary Hypothesis of Torah authorship

documents according to *style*, have a long history in the NLP research community (Potthast et al., 2017; Stamatatos, 2009; Potthast et al., 2010) as a text classification (Sari et al., 2018) or clustering/outlier detection (Seidman and Koppel, 2017; Lippincott, 2009) task. They typically consider the situation where the data are isolated document-label pairs without inter- or intra-document structure (Stamatatos, 2009; Seroussi et al., 2011). In contrast, the DH labels are embedded in the book-chapter-verse structure of the Torah. The basic premise remains the same: the labeled texts should contain linguistic features that, in some fashion, reflect their source. Our intuition is that structural information, which is often isomorphic to other modalities (narrative, time of composition, rhetorical role, etc) is a useful signal that can be exploited by a suitable model. For example, one source might tend to make word-level edits distributed evenly across a document, another might insert narrative elements constituting entire chapters, while a third might make ideologically-motivated changes only to the work of an earlier source. These observations all require some awareness of position inside a larger structure, in

---

[1] The DH has 150 years of history, exists in several forms, and is by no means universally accepted: for the purposes of this study, it is a reasonable starting point.

Proc. of the 3rd Joint SIGHUM Workshop on Computational Linguistics for Cultural Heritage, Social Sciences, Humanities and Literature, pp. 76–81
Minneapolis, MN, USA, June 7, 2019. ©2019 Association for Computational Linguistics

addition to the linguistic features.

Linguistic features for determining a document's source are often designed for robustness and generalization, e.g. word length, puctuation, function words (Mosteller and Wallace, 1963; Sundararajan and Woodard, 2018). Some studies employ full vocabulary or character n-gram features (Sari et al., 2018), which increase the potential for overfitting on topic and open-class vocabulary, but can also capture additional stylistic aspects. Recent work has begun to apply neural models to the author attribution task: Sari et al. (2018), for example, combine character n-gram embeddings with a single hidden layer feedforward network. These features and models do not take into account document structure.

	A	B	C	D
A	1	1	0	1
B	1	1	1	0
C	0	1	1	0
D	1	0	0	1

Figure 1: In a GCN, each layer receives input from the previous according to the node adjacency matrix. Initially, node C's representation is based only on it's own features. After the first convolutional layer, it is also based on features from its predecessor B. By the third layer, it has access to information propagated from its two-hop ancestor A.

The recently-introduced *graph convolutional network* (GCN) (Kipf and Welling, 2016) allows nodes, with L layers of convolution, access to representations of their neighbors up to L hops away. This is accomplished by using a function of the adjacency matrix $A' = f(A)$, which describes the connections between nodes, to determine how the representations from one layer feed into the next. Figure 1 shows a four-node graph and its associated adjacency matrix, plus self-connections (the diagonal) so that nodes employ their own features. Each layer n in the corresponding GCN has a $4xH_n$ output, where H_n is the size of that layer's representations. Before passing the output of layer n to layer $n + 1$, it is multiplied by A', which for suitable functions (e.g. $f = norm$) effectively mixes the output for a given node with that of its neighbors. Thus, at layer l, each node's representation has been combined to some degree with it's l-size neighborhood.

2   Experimental setup

Our goal is to train a model to recover the DH using stylistic features: the following sections describe our data, features, and models.

Data

Our experiments use the Westminster Leningrad Codex (WLC) (Lowery, 2016), available at `http://tanach.us/Tanach.zip`, a publicly-available TEI document (editors, 2019) of the oldest complete Masoretic text of the Hebrew Bible. The WLC encodes the DH as described in Friedman (2003), mapping spans (fragments of the Torah document tree) to sources. Spans can be at different levels of granularity, from book down to token, e.g "Num:20:1.1-Num:20:1.5" or "Lev:23:44-Lev:26:38". Each span corresponds to one or more consecutive nodes in the WLC tree and their children. There are 378 spans with associated source labels, covering the entire Torah. The Torah portion of the WLC consists of 5 books, split into 929 chapters, 5,853 verses, and 79,915 tokens. Furthermore, tokens are segmented into morphs (stems, prefixes, and suffixes), with 6,625 unique morphs averaging 1.5 per token. Our most significant data preprocessing is the removal of vowel pointing, which was not introduced until the middle of the first millenium A.D., at earliest. The WLC is tree-structured, and any location can be specified with a tuple of $(book, chapter, verse, token, morph)$, where the latter two are indices calculated from the data. In this paper we construct our features from morphs, not tokens, as most Hebrew function-words occur at the prefix/suffix level.

The data points are the labeled spans of the DH: the categorical source value, and some linguistic or structural features extracted from the corresponding fragment of the WLC. As recognized by much previous work (Mosteller and Wallace, 1963), authors can often be trivially distinguished using naive vocabulary features, and care must be taken to avoid this uninformative result. We therefore construct bag-of-morph distributions limited to those morphs that occur in every source, as a simple heuristic to focus on the distribution of function-words and widely-used open class vocabulary. This reduces the morph vocabulary from 6,625 to 70. On inspection, these appear to be ~50% function-morphs, ~20% verbs, ~20% common nouns, and three proper names: Moses, Israel, and Jehovah.

We also consider two structural features: first, indicator variables for the span's level of **granularity** (books, chapters, verses, or words), with the idea that sources differ in the processes that inserted them, e.g. broad original narratives versus surgical edits. Second, and separate from the feature vectors, we construct a **sibling** adjacency matrix for the spans, where a span is connected to another if they share the same parent in the WLC (e.g. if the span is a sequence of chapters in Genesis, the parent is the Genesis book node). This will allow graph-aware models to consider how a source is situated relative to nearby sources.

Models[2]

Our baseline models are logistic regression (LR), a standard non-neural classification model capable of handling heterogeneous and potentially-correlated features, and multi-layer perceptrons (MLP), the structure-unaware corrolary to the simple GCN architecture we employ:

LR Logistic regression is equivalent to a neural network with a single fully-connected linear mapping feature vector to label distribution

MLP A multi-layer perceptron maps the input feature vector through L fully-connected hidden layers of dimensionality $d_1, d_2 \ldots d_L$, each followed by an activation function

GCN Graph convolutional networks (Kipf and Welling, 2016) are similar to MLPs, but at each hidden layer the current *matrix* containing hidden states of *all* data points is multiplied by the adjacency matrix, allowing a data point to take its neighbors' states into account

The final layer (or, in the case of **LR**, the input) is fed to a fully-connected linear layer that projects it to the number of labels, followed by softmax to get a valid distribution. For **MLP** and **GCN**, We experiment with linear and non-linear (ReLU) activations, with 32-unit hidden representations based on dev set grid search over possible sizes in $(16, 32, 64, 128)$. All models can be trained with or without the granularity indicator variables (**gran**). The **GCN** models are also passed the sibling adjacency matrix: combined with one hidden layer, this allows the models to take into account properties of adjacent spans.

The labeled spans are randomly split into 80/10/10 train/dev/test. Because the data set is very small, we can treat it as a single large batch, which also simplifies the GCN approach, and train by only back-propagating error from the training set loss. We use the Adam optimizer with default parameters ($lr = 0.001, betas = (0.9, 0.999)$) and allow up to 10k epochs, and monitor the dev set loss for early stopping after 100 epochs without improvement. We report macro F-scores on the test set, which gives equal weight to the eight source labels.

3 Results

Table 2 shows the performance of the model and feature combinations described in Section 2. Our primary result is that **GCN**, with ReLU activation and the granularity features, outperforms the other configurations. Perhaps most striking is the importance of the granularity features for the models with hidden layers. While these indicator variables hurt performance of logistic regression, the rest of the models all see ~10-20 point improvements. Interestingly, when using the full feature set (i.e. allowing the model to consider topic), including granularity features dramatically and consistently *lowers* performance: with only word features, all GCN and MLP models manage an F-score ~77, but with the granularity indicators this drops to ~56. The granularity features may allow for particularly damaging overfitting, and we plan to explore this in follow-up work.

Model	F-score
LogisticRegression	45.80
LogisticRegression+gran	41.39
GCNstruct+lin	11.24
GCNstruct+relu	7.92
MLP+lin	27.79
MLP+lin+gran	45.22
MLP+relu	24.97
MLP+relu+gran	47.45
GCN+lin	31.38
GCN+lin+gran	46.64
GCN+relu	28.77
GCN+relu+gran	**48.60**

Table 2: Performance of different model and feature configurations on the test set, in terms of macro F-score

[2]Code available at www.github.com/ FirstAuthor/documentary-hypothesis

Table 3 shows the confusion matrix of the best model (GCN+relu+gran). The P source is more than twice as likely to be misclassified as J than as E, perhaps reflecting their shared provenance in Judah and concern with the Aaronic priesthood. The P and R sources also show affinity, again, with the latter thought to have arisen in Judah (or Babylon) long after Israel ceased to exist.

Gold	Guess							
	J	E	P	1D	2D	nD	R	O
J	100	8	7	0	0	0	3	0
E	22	53	8	0	0	0	0	0
P	13	5	77	0	1	0	4	0
1D	2	0	2	7	1	0	0	0
2D	2	2	1	0	5	0	0	0
nD	0	0	0	1	0	0	0	0
R	3	3	11	0	0	0	33	0
O	2	0	1	0	0	0	1	0

Table 3: Confusion matrix of the eight labels for GCN+relu+gran, where entry (r, c) is the number of times label r was misclassified as label c

Table 4 lists the ten most-misclassified spans, based on the difference between the probability of the guessed label and the correct label. Looking closely at a few misclassified spans, we make some (amateur) observations: the P and J sources share an affinity for the word "wife",[3] sometimes inserting a clarification of the E source that otherwise paints a less-than-monogamous picture. However, combined with our bag-of-words assumption this can create problems: Genesis:25:1-4 is labeled E but misclassified P, using the word "wife" in the context of "took an additional wife". For Numbers:13:21-22 (P, misclassified as J), the model misses the discontinuity introduced between the preceding and succeeding spans, whose specific focus on "grapes" is strangely interrupted (though this feature is also inaccessible due to the initial feature selection). Finally, Deuteronomy:32:48-52 (O, misclassified as P) is interesting because it is a direct copy of Numbers:27:12-14, which is indeed P.

4 Future work

Along with graph convolutional networks, several graph-aware neural models have recently been introduced (e.g. graph attention networks

Span	True	Guess	Diff
Exodus:14:8	P	R	88.42
Numbers:13:21-22	P	J	88.10
Genesis:37:28.11-20	J	P	83.88
Genesis:30:4.1-6	J	P	81.32
Deuteronomy:32:48-52	O	P	78.96
Genesis:21:2.1-6	J	P	66.48
Genesis:25:1-4	E	P	62.54
Numbers:26:9-11	R	P	60.95
Exodus:14:25.1-6	E	J	60.61
Genesis:22:11.1-16.5	R	J	59.36

Table 4: Top ten misclassifications based on difference between the probability of the true label and the probability of the (incorrectly) guessed label

(Veličković et al., 2017), tree-structured variational autoencoders (Yin et al., 2018)), and their effectiveness should be tested on this task. In particular, vanilla GCNs are limited in how they integrate information from other nodes, and the expressivity of these models may prove useful for the more complex relationships involved in compositional forces. Active research into augmented GCNs (Lee et al., 2018) is another avenue for addressing the current limitations.

There are existing resources for Hebrew NLP (Multiple, 2019) that, in principle, could facilitate feature engineering. Authors often have strong positive or negative dispositions regarding people, places, activities, and the like. Moses vs. Aaron is the most obvious for the DH, but characters like Baalam and many of the pre-exilic judges/kings have striking mixtures of praise and condemnation. Sentiment detection (Amram et al., 2018) might provide a window into these differences. Several DH justifications involve concept-realization (most famously, the use of Elohim vs Jehovah for the Deity), and being able to tie two words as alternate expressions of the same concept would be very useful. However, we are hesitant to incorporate modern resources due to potential bias, both in general language (given Hebrew's long existence as a liturgical language and subsequent revival) and specific resources created by scholars who may unintentionally encode their own conclusions. We therefore are experimenting with training unsupervised distributional models (Blei et al., 2003; Mikolov et al., 2013; Lippincott et al., 2012; Rasooli et al., 2014) directly on Biblical and contem-

---

[3]One of the common nouns that met the filter criterion.

porary texts to produce low-bias probablistic linguistic resources.

There is a far richer space of traditional scholarly hypotheses regarding the Bible that we plan to consider in future work. For example, the Deuteronomist sources are historically entangled with the historical books (Judges through Kings), and the prophet Jeremiah and his scribe, Baruch, which ties them to a number of spans outside the Torah (Friedman, 1987). Other annotations include: spans thought to be written in the closely-related Aramaic language, links between narrative doublets, information on poetic meter, and observations on antiquated linguistic markers. We are augmenting the initial TEI document with these annotation layers.

We framed our task as supervised span classification of a source-critical hypothesis, with the spans themselves (and hence their structural relations) taken for granted. Our longer-term goal is hypothesis *generation*, in which a model can be applied to unseen documents and propose their compositional structure. This will involve combining a linguisticly-driven model with a structural model that encourages parsimonious hypotheses. Data for training such a structural model is an open question: version control for collaborative writing is a natural modern choice, but only partially overlaps with the phenomena in the centuries-long transmission of historical text.

5 Conclusion

We have demonstrated that a simple graph convolutional network outperforms graph-unaware models on a task from traditional source criticism. Our error analysis revealed several characteristic shortcomings of the model and feature set, and we discussed future directions to address these.

This study is also a first step towards a more general approach to studying compositional forces in richly-structured historical texts. The basic assumptions of a tree-structured document with traditional annotations attached to nodes fits many situations, and in fact an immediate next step is to adopt these procedures to arbitrary TEI-encoded data sets and metadata. This will open up a broad range of existing documents and hypotheses (Smith et al., 2000; Tom Elliott, 2017; Association for Literary and Linguistic Computing, 1977; University of Ulster, 2017), and encourage collaboration with domain experts via e.g. common visualization and annotation tools.

References

Adam Amram, Anat Ben-David, and Reut Tsarfaty. 2018. Representations and Architectures in Neural Sentiment Analysis for Morphologically Rich Languages: A Case Study from Modern Hebrew. In *Proceedings of the 27th International Conference on Computational Linguistics*, pages 2242–2252.

Association for Literary and Linguistic Computing. 1977. Oxford Archive of Electronic Literature.

David M Blei, Andrew Y Ng, and Michael I Jordan. 2003. Latent Dirichlet allocation. *Journal of machine Learning research*, 3(Jan):993–1022.

TEI Consortium editors. 2019. TEI P5: Guidelines for Electronic Text Encoding and Interchange.

Richard Elliott Friedman. 1987. *Who Wrote the Bible?* Simon and Schuster.

Richard Elliott Friedman. 2003. *The Bible with Sources Revealed*. HarperCollins.

Thomas N Kipf and Max Welling. 2016. Semi-supervised classification with graph convolutional networks. *arXiv preprint arXiv:1609.02907*.

John Boaz Lee, Ryan A Rossi, Xiangnan Kong, Sungchul Kim, Eunyee Koh, and Anup Rao. 2018. Higher-order graph convolutional networks. *arXiv preprint arXiv:1809.07697*.

Thomas Lippincott. 2009. A Framework for Multilayered Boundary Detection. *Digital Humanities 2009*.

Thomas Lippincott, Diarmuid O Séaghdha, and Anna Korhonen. 2012. Learning syntactic verb frames using graphical models. In *Proceedings of the 50th Annual Meeting of the Association for Computational Linguistics: Long Papers-Volum e 1*, pages 420–429. Association for Computational Linguistics.

Kirk E. Lowery. 2016. A Reference Guide to the Westminster Leningrad Codex.

Tomas Mikolov, Ilya Sutskever, Kai Chen, Greg S Corrado, and Jeff Dean. 2013. Distributed Representations of Words and Phrases and their Compositionality. In C. J. C. Burges, L. Bottou, M. Welling, Z. Ghahramani, and K. Q. Weinberger, editors, *Advances in Neural Information Processing Systems 26*, pages 3111–3119. Curran Associates, Inc.

Frederick Mosteller and David L. Wallace. 1963. Inference in an Authorship Problem. *Journal of the American Statistical Association*, 58(302):275–309.

Multiple. 2019. Hebrew NLP Resources.

Martin Potthast, Francisco Rangel, Michael Tschugnall, Efstathios Stamatatos, Paolo Rosso, and Benno Stein. 2017. Overview of PAN'17: Author Identification, Author Profiling, and Author Obfuscation. In *Experimental IR Meets Multilinguality, Multimodality, and Interaction. 7th International Conference of the CLEF Initiative (CLEF 17)*, Berlin Heidelberg New York. Springer.

Martin Potthast, Benno Stein, Alberto Barrón-Cedeño, and Paolo Rosso. 2010. An evaluation framework for plagiarism detection. In *Proceedings of the 23rd international conference on computational linguistics: Posters*, pages 997–1005. Association for Computational Linguistics.

Mohammad Sadegh Rasooli, Thomas Lippincott, Nizar Habash, and Owen Rambow. 2014. Unsupervised Morphology-Based Vocabulary Expansion. In *ACL (1)*, pages 1349–1359.

Yunita Sari, Mark Stevenson, and Andreas Vlachos. 2018. Topic or Style? Exploring the Most Useful Features for Authorship Attribution. In *Proceedings of the 27th International Conference on Computational Linguistics*, pages 343–353.

Shachar Seidman and Moshe Koppel. 2017. Detecting pseudepigraphic texts using novel similarity measures. *Digital Scholarship in the Humanities*, 33(1):72–81.

Yanir Seroussi, Ingrid Zukerman, and Fabian Bohnert. 2011. Authorship attribution with latent Dirichlet allocation. In *Proceedings of the fifteenth conference on computational natural language learning*, pages 181–189. Association for Computational Linguistics.

DA Smith, JA Rydberg-Cox, and GR Crane. 2000. The Perseus Project: a digital library for the humanities. *Literary and Linguistic Computing*, 15(1):15–25.

Efstathios Stamatatos. 2009. A survey of modern authorship attribution methods. *Journal of the American Society for information Science and Technology*, 60(3):538–556.

Kalaivani Sundararajan and Damon Woodard. 2018. What represents "style" in authorship attribution? In *Proceedings of the 27th International Conference on Computational Linguistics*, pages 2814–2822.

Hugh Cayless et al. Tom Elliott, Gabriel Bodard. 2017. EpiDoc: Epigraphic Documents in TEI XML.

University of Ulster. 2017. CELT: Corpus of Electronic Texts.

Petar Veličković, Guillem Cucurull, Arantxa Casanova, Adriana Romero, Pietro Lio, and Yoshua Bengio. 2017. Graph attention networks. *arXiv preprint arXiv:1710.10903*.

Pengcheng Yin, Chunting Zhou, Junxian He, and Graham Neubig. 2018. StructVAE: Tree-structured latent variable models for semi-supervised semantic parsing. *arXiv preprint arXiv:1806.07832*.

Semantics and Homothetic Clustering of Hafez Poetry

Arya Rahgozar **Diana Inkpen**
School of Engineering and Computer Science
University of Ottawa, Canada
800 King Edward Ave. Ottawa, ON, K1N 6N5
arahgoza@uottawa.ca diana@site.uottawa.ca

Abstract

We have created two sets of labels for Hafez[1] (1315-1390) poems, using unsupervised learning. Our labels are the only semantic clustering alternative to the previously existing, hand-labeled, gold-standard classification of Hafez poems, to be used for literary research. We have cross-referenced, measured and analyzed the agreements of our clustering labels with Houman's chronological classes. Our features are based on topic modeling and word embeddings. We also introduced a similarity of similarities' features, we called homothetic clustering approach that proved effective, in case of Hafez's small corpus of ghazals[2]. Although all our experiments showed different clusters when compared with Houman's classes, we think they were valid in their own right to have provided further insights, and have proved useful as a contrasting alternative to Houman's classes. Our homothetic clusterer and its feature design and engineering framework can be used for further semantic analysis of Hafez's poetry and other similar literary research.

1 Introduction

Chronological classification of Hafez poetry was done by Houman, in his book (Houman, 1938). He partly hand-classified Hafez's poems in 1938, based on the semantic attributes engraved and encrypted in the ghazals. Houman's labeling has been the gold-standard of chronological classification for Hafez, and Rahgozar and Inkpen (2016b) used them as training data for supervised learning to predict the rest of the ghazals. We used similar semantic features, but instead we conducted unsupervised learning (clustering experiments) to

create alternative labels to those of Houman. Houman's classification was based on the premise that artist's mindset and worldview changed throughout his lifetime and this change was reflected in his art, in this case, poetry. Hypothesising about the evolutionary reflection of this chronological worldview in the semantics of Hafez's art and capturing it, was Houman's intension; so was ours, but by using machine learning. For example, Houman believed that the old Hafez was more introverted than the young. Houman explained in detail that these worldview characteristics and their interpretations were buried in the semantic attributes of Hafez's highly indirect, multilayered and equivocal ghazals, intertwined among couplets' and hemistiches' surface meaning, but differently throughout his life.

1.1 Problem Statement

We hope that the chronological classification of Hafez would facilitate interpretations and demystify the depth of meaning in his majestic poetry. In this work, we used clustering as a semantic analysis tool to assist with literary investigations of Hafez's poetry. As a result, we have produced new unsupervised labeling standards for Hafez corpus[3]. We have also conducted what we refer to as *homothetic clustering* experiments, using similarity transformations as features, discussed in Section 2.5. We have performed semantic analysis, partly discussed in Section 4, using a topic-modelling visualization interactive tool.

Although the fundamental question was to find out how consistent our semantic-based clustering would be with Houman's chronological classification, and to establish a verification experiment

---

[1]Persian philosopher and poet.

[2]Popular form of Persian poetry with specific rhyme and rhythm, consisting of about ten, seemingly independent couplets; Ghazal is interchangably used with the word poem here.

[3]Our Hafez corpus will be available, alternative sources for Hafez corpus are https://ganjoor.net/hafez/, http://www.nosokhan.com/ and https://www.hafizonlove.com/

Proc. of the 3rd Joint SIGHUM Workshop on Computational Linguistics for Cultural Heritage, Social Sciences, Humanities and Literature, pp. 82–90
Minneapolis, MN, USA, June 7, 2019. ©2019 Association for Computational Linguistics

against Houman's labeling, we set to achieve the following objectives:

- Semantic Feature Engineering;

- K-Means Clustering: Automatic Semantic Labeling;

- Similarity Feature Transformation as Homothetic Clustering;

- Multi-label Semantic Analysis and Visualization: Houman's, plus Machine Labeling.

We also wanted to see if homothetic features could qualify our unsupervised method as a guided or quasi-semi-supervised labeling.

2 Methodology

Our focus was to observe the performance and identify the semantic features that provided us with the best clustering results, measured by *Silhouette*. We were also interested to find out which features produced more consistent results with Houman labels. To measure interagreements we used *kappa* and other measures. In all the experiments, the clustering algorithm was K-Means to focus on the effects of features.

2.1 Corpus Work

Our bilingual[4] Hafez corpus had six chronological classes labeled by Dr. Houman[5] that were logically enumerated from *Youth* to *Senectitude*, therefore they could be logically consolidated into valid three classes, while maintaining their sequential order. Houman only labeled 248 poems out of 460 total confirmed Hafez ghazals, and we only considered those poems for clustering, so that we could cross-reference, verify and compare their Houman-classifications with our clustering generated labels or classes.
We applied the *white-space*[6] character and zero-width joiner (ZWJ), wherever it was needed in our corpus, so that the linguistic properties of Persian words and their inflections were maintained consistently.

2.2 Preprocessing

We followed (Asgari and Chappelier, 2013) for our preprocessing steps:

- Tokenization

- Normalization

- Lemmatization

- Filtering

In our preprocessing we removed the stop-words and the tokens that occured only once. We built the dictionary of documents, every document being a poem (ghazal). Then using the bag-of-words, we set up and transformed the corpus into vector representations. We built the TF-IDF[7] vectors accordingly. We initialized LSI, LDA[8], Log-Entropy (Lee et al., 2005) and Doc2Vec (Le and Mikolov, 2014) objects using both the Persian and Persian-English corpus as training. We used gensim library (Řehůřek and Sojka, 2010) and used HAZM[9] Python library for Persian pre-processing tasks, such as *lemmatization*.

2.3 Clustering Evaluation Indices

We followed metrics and clustering agreement techniques and scores[10] to measure our performance results in comparison with Houman's chronological labels. A value of one indicated perfect consistency.

- *Inertia*: Within-cluster sum of squared criterion, which K-Means clustering tries to minimize; the lower the inertia is the better.

- *Homogeneity*: Average single Houman class poems' distance to the center of the clusters; clusters are homogeneous if they only contain poems of a single Houman-class;

- *Completeness*: A measure of parallel correspondence between Houman classes and our clusters;

---

[4]Persian-English

[5]Dr. Houman labeled Hafez in about 1317 SH (1939 AD).

[6]Persian words can be multi-words; white-space is a transparent character linking the sub-tokens, for example **daneʃ âmuz** means student, is one word, but is written as two.

[7]Term frequency/inverse document frequency is a measure of term's importance among documents in the corpus.

[8]A high number of topics were pointless given our small corpus size, but we chose $(5 < Topics - Number < 20)$, based on Silhouette convergence, in each experiment setting.

[9]https://pypi.org/project/hazm/

[10]http://scikit-learn.org/

- *V Measure*: Homogeneity = HOM, Completeness = COM:

$$2 * (HOM * COM)/(HOM + COM)$$

- *Adjusted Random Index* (ARI): Is a similarity measure between clusters by pairwise comparisons of cluster and Houman class poems, E = Expected:

$$ARI = (RI - E(RI))/(max(RI) - E(RI))$$

- *Adjusted Mutual Info*: Is a symmetric measure of dependence between our cluster membership and the Houman-class:

$$\frac{MI(U,V) - E(MI(U,V))}{max(H(U),H(V)) - E(MI(U,V))}$$

- *Silhouette*: Is a measure of cohesion and distinctive quality to separate clusters, that is the mean of a and b, $(b - a)/max(a,b)$, where a and b are aggregated intra-cluster and nearest-cluster distances of each poem.

- *Cohen's kappa* measures the consistencies between two sets of labels, generated by classification or clustering[11]:

$$\kappa = \frac{p_o - p_e}{1 - p_e} = 1 - \frac{1 - p_o}{1 - p_e}$$

2.4 Feature Engineering

The variant of TFIDF we used was based on a logarithmically scaled frequencies of term i in document j in a corpus of D documents:

$$weight_{i,j} = frequency_{i,j} * log_2 \frac{D}{document-freq_i}$$

The LDA[12] implementation followed (Hoffman et al., 2010); base code was found here[13]. We kept the default parameters when initialized the LDA model, except setting wokers equal to 8. For the LDA driven similarities, we only set the number of topics and passes to 5.

Doc2Vec[14] implementation followed (Mikolov et al., 2013). We set the parameters as follows: vector size=249, window=8, min count=5, workers=8, dm = 1, alpha=0.025, min alpha=0.001, start alpha=0.01, infer epoch=1000.

---

[11]en.wikipedia.org

[12]https://radimrehurek.com/gensim/models/ldamulticore.html

[13]https://github.com/blei-lab/onlineldavb

[14]https://radimrehurek.com/gensim/models/doc2vec.html

2.5 Homothetic Features: Sim^2

Homothetic transformations are frequently used in transferring arguments amongst economic models. Intuitively, one could think of the concept as similarity of similarities. In our case, for every poem in the corpus, represented as LDA-driven vector, we derived and formed a new vector, consisting of calculated *Cosine* similarities or distances from that poem to a subset of hand-picked poems, we refer to as anchors. Anchors were chosen for semantic reasons to guide the clustering towards Houman's classes. By these similarity measures to the anchors, we formed a new vectorized corpus. In other words, we used *Cosine* similarity as a transformation function from one vector space to another, before we measured their Euclidean distances, in a clustering procedure such as K-Means.

Data: Hafez Corpus
Result: Generate labels
read corpus and anchor instances;
tokenize, remove stop-words and tokens-once;
normalize, lemmatize;
create *bag-of-words, TF-IDF*;
initialization LDA;
create *LDA-driven* similarity index;
while *not at end of the corpus* **do**
    while *not at end of the anchors* **do**
        calculate *similarity* Measure;
        append to vector list;
        go to the next anchor;
    end
    write document similarities: *Sim-Corpus*;
    go to the next document;
end
set k clusters;
cluster (*Sim-Corpus*);
produce predictions;
Algorithm 1: Homothetic Clustering, Sim^2

2.5.1 Homothetic Properties

Similarity transformations are not necessarily linear, as we ran into the equality contradiction of summation of two square roots of polynomials and that of one, which proves the nonlinearity property, in a 3D Euclidean space:

$$f(u) + f(v) \neq f(u + v)$$

Similarity transformations also maintain *homothetic* properties, a monotonic transformation of a

Feature	Inertia	Homog.	Comp.	v-meas.	ARI	AMI
LogEntropy	238	0.017	0.015	0.016	-0.004	0.008
LSI	237	0.004	0.004	0.004	-0.003	-0.004
LDA-TFIDF	233	0.003	0.009	0.005	0.013	-0.007
LDA	233	0.006	**0.023**	0.009	-0.007	-0.004
Doc2Vec-P	1445	0.010	0.010	0.010	-0.008	-0.002
Doc2Vec-PE	338	0.020	0.017	0.018	0.018	**0.010**

Table 1: K-Means Performance, $(k = cls = 3)$
cls = number of classes

Feature	3cls-Silhouette	6cls-Silhouette
LogEntropy	0.001	-0.000
LSI	0.001	-0.002
LDA-TFIDF	0.037	0.097
LDA	0.059	0.109
Doc2Vec-P	**0.560**	**0.528**
Doc2Vec-PE	0.530	0.471

Table 2: K-Means Performance
P=Persian, E=English

Feature	Inertia	Homog.	Comp.	v-meas.	ARI	AMI
HRP	0	0.034	0.035	0.034	-0.001	0.004
HEP	0	0.024	0.024	0.024	-0.006	-0.006
RND	0	0.021	0.022	0.021	0.001	-0.009

Table 3: Sim^2 Performance
$(k = anchors = cls = 6)$

homogenous function for which the level sets were radial expansions of one another. In Euclidean geometry, a homothety of factor k magnifies or *dilates* distances between points by $|k|$ times, in the target vector-space. Risk of overfitting and its divergence was also empirically suspected to be higher and quicker. The properties of Homothetic functions were proven by (Simon and Blume, 1994):

$$v(tx) = g(u(tx))$$

$$g(t^k u(x)) = g(t^k u(y)) = g(u(ty)) = v(ty)$$

We have demonstrated empirically, that the homothetic clustering procedure we used here, was effective to increase Silhouette score and showed tractable interpretations, when used against our small poetry corpus of Hafez. The average complexity of the homothetic clustering was the same as the complexity of the clustering method it uses. In this case, we used K-Means with polynomial smoothed running time, therefore the complexity was the number of samples n, times the number of iterations i, times the number of clusters k:

$$Complexity(Sim^2) = O(n.i.k)$$

3 Experiments

In the first set of experiments, we used different semantic features for clustering. We then passed the vector representation of the labeled portion of the corpus to K-Means[15] for clustering ($k = 3, 6$). Then we compared the clustering labels with Houman labels. The Table 1 shows the results. As we see, the Doc2VecPE feature ranked at the top in *Homogeneity, V-measure, ARI* and *AMI*. The LDA feature obtained the best in *Completeness* compared to other features. As we see in Table 2 The pure Persian *Embedding, (Doc2Vec-P)* showed the highest *Silhouette*[16], while adding English[17] to the

---

[15] http://scikit-learn.org/

[16] Defined in Section 2.3

[17] English translation of the poems by Shahriari, were inline with the Persian version, when the translation was available.

corpus brought this measure a bit lower and still maintained second rank compared to all other features.

3.1 Homothetic Clustering Experiments

Houman (1938) picked a representative poem for each of his classes. For every poem of the labeled portion of the corpus, we calculated the LDA-based similarities to either three (or six) anchor poems, depending on the intended clusters. The resulting vector-space had three (or six) dimensions. We called this Houman Representative Picks (HRP). In a separate set of experiments, we also picked six poems as anchors, three poems from either extreme peripheries of the Houman's labeled poem classes, that is three from the earliest *Youth* class, and three from the latest period ranked in the *Senectitude*. We referred to this experiment's feature set, Houman Extremal Picks (HEP). Or in case of the three classes HEP, we picked two extremal poems and one from central poem from class two, mid-age. RND stands for random picks. We always maintained that the number of anchors matched with the number of intended clusters: ($anchors = k = 3, 6$), shown in the tables.

As we see in Table 3, HEP, HRP and RND maintain zero *Inertia*, which is an indication of perfect inner cohesion of the clusters. HRP has about 3% as the highest *Homogeneity*, which was higher than that of the challenger, Table 1. LDA had the highest *completeness* as challenger, while Doc2Vec-PE had the highest *AMI*. Both HRP and HEP champion models with similarity features also entailed higher *Silhouette* scores in clustering (Table 4) than the one achieved by

Feature	6cls-Sil.	6cls-Kap.	3cls-Sil.	3cls-Kap.
HEP	0.837	0.004	0.695	-0.014
HRP	0.903	**0.034**	0.824	-0.006
RND	**0.945**	-0.052	0.821	-0.001

Table 4: Sim^2 Performance, (kappa with Houman)

the challenger model, with word-embedding features. Only HRP showed slight resemblance with Houman's classes, as kappa indicated in the same Table. This means that Houman's poems that he mentioned in his book as their class representatives, while explaining his methodology, had a better homothetic guiding power than the actual extremal poems of his classified corpus, when we used them as anchors.

The number of LDA topics in multiple K-Means runs, affected the Silhouette score, but mostly converged in around 5 to 15 topics, depending on the feature set. To avoid local-optima, it was also important to iterate through K-Means algorithm enough times to attain an optimum Silhouette score while targeting the right number of LDA topics, to achieve the best possible clustering quality. Our Homothetic experiments achieved best *Silhouette* scores with 6 LDA topics. In all homothetic and non-homothetic clustering experiments, number of clusters $k = 6$ and $k = 3$, achieved the highest silhouette scores, in their experiments group respectively, $k = anchors$. In homothetic experiments, $k = 6$ clusters always produced both better kappa[18] and silhouette, regardless of the number of anchors being 3 or 6.

We also compared the consistency of HEP Sim^2 clusterer with the challenger (Doc2VecP) model. The Spearman correlation was 0.86. Noteworthy, the Cohen's linear and nonlinear *Kappa* were 0.58 and 0.43 respectively, between these two independent clusterers.

Our Student's t-test did not support the claim that anchors guided the Sim^2 clustering to have a significant consistency with Houman classifications, when we compared the effects of HEP and HRP anchors with randomly selected 6 anchors instead, using *kappa*. Although random anchors were selected with the proviso that they came from different Houman classes.The *Silhouette* of Sim^2 clusterer with random anchors was close to that of HEP and HRP, very high.

<hr>

[18]Comparing only when $k = cls$.

Duplicity, Sufi and Abstemious	A	B	C
Doc2Vec-P	56, 19, 22	12, 2, 3	17, 3, 4
HRP	31, 11, 13	30, 5, 6	24, 8, 6
HCEP	19, 4, 5	53, 15, 13	13, 5, 7
Vision, Barmaid, Knave	B	A	C
Doc2Vec-P	18, 11, 17	58, 39, 67	8, 10, 0
HRP	17, 19, 19	29, 26, 29	38, 15, 0
HCEP	51, 38, 63	18, 11, 14	15, 11, 0
Expedient, Guru, Pub	C	A	B
Doc2Vec-P	1, 9, 0	6, 44, 1	2, 11, 0
HRP	4, 22, 5	1, 21, 0	4, 21, 1
HCEP	3, 14, 1	0, 14, 0	6, 36, 0

Figure 1: Tracing Clusters of Terms

4 Analysis and Discussion

We used the Persian part of the corpus for this section, suffices to demonstrate the semantic values of our new sets of labels.

4.1 Cycle of Words

More rigorous analysis should be done by literary scholars, but as a sample of examination, we constructed in Figure 1 as follows. We counted the Houman labeled poems in each cluster and calculated their percentages to decide the highest resemblance of each cluster with its closest Houman class. In case of a tie, we did the same for the other clusters and then tracked back to maximize an overall resemblance. HRP and HEP were constructed as explained in Section 3.1. Then we considered a cluster of terms, relevant to Houman's representative poems and his semantic constructs (Houman, 1938). For Youth class (A), we chose three terms: Duplicity (*riâ*), Sufi (*sufi*) and Abstemious (*zâhəd*), and for Mid-age class (B), we chose Vision (*nazar*), Barmaid (*sâqi*), Knave (*rənd*) and finally for the Senectitude (C), we chose three representative terms of Expedient (*masləhat*), Guru (*pir*), Pub (*meikade*). Then we counted the frequency of the terms in each cluster, as per the closest Houman-class. Each cell in Figure 1 contains frequencies of three terms respectively.

If we trace any effect of anchors' semantics in the final homothetic clustering result, we observed that HRP had slightly stronger resemblance with the Houman classes as it was also measured by higher homogeneity and completeness in Section 3.1. Both HEP and HRP showed better overall balanced distribution in terms of size of each cluster compared to Doc2Vec-P, which was also reflected in the higher silhouette score from Section 3.1. Although both HEP and HRP showed stronger correlation with Houman-classes than Doc2Vec did. HEP was also stronger in discriminating against class A and C which was attributed to its original anchor poems purposely picked from the same peripheries of the chronological Hafez corpus. This simple example, therefore, was consistent with the assumption that similarity measures transferred the information to the clustering and guided it as per the semantics of the *anchored* poems.

4.2 Semantic Analysis

Each poem's new label provided new perspective and insights, to enable us interpret Hafez's poem better, by investigating the semantic characteristics of its associated cluster, in conjunction with its Houman classification. We could visualize the corresponding cluster, using *LDAvis* topic modelling (Sievert and Shirley, 2014) who introduced and used *Relevance* measure. (2012) defined and developed *Saliency* as part of Termite visualization tool.

For example, we selected to analyze a poem, number 230 from the Houman labeled portion of the corpus, which was the number 143 in Ganjour[19]. On the one hand, we saw that this poem belonged to class 5 or *before-senectitude* of Houman's classification. On the other hand, we looked at the top 30 terms of the topic 3 which was central in PCA depiction of 5 LDA topics, Figure 2, which corresponded with our new label 1 cluster poems generated by Sim^2 clusterer. The words *old (pɪr), Heart (dəl), Love (əʃq), Guru (pɪr ə moqân), Sadness (qam), Ocean (dariâ), Circle (dâyərə), Want (talab), Destiny (kâr), Sigh (âh)* were not only semantically consistent between the two classifications, but they also provided us with a tangible context to better understand and associate with the poem.

Interacting with the visualization tool revealed other themes associated with this previously known as *before-senectitude* poem, that for example, showed a topic 2 at the left of PC1 line, having top salient words such as *jewel (laəl), gal (iâr), sun (xorʃɪd), earth (xâk), hand (dast), heart (dəl), joy (xoʃ), laughter (xandân), love (əʃq), flaw*

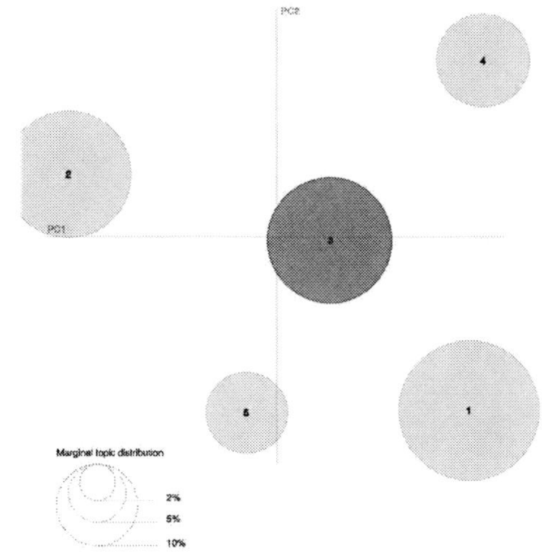

Figure 2: Intertopic Distance Map

(əib). This indicated that the traces of material world and its desires still equally existed and decorated Hafez's poetry, even during those mature years of his life, but he perhaps used these words more metaphorically and mystically.

For years my heart was in search of the Grail What was inside me it searched for on the trail

That pearl that transcends time and place Sought of divers whom oceans sail

My quest to the Magi my path trace One glance solved the riddles that I Braille

Found him wine in hand and happy face In the mirror of his cup would watch a hundred detail

I asked "when did God give you this Holy Grail?" Said "on the day He hammered the worlds first nail!"

Even the unbeliever had the support of God Though he could not see Gods name would always hail.

All the tricks of the mind would make God seem like fraud Yet the Golden Calf beside Moses rod would just pale.

And the one put on the cross by his race His crime secrets of God would unveil

Anyone who is touched by Gods grace Can do what Christ did without fail.

And what of this curly lock that's my jail Said this is for Hafiz to tell his tale.

5 Related Work

Semi-supervised concepts, prototype and anchors have been discussed in the literature (Zhang et al., 2015), but our approach was new in that no label was directly used in the algorithm. Instead, instance similarities to a few labeled instances formed the entire vector space as their feature set,

---

[19]https://ganjoor.net/hafez/ghazal/sh143/

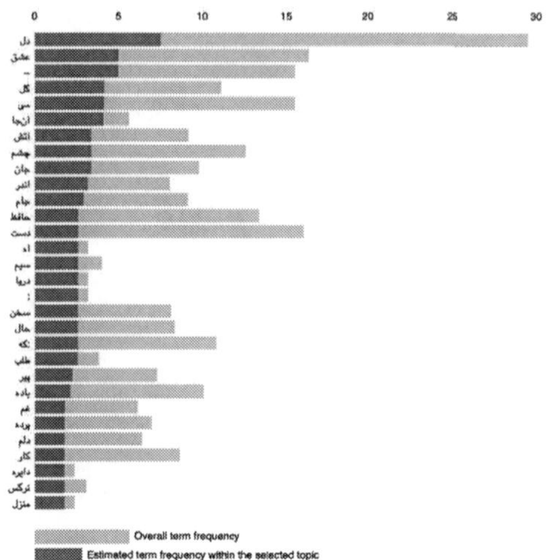

Figure 3: Top 30 Most Relevant Terms

which were then used in clustering. Rahgozar and Inkpen (2016a) used supervised learning to classify Hafez. We tried an unsupervised method and did not use master-labels by Houman (1938) as training, but we used his labels to evaluate our clusters. For a long time, researchers tried to extract what was implied in the context, by applying generative models and collocation of the words. For example Brown et al. (1992) assumed word clustering carried semantic groupings. Our corpus was considerably smaller than those in the literature, none-the-less, hand-labeling or human annotation is an expensive, rare and slow process. Therefore, similar to many NLP researchers, we used clustering to augment annotated data based on the assumption that word clusters contained specific semantic information (Miller et al., 2004). Capturing semantic latent properties has been a long and continuous effort in Computational Linguistics. (Deerwester et al., 1990) used *singular-value decomposition* as pseudo-document vectors to detect implicit semantic properties, referred to as latent semantic analysis (LSA) in text. This was what we intended to do but in poetic text. In the continuation of semantic endeavour, (Blei et al., 2003) later developed latent Dirichlet allocation (LDA), an unsupervised generative probabilistic model to extract topics and their important associated terms. We used LDA driven features, before passing them as vectorized corpus to the K-Means clustering algorithm. Inkpen and Razavi (2013) used LDA driven features for semantic classifications of news group texts. Asgari et al. (2013)

used topic models (unsupervised learning) to cluster Persian poetry by genre and then compared the results with SVM (supervised learning) classifications. Similarly, we used latent semantic indexing (LSI) and LDA-driven features for clustering. Saeedi et al. (2014) also used unsupervised semantic role labeling in Persian, but used different clustering scores than ours, such as purity and inverse-purity. We also used word embedding as features (Mikolov et al., 2011), which was the basis of our challenger model, against the top champion, the homothetic model. Zhang and Lapata (2014) used word embedding in poetry generation task and found it an effective feature for capturing the context.

The concept of *similarity*, mostly translated to *distance* in mathematics, is inherent and fundamental, especially in clustering and unsupervised learning algorithms. Kaplan and Blei (2007) for example, used vector space and principal components analysis (PCA), to depict style similarities in American poetry. Correlation was also used as a similarity measure to detect topics in poetry (Asgari and Chappelier, 2013). Lee et al. (2005) concluded that measures such as correlation, Jaccard and Cosine similarities performed almost the same in clustering documents. Similar to our research, Chambers and Jurafsky (2009) used but chain-similarities in an unsupervised learning algorithm, to determine narrative schemas and participants of semantic roles, instead of relying on any hand-built classes or knowledgebase. Their similarity definition was based on a pairwise summation of PMI and Log-Frequency of their narrative schema's vector representations. Then they maximized those similarities to score and determine semantic-role labels. Herbelot (2014) used similarity of word distributions, in pursuit of detecting semantic coherence in modern and contemporary poetry.

6 Conclusion

Capturing semantic attributes of text by machine learning has been an open research area. Houman's (1938) chronological and semantic classification of Hafez, unique up to now, assumed the young poet had a different world-view than the old, hence the difference would be reflected in his poetry, in terms of meaning. We created the first series of unsupervised semantic classifications of Hafez; using LDA, LSI, Log-

Entropy, Doc2Vec and similarity-driven features to capture such nuances of meaning. We showed that these NLP tools could help to produce different clusters of poems, to complement their scholarly hand-labeled version. We introduced the similarity-based features to build our champion models. We observed that our homothetic clustering had a slightly higher homogeneity, completeness and much better silhouette scores compared with our other features, but kappa distribution with Houman labels, was not statistically significant. Yet, in the analysis of our homothetic clustering results, we could trace the effect of similarity to the anchor poems. In case of HEP for example, clusters seemed to be more "aware" of classes "Youth" and "Senectitude", from which the anchors had been chosen.

Using LSI and LDA-driven features, similar to those Rahgozar and Inkpen (2016b) proved effective in chronological classification of Hafez poems, plus other semantically effective features, we created new sets of labels, not necessarily chronological, yet semantically different.

We applied our top homothetic feature engineering that proved the most effective in our clustering, to predict the whole Hafez corpus as a parallel labeling to Houman's. We investigated semantic differences, using both labels while comparing and tracing the consistencies through visualizations. We developed rigorous semantic analysis, refined and guided our homothetic clustering framework to get closer to Houman's ground-truth if possible. We provided multiple perspectives by our automatic labeling results and framework to support semantic analysis in literary scholarship.

6.1   Results

- Doc2Vec-P word-embedding scored higher coherence[20] and silhouette than other non-homothetic features used in Hafez automatic clustering experiments;

- We created two new sets of automatic labeling for Hafez corpus, by Doc2Vec as challenger and Sim^2 as champion clusterers, which had 0.58 *kappa* and 0.86 correlations but had insignificant resemblance with the Houman labels, 0.034 kappa at best(HRP-6cls);

- Sim^2 did not fully qualify as a quasi-semi-supervised[21] algorithm, given the low linear kappa with Houman, but proved to be a powerful clusterer, reaching (high coherence and) silhouette scores, of up to 95%;

- Sim^2 was the only clusterer to perform at its best with 6 clusters, equal to Houman classes, $k = cls$;

- None of the automatically generated labels were showing signigicant consistency with Houman's classification, but provided with new semantic perspectives to Hafez studies;

- Semantic evaluations and visulaizations helped validate the clustering results, using random poems;

- Visualizations in conjunction with homothetic clustering could be used to build a poetry analysis tool to support literary scholarship and research, even with small corpora such as ours.

Inspired by Houman's (1938) semantic approach, one can replicate and apply our poetry clustering framework to other poetic texts, as a means of assisting and enabling literary research and scholarly analysis of poetic text by clustering. We have also made the results of our clustering and new labels available for literary research and public use. Our guide is with refernce to the Houman's order of poems, which is based on Ghazvini copy[22] (see Appendix A).

References

Ehsaneddin Asgari and Jean-Cédric Chappelier. 2013. Linguistic resources and topic models for the analysis of persian poems. In *Proceedings of the Workshop on Computational Linguistics for Literature*, pages 23–31.

Ehsaneddin Asgari, Marzyeh Ghassemi, and Mark Alan Finlayson. 2013. Confirming the themes and interpretive unity of ghazal poetry using topic models. In *Neural Information Processing Systems (NIPS) Workshop for Topic Models*.

---

[20]*Coherences* were not reported here specifically as they were reflected in *Silhouette* scores by definition.

[21]Handpicked anchors did not significantly increase kappa with Houman labels.

[22]An old reliable source of Hafez poems.

David M Blei, Andrew Y Ng, and Michael I Jordan. 2003. Latent dirichlet allocation. *Journal of machine Learning research*, 3(Jan):993–1022.

Peter F Brown, Peter V Desouza, Robert L Mercer, Vincent J Della Pietra, and Jenifer C Lai. 1992. Class-based n-gram models of natural language. *Computational linguistics*, 18(4):467–479.

Nathanael Chambers and Dan Jurafsky. 2009. Unsupervised learning of narrative schemas and their participants. In *Proceedings of the Joint Conference of the 47th Annual Meeting of the ACL and the 4th International Joint Conference on Natural Language Processing of the AFNLP: Volume 2-Volume 2*, pages 602–610. Association for Computational Linguistics.

Jason Chuang, Christopher D Manning, and Jeffrey Heer. 2012. Termite: Visualization techniques for assessing textual topic models. In *Proceedings of the international working conference on advanced visual interfaces*, pages 74–77. ACM.

Scott Deerwester, Susan T Dumais, George W Furnas, Thomas K Landauer, and Richard Harshman. 1990. Indexing by latent semantic analysis. *Journal of the American society for information science*, 41(6):391.

Aurélie Herbelot. 2014. The semantics of poetry: A distributional reading. *Digital Scholarship in the Humanities*, 30(4):516–531.

Matthew Hoffman, Francis R Bach, and David M Blei. 2010. Online learning for latent dirichlet allocation. In *advances in neural information processing systems*, pages 856–864.

Mahmoud Houman. 1938. *Hafez*. Tahuri.

D. Inkpen and A. H. Razavi. 2013. *Topic Classification using Latent Dirichlet Allocation at Multiple Levels*. School of Electrical Engineering and Computer Sci. University of Ottawa.

David M Kaplan and David M Blei. 2007. A computational approach to style in american poetry. In *Data Mining, 2007. ICDM 2007. Seventh IEEE International Conference on*, pages 553–558. IEEE.

Quoc Le and Tomas Mikolov. 2014. Distributed representations of sentences and documents. In *International Conference on Machine Learning*, pages 1188–1196.

Michael D Lee, Brandon Pincombe, and Matthew Welsh. 2005. An empirical evaluation of models of text document similarity. In *Proceedings of the Annual Meeting of the Cognitive Science Society*, volume 27.

Tomas Mikolov, Kai Chen, Greg Corrado, and Jeffrey Dean. 2013. Efficient estimation of word representations in vector space. *arXiv preprint arXiv:1301.3781*.

Tomáš Mikolov, Anoop Deoras, Daniel Povey, Lukáš Burget, and Jan Černocký. 2011. Strategies for training large scale neural network language models. In *Automatic Speech Recognition and Understanding (ASRU), 2011 IEEE Workshop on*, pages 196–201. IEEE.

Scott Miller, Jethran Guinness, and Alex Zamanian. 2004. Name tagging with word clusters and discriminative training. In *Proceedings of the Human Language Technology Conference of the North American Chapter of the Association for Computational Linguistics: HLT-NAACL 2004*.

Arya Rahgozar and Diana Inkpen. 2016a. Bilingual chronological classification of hafez's poems. In *Proceedings of the Fifth Workshop on Computational Linguistics for Literature*, pages 54–62.

Arya Rahgozar and Diana Inkpen. 2016b. Poetry chronological classification: Hafez. In *Canadian Conference on Artificial Intelligence*, pages 131–136. Springer.

Radim Řehůřek and Petr Sojka. 2010. Software Framework for Topic Modelling with Large Corpora. In *Proceedings of the LREC 2010 Workshop on New Challenges for NLP Frameworks*, pages 45–50, Valletta, Malta. ELRA. http://is.muni.cz/publication/884893/en.

Parisa Saeedi, Heshaam Faili, and Azadeh Shakery. 2014. Semantic role induction in persian: An unsupervised approach by using probabilistic models. *Literary and Linguistic Computing*, 31(1):181–203.

Carson Sievert and Kenneth Shirley. 2014. Ldavis: A method for visualizing and interpreting topics. In *Proceedings of the workshop on interactive language learning, visualization, and interfaces*, pages 63–70.

Carl P Simon and Lawrence Blume. 1994. *Mathematics for economists*, volume 7. Norton New York.

Kai Zhang, Liang Lan, James T Kwok, Slobodan Vucetic, and Bahram Parvin. 2015. Scaling up graph-based semisupervised learning via prototype vector machines. *IEEE transactions on neural networks and learning systems*, 26(3):444–457.

Xingxing Zhang and Mirella Lapata. 2014. Chinese poetry generation with recurrent neural networks. In *Proceedings of the 2014 Conference on Empirical Methods in Natural Language Processing (EMNLP)*, pages 670–680.

A Appendix

The most reliable print of Hafez is by Ghazvini, in which poems are organized alphabetically. The mapping table of the alphabetical order of poems to Houman classification can be found in (Houman, 1938).

Computational Linguistics Applications for Multimedia Services

Kyeongmin Rim   **Kelley Lynch**   **James Pustejovsky**

Department of Computer Science
Brandeis University
Waltham MA USA
{krim,kmlynch,jamesp}@brandeis.edu

Abstract

We present Computational Linguistics Applications for Multimedia Services (CLAMS), a platform that provides access to computational content analysis tools for archival multimedia material that appear in different media, such as text, audio, image, and video. The primary goal of CLAMS is: (1) to develop an interchange format between multimodal metadata generation tools to ensure interoperability between tools; (2) to provide users with a portable, user-friendly workflow engine to chain selected tools to extract meaningful analyses; and (3) to create a public software development kit (SDK) for developers that eases deployment of analysis tools within the CLAMS platform. CLAMS is designed to help archives and libraries enrich the metadata associated with their mass-digitized multimedia collections, that would otherwise be largely unsearchable.

1   Introduction and Motivation

Since the invention of the phonograph and moving pictures, audiovisual materials have been one of the primary methods of recording modern history alongside textual records. Many historical events, important persons, social issues, and major conflicts over the last several decades have been recorded on such mass media. Researchers in both media studies and the social sciences, as well as historians have long recognized the value of audio and visual records as evidence about the past (e.g., Boykoff and Boykoff, 2007; Dalton and Charnigo, 2004; Doms and Morin, 2004). Likewise, educators have appreciated the ability of multimedia materials to make history and cultural heritage artifacts come alive in the classroom setting (e.g. Ott and Pozzi, 2011; Antonaci et al., 2013). Recently, with the advent of large digital storage, there have been many large-scale projects aimed at the mass-digitization of books (Christenson, 2011), newspapers (NDNP, 2005), oral history (Oard et al., 2002; NYPL, 2013), and public broadcasting (MDPI, 2014; AAPB, 2015). Selections of results from these projects are publicly available through web-based *digital libraries*, often accompanied by a search interface. However, users of such digital library resources can be frustrated by the difficulties associated with accessing these historical audiovisual records, not because of any lack of accessibility to the digital media themselves, but because of the lack of accessibility to the *contents* of the media (Schaffner, 2009). Audiovisual media, unlike textual records, are opaque to even the simplest text-based search capability. Finding content relevant to one's research question among thousands of hours of audiovisual records, hence, is time-consuming, involving watching or listening to hours of contents. Therefore, a key to making a digital multimedia archive useful and accessible is to generate and deploy rich metadata of collection items (Cariani et al., 2015). The availability of such descriptive, structured, textual metadata about the content of the collections and the included items radically improve the searchability and discoverability of the material (Pustejovsky et al., 2017). Yet, manually cataloging meaningful and suitably robust metadata is a general challenge across digital archives, as it will also be time-consuming and laborious, involving archivists watching and listening to items.

In this paper, we describe the CLAMS[1] platform, developed for libraries and archivists to help enrich item-level descriptive metadata by providing with automatically extracted information from time-based multimedia collections utilizing computational analysis tools for text, audio, and video (Pustejovsky, 2018). These tools for different modalities will be orchestrated via CLAMS work-

---

[1] http://www.clams.ai

Proc. of the 3rd Joint SIGHUM Workshop on Computational Linguistics for Cultural Heritage, Social Sciences, Humanities and Literature, pp. 91–97
Minneapolis, MN, USA, June 7, 2019. ©2019 Association for Computational Linguistics

flow engine that provides a common interchange format ensuring syntactic and semantic interoperability between these tools.

2   Prior Work

Multilingual Access to Large Spoken Archives (MALACH) (Oard et al., 2002) was one of the early studies that used computational linguistics tools to build an automatic metadata extraction system. In MALACH, oral history recording data was processed through automatic speech recognition (ASR) and natural language processing (NLP) pipelines that extracted relevant information for cataloging. In prototyping its World Service Archive (Raimond et al., 2014), the BBC developed COMMA, an metadata extraction and linked data-based interlinking system for public radio broadcasts. Its outcome is now in use by the BBC (BBC, 2015), however it is not publicly available. More recently, the EU funded Media in Context (MiCO) project (Aichroth et al., 2015). This project aimed at accomplishing a media analysis platform for multimodal media that supports customized workflows leveraging on assorted open and closed source content analysis tools. An interoperability layer, MiCO Broker, was developed based on RDF and XML structures to chain different tools. Among the latest work, Audiovisual Metadata Platform (AMP) is noteworthy as it plans to design and develop a platform that exploits chains of automated tools and human-in-the-loop to generate and manage metadata at institutional scale (Dunn et al., 2018). We actively seek collaboration with others in order to move closer to achieving a "global laboratory" for language applications.

In the computational linguistics (CL) community, UIMA (Ferrucci et al., 2009) and GATE (Cunningham et al., 2013) have been longstanding popular tool-chaining platforms for researchers and NLP developers. Particularly, UIMA provides an extremely general model of type systems and annotations that can be applied upon multimedia source data. However, there is stiff learning curve behind its high generality, combined with its tight binding with XML syntax and Java programming language. More recently, web-based workflow engines such as the LAPPS Grid (Ide et al., 2014) and WebLicht (Hinrichs et al., 2010) provide user friendly web interfaces. Particularly, these web-based platforms not only offer tool repositories of various levels of state-of-the-art NLP tools for textual data, such as CoreNLP (Manning et al., 2014), OpenNLP (OpenNLP, 2017), but also implement open source SDK for tool developers to promote adoption. These workflow engines can operate different tools which are separately developed only because of the underlying data interchange formats that impose common I/O language between those tools. For such an interchange format, The LAPPS Grid uses LAPPS Interchange Format (LIF) rooted on JSON-LD serialization (Verhagen et al., 2015), while the WebLicht uses XML-based Text Corpus Format (TCF) (Heid et al., 2010). Additionally the LAPPS Grid defines a semantic linked data vocabulary that ensures semantic interoperability (Ide et al., 2015). Having implemented in-platform interoperability has led to a multi-platform collaboration between LAPPS and CLARIN (Hinrichs et al., 2018).

3   Project Description

Figure 1 shows the overall structure of the platform in a working environment as delivered to an archive. As a platform, the primary goals of CLAMS are 1) to develop an interchange format between multimodal annotations that allows analysis tools for different modalities to work together when chained into a single workflow, and 2) to provide libraries and archivists a portable workflow engine software with a user-friendly interface to select available tools and create workflows and run them, and lastly 3) to offer various analysis tools alongside a public SDK for developers of the tools that allows easy adoption of the interchange format and streamlined deployment to the workflow engine. In the rest of this section, we will discuss how we address each of aforementioned goals.

3.1   Multimodal Interoperability

To implement the platform with interoperating analysis tools, we developed Multi-Media Interchange Format (MMIF) as the *common tongue* of CLAMS. MMIF consists of two parts – it adopts the already successful JSON-LD as syntax, and an open linked data vocabulary for the semantics of the terminology. The vocabulary is re-using the LAPPS Grid vocabulary as its linguistic terminology, while extending it further to cover audiovisual concepts such as `timeFrame`, or `boundingBox`.

Typologically, multimodal annotations in

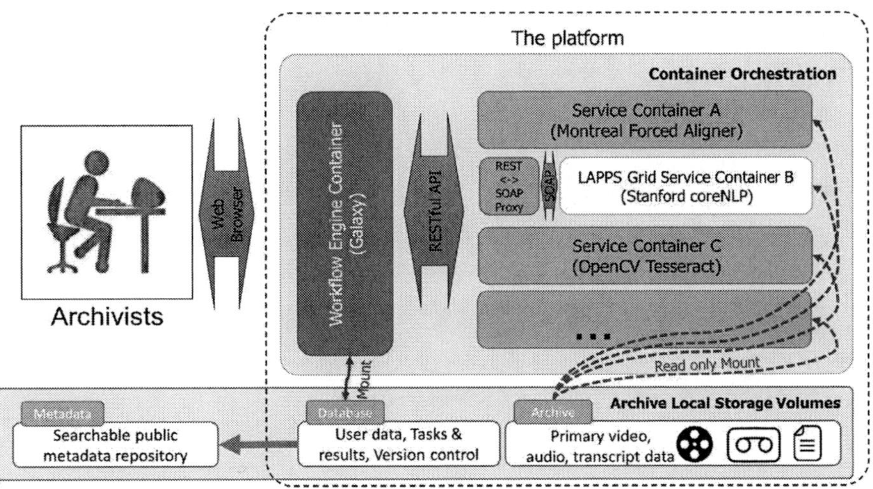

Figure 1: Architectural sketch of CLAMS platform. Archives pull the containerized platform and services. The platform runs as an orchestrated set of containers that are connected to local storage to grant access to the data repository. Archivists interact with services to create, edit, and execute workflows only via the web-based front-end workflow engine.

CLAMS are first categorized by the anchor type on which the annotation is placed. That is, an annotation can be placed on 1) character offsets of a text, 2) time segments of time-based media, 3) two-dimensional (width × height) or three-dimensional (w × h × duration) bounding boxes on video frames, and 4) other annotation. For instance, a `named entity recognition` `(NER)` annotation can anchor on a `token` annotation that in turn anchored on character offsets. Furthermore, the characters can be from primary text data or from other annotations (such as ASR or optical character recognition (OCR)). Next, annotations are further categorized by the semantic types that are hierarchically defined in CLAMS vocabulary. For example, white noise detection and blank screen detection tools both produce subcategories of the `noisyFrame` annotation.

To address the complexity of additional annotation types and I/O constraints on tools, a layered annotation structure proved to be the best implementation choice for the interchange format based on many precedents, including LIF and TCF. Specifically, in MMIF, each tool generates a `view` object that contains all annotations as well as information about the production of the view (producer, production time, version, included annotation types, etc.). As a result, downstream tools can precisely locate any required input annotations from the input MMIF.

Last but not least, each tool deployed as a service on CLAMS must expose an application programming interface (API) to return its tool metadata, which contains information of the I/O constraints it poses. This tool metadata is used by the workflow engine to validate tool chains before creation and execution of workflows.

3.2 Workflow Engine

In order to facilitate the development of metadata generation workflows, we are using the Galaxy platform. The Galaxy platform was originally developed for genomic research, but has successfully been used for the deployment and integration of NLP tools (Giardine et al., 2005; Ide et al., 2016). Galaxy provides a web-based graphical user interface which will allow archivists to import data, construct complex multimodal workflows, and explore and visualize the metadata generated by applying workflows to their data.

3.3 CLAMS SDK and Services

We start with a number of fundamental analysis tools for text, image, audio, and video as CLAMS microservices. Users can easily configure a CLAMS instance with various tools based on specific needs, and then deploy it on a server where the archival data is stored. Figure 2 shows an example of a CLAMS instance configured with a set of video services. It also shows creation of a workflow of an ordered application of services to a specific set of input data.

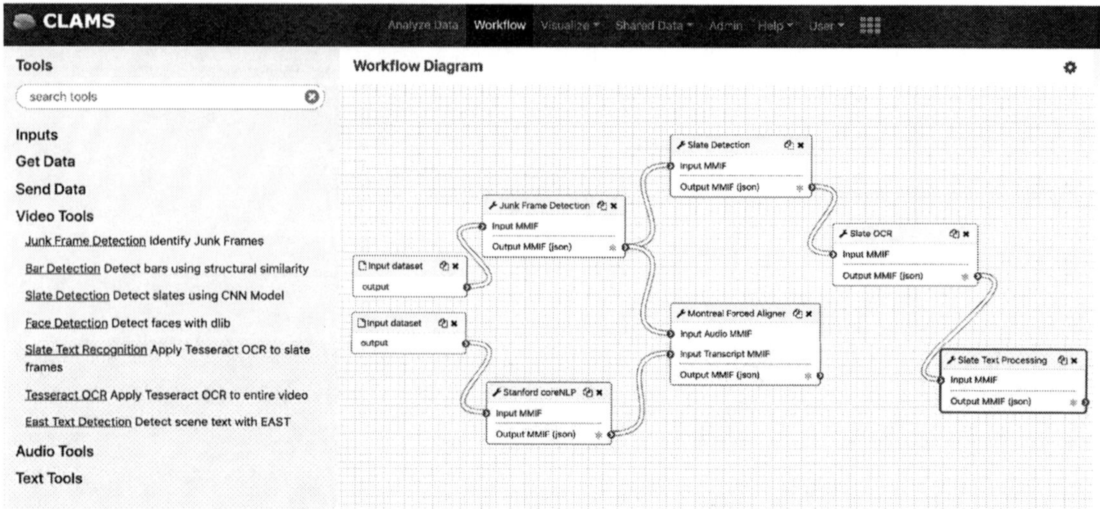

Figure 2: An example workflow created using the Galaxy workflow engine

The SDK including core APIs used in the development and deployment of tools will release on an open repository under open source license.

3.3.1 Text Services

As the design of the interoperability layer, the MMIF, of CLAMS is largely inspired by and expanding that of the LAPPS Grid platform (LIF). The LAPPS Grid offers a wide range of text analysis services via its web-based SOAP API, and re-using them in CLAMS can be done by mapping these SOAP messages out to CLAMS API. These text analysis services include NER, parsing, relation extraction, and coreference resolution. Used on audio transcripts and OCR results, they will capture important entities, events, participants, and relations that can be included in the descriptive metadata.

3.3.2 Audiovisual Filtering Services

In spite of recent achievements in computer vision (CV) and ASR, such tools are still very expensive with respect to time and space to run. However, a video clip can include completely contentless blank frames or SMPTE bars as well as non-speech audio (music, natural sounds, beep, etc). Thus, blindly feeding those expensive CV and ASR tools with the entire clip can be not only a waste of computing resources, but can also result in introducing unnecessary noisy annotations. To address this problem, we added a range of less expensive *filtering* services such as blank screen detection, SMPTE bar detection, and HiPSTAS audio tagger (Clement et al., 2014).

3.3.3 ASR and Forced Alignment

The platform will include open source tools to process speech and audio from video and audio data. Audio processing will include Kaldi-based ASR which generates a transcript of the data that can then be processed with NLP tools. Additionally, CLAMS can provide forced alignment services such as the Montreal Forced Aligner, which generates time-aligned transcriptions from raw text transcripts (McAuliffe et al., 2017). These speech services in particular are very important for multimodal annotation, as they provide alignment between a time-based modality and a character-based modality.

3.3.4 Computer Vision Tools

Various types of metadata can be found in text displayed in frames of a video. Slates are video frames which display metadata such as air date, director, producer, and title. This metadata can be extracted by constructing a pipeline of computer vision and NLP tools. Text localization tools can detect the bounding boxes of text in a frame which can then be used to label a section of a video as a slate. Slate frames are then fed to a preprocessing tool and an OCR tool. The OCR tool generates unstructured text. Since the text generated through OCR is likely to contain significant errors, a subsequent tool processes this text to correct spelling errors and extract structured metadata from the corrected text.

In news programs, when a reporter or guest is introduced, it is common for their name and title to be displayed at the bottom of the frame in a chyron or "lower-third". By applying OCR to chyrons, we can identify names of people appearing in a video. End credits contain production metadata such as cast and crew which can also be recognized by applying OCR tools.

Face detection and recognition (FDR) can be used to detect the location of faces in frames of video and to cluster detected faces so that individuals can be identified across different scenes within a video.

By integrating multiple vision and text based tools into a pipeline, it is possible to generate more robust metadata. For example, once clusters of detected faces are identified, this metadata can be combined with metadata from applying OCR to chyrons. By combining these two metadata sources, it will be possible to identify people in a video even after the chyron is no longer displayed. This metadata will be useful for researchers and archivists who are searching for all of the video segments in a dataset in which a particular person appears.

4   On-going and Future Work

We are currently collaborating with the American Archive of Public Broadcasting (AAPB) at WGBH Boston. The expertise of their archivists and librarians, as well as their perspective as target users, can provide us with insight towards selecting the analysis tools and phenomena of interest that can potentially push forward the state-of-the-art CL and CV technologies, within the vast unexplored collections of multimedia data. We actively seek collaboration with others in order to move closer to achieving an open platform for multimeida analysis.

We also believe that the platform can be used in academic settings with multimodal research datasets, such as MPII Movie Description dataset (Rohrbach et al., 2015), oral histories (StoryCorps, 2003; Telling Their Stories, 2005), and the The CHILDES Project (MacWhinney, 2014). For more technically literate users in research communities, we plan to develop a scriptable workflow engine extending the current SDK.

5   Conclusion

In this paper, we have presented CLAMS, a platform for multimodal computational analysis tools that provides interoperability between tools and a portable graphical user interface (GUI) workflow engine. Together, these tools can be used to automatically extract important information, such as timestamps (airing time, event time), people, companies, or historical events and relations, from time-based audiovisual material. We believe that archivists can use CLAMS over the digital multimedia collections they have to enrich item-level metadata of their collections and, in turn, greatly enhance the searchability and discoverability of their assets.

References

AAPB. 2015. American Archive of Public Broadcasting. http://americanarchive.org/. Accessed: 2019-02-20.

Patrick Aichroth, Christian Weigel, Thomas Kurz, Horst Stadler, Frank Drewes, Johanna Björklund, Kai Schlegel, Emanuel Berndl, Antonio Perez, Alex Bowyer, et al. 2015. Mico-media in context. In *2015 IEEE International Conference on Multimedia & Expo Workshops (ICMEW)*, pages 1–4. IEEE.

Alessandra Antonaci, Michela Ott, and Francesca Pozzi. 2013. Virtual museums, cultural heritage education and 21st century skills. *Learning & Teaching with Media & Technology*, 185.

BBC. 2015. COMMA - BBC R & D. https://www.bbc.co.uk/rd/projects/comma. Accessed: 2019-02-20.

Maxwell T Boykoff and Jules M Boykoff. 2007. Climate change and journalistic norms: A case-study of us mass-media coverage. *Geoforum*, 38(6):1190–1204.

Karen Cariani, Sadie Roosa, Jack Brighton, and Brian Grane. 2015. Accelerating exposure of audiovisual collections: What's next? In *Innovation, Collaboration, and Models: Proceedings of the CLIR Cataloging Hidden Special Collections and Archives Symposium*.

Heather Christenson. 2011. Hathitrust. *Library Resources & Technical Services*, 55(2):93–102.

Tanya E Clement, David Tcheng, Loretta Auvil, and Tony Borries. 2014. High performance sound technologies for access and scholarship (hipstas) in the digital humanities. *Proceedings of the American Society for Information Science and Technology*, 51(1):1–10.

Hamish Cunningham, Valentin Tablan, Angus Roberts, and Kalina Bontcheva. 2013. Getting more out of biomedical documents with gate's full lifecycle open source text analytics. *PLoS computational biology*, 9(2):e1002854.

Margaret Stieg Dalton and Laurie Charnigo. 2004. Historians and their information sources. *College & Research Libraries*, 65(5):400–425.

Mark Doms and Norman J. Morin. 2004. Consumer sentiment, the economy, and the news media. Finance and Economics Discussion Series 2004-51, Board of Governors of the Federal Reserve System (US).

Jon W Dunn, Juliet L Hardesty, Tanya Clement, Chris Lacinak, and Amy Rudersdorf. 2018. Audiovisual metadata platform (amp) planning project: Progress report and next steps. Technical report.

David Ferrucci, Adam Lally, Karin Verspoor, and Eric Nyberg. 2009. Unstructured information management architecture (UIMA) version 1.0. OASIS Standard.

Belinda Giardine, Cathy Riemer, Ross C Hardison, Richard Burhans, Laura Elnitski, Prachi Shah, Yi Zhang, Daniel Blankenberg, Istvan Albert, James Taylor, et al. 2005. Galaxy: a platform for interactive large-scale genome analysis. *Genome research*, 15(10):1451–1455.

Ulrich Heid, Helmut Schmid, Kerstin Eckart, and Erhard Hinrichs. 2010. A corpus representation format for linguistic web services: The d-spin text corpus format and its relationship with iso standards. In *LREC2010*, Valletta, Malta. European Language Resources Association (ELRA).

Erhard Hinrichs, Marie Hinrichs, and Thomas Zastrow. 2010. Weblicht: Web-based LRT services for german. In *Proceedings of the ACL 2010 System Demonstrations*, pages 25–29. Association for Computational Linguistics.

Erhard Hinrichs, Nancy Ide, James Pustejovsky, Jan Hajic, Marie Hinrichs, Mohammad Fazleh Elahi, Keith Suderman, Marc Verhagen, Kyeongmin Rim, Pavel Stranak, and Jozef Misutka. 2018. Bridging the LAPPS Grid and CLARIN. In *LREC2018*, Miyazaki, Japan. European Language Resources Association (ELRA).

Nancy Ide, James Pustejovsky, Christopher Cieri, Eric Nyberg, Di Wang, Keith Suderman, Marc Verhagen, and Jonathan Wright. 2014. The language application grid. In *LREC2014*, Reykjavik, Iceland. European Language Resources Association (ELRA).

Nancy Ide, James Pustejovsky, Keith Suderman, Marc Verhagen, Christopher Cieri, and Eric Nyberg. 2016. The Language Application Grid and Galaxy. In *LREC 2016*, pages 51–70.

Nancy Ide, Keith Suderman, Marc Verhagen, and James Pustejovsky. 2015. The language application grid web service exchange vocabulary. In *International Workshop on Worldwide Language Service Infrastructure*, pages 18–32. Springer.

Brian MacWhinney. 2014. *The CHILDES project: Tools for analyzing talk, Volume I: Transcription format and programs*. Psychology Press.

Christopher D. Manning, Mihai Surdeanu, John Bauer, Jenny Finkel, Steven J. Bethard, and David McClosky. 2014. The Stanford CoreNLP natural language processing toolkit. In *Association for Computational Linguistics (ACL) System Demonstrations*, pages 55–60.

Michael McAuliffe, Michaela Socolof, Sarah Mihuc, Michael Wagner, and Morgan Sonderegger. 2017. Montreal forced aligner: Trainable text-speech alignment using kaldi. In *INTERSPEECH*.

MDPI. 2014. Media Digitization & Preservation Initiative. https://mdpi.iu.edu/. Accessed: 2019-02-20.

NDNP. 2005. National digital newspaper program ndnp: a partnership between the library of congress and the national endowment for the humanities. https://lccn.loc.gov/2005567119. Accessed: 2019-02-20.

NYPL. 2013. The New York Public Library's Community Oral History Project. http://oralhistory.nypl.org/. Accessed: 2019-02-20.

Douglas W Oard, Dina Demner-Fushman, Jan Hajič, Bhuvana Ramabhadran, Samuel Gustman, William J Byrne, Dagobert Soergel, Bonnie Dorr, Philip Resnik, and Michael Picheny. 2002. Cross-language access to recorded speech in the malach project. In *International Conference on Text, Speech and Dialogue*, pages 57–64. Springer.

OpenNLP. 2017. Apache OpenNLP. https://opennlp.apache.org/. Accessed: 2019-02-20.

Michela Ott and Francesca Pozzi. 2011. Towards a new era for cultural heritage education: Discussing the role of ict. *Computers in Human Behavior*, 27(4):1365–1371.

James Pustejovsky. 2018. Enhancing access to media collections and archives using computational linguistic tools. In *Proceedings of Enhancing Exploration of Audiovisual Collections with Computer-based Annotation Techniques, Workshop at AMIA*.

James Pustejovsky, Nancy Ide, Marc Verhagen, and Keith Suderman. 2017. Enhancing access to media collections and archives using computational linguistic tools. In *Proceedings of the Corpora for Digital Humanities Workshop*, pages 19–28. Association for Computational Linguistics.

Yves Raimond, Tristan Ferne, Michael Smethurst, and Gareth Adams. 2014. The bbc world service archive prototype. *Web Semantics: Science, Services and Agents on the World Wide Web*, 27:2–9.

Anna Rohrbach, Marcus Rohrbach, Niket Tandon, and Bernt Schiele. 2015. A dataset for movie description. In *Proceedings of the IEEE Conference on Computer Vision and Pattern Recognition (CVPR)*.

Jennifer Schaffner. 2009. The metadata is the interface: Better description for better discovery of archives and special collections, synthesized from user studies. `http://www.oclc.org/programs/publications/reports/2009-06.pdf`.

StoryCorps. 2003. Storycorps - stories from people of all backgrounds and beliefs. `https://storycorps.org/`. Accessed: 2019-04-04.

Telling Their Stories. 2005. Telling their stories oral history archives project. `http://www.tellingstories.org/`. Accessed: 2019-04-04.

Marc Verhagen, Keith Suderman, Di Wang, Nancy Ide, Chunqi Shi, Jonathan Wright, and James Pustejovsky. 2015. The lapps interchange format. In *International Workshop on Worldwide Language Service Infrastructure*, pages 33–47. Springer.

Correcting Whitespace Errors in Digitized Historical Texts

Sandeep Soni and **Lauren F. Klein** and **Jacob Eisenstein**
Georgia Institute of Technology
sandeepsoni@gatech.edu lauren.klein@lmc.gatech.edu jacobe@gmail.com

Abstract

Whitespace errors are common to digitized archives. This paper describes a lightweight unsupervised technique for recovering the original whitespace. Our approach is based on count statistics from Google n-grams, which are converted into a likelihood ratio test computed from interpolated trigram and bigram probabilities. To evaluate this approach, we annotate a small corpus of whitespace errors in a digitized corpus of newspapers from the 19th century United States. Our technique identifies and corrects most whitespace errors while introducing a minimal amount of oversegmentation: it achieves 77% recall at a false positive rate of less than 1%, and 91% recall at a false positive rate of less than 3%.

1 Introduction

The application of natural language processing to digitized archives has the potential for significant impact in the humanities. However, to realize this potential, it is necessary to ensure that digitization produces accurate representations of the original texts. Most large-scale digital corpora are produced by optical character recognition (OCR; e.g., Smith, 2007), but even the best current methods yield substantial amounts of noise when applied to historical texts, such as the nineteenth-century newspaper shown in Figure 1. Alternatively, with substantial effort, digitization can be performed manually, or by manual correction of OCR output (Tanner et al., 2009). However, even for manually "keyed-in" corpora, noise can be introduced due to errors in workflow (Haaf et al., 2013).

Whitespace is a particularly common source of digitization errors in both OCR and manually digitized corpora. Such errors, also known as *word segmentation errors* or *spacing errors*, can arise during OCR as well as during the post-digitization handling of the data (Kissos and Der-

Figure 1: An example front page from the *Accessible Archives* corpus.

showitz, 2016). These errors can result in the elimination of whitespace between words, leading to out-of-vocabulary items like *senatoradmits* and *endowedwith*. This paper presents a set of unsupervised techniques for the identification and correction of such errors.

To resolve these errors, we apply large-scale n-gram counts from Google Books (Michel et al., 2011; Lin et al., 2012). The basic premise of this approach is that additional whitespace should be introduced in cases where a token is out-of-vocabulary, yet can be decomposed into two or more in-vocabulary tokens. By using bigram and unigram counts, it is possible to distinguish these cases, without treating membership in a predefined vocabulary as the sole and determinative indicator of whether a token should be segmented. Furthermore, by using higher-order n-gram counts, it is possible to make a contextualized judgment about whether and how whitespace

Proc. of the 3rd Joint SIGHUM Workshop on Computational Linguistics for Cultural Heritage, Social Sciences, Humanities and Literature, pp. 98–103
Minneapolis, MN, USA, June 7, 2019. ©2019 Association for Computational Linguistics

should be introduced. We show that contextualization yields significant improvements in segmentation accuracy.

Our research is motivated by our own experience working with historical texts. We were fortunate to obtain access to a manually-digitized corpus of nineteenth-century newspapers from the United States.[1] However, the digitization process introduced whitespace errors, and the original tokenization was unrecoverable. These errors were sufficiently frequent as to substantially impact downstream analyses such as topic models and word embeddings. We undertook this research to solve this practical problem, but because we believe it generalizes beyond our specific case, we systematically analyze the performance of our solution, and release a trained system for whitespace recovery. To summarize our contributions:

- We present a new method for correcting common whitespace errors in digitized archives.

- We evaluate on new annotations of manual whitespace error corrections in a digitized historical corpus.

- We release a trained system for other researchers who face similar problems.[2]

2 Unsupervised Token Segmentation

A token is likely to contain missing whitespace if (a) the token is out-of-vocabulary; and (b) there is some segmentation of the token into substrings that are all in-vocabulary. By these conditions, the term *applebanana* is likely to contain missing whitespace. The term *watermelon* is excluded by condition (a), and *cherimoya* is excluded by condition (b).

In real scenarios, membership in a predefined vocabulary of terms is not the sole indicator of whether a token should be segmented: in some contexts, an "in-vocabulary" term should be segmented; in other cases, an out-of-vocabulary term, such as a name, should not be segmented. The premise of our approach is to approximate the notion of vocabulary inclusion with n-gram probabilities. Specifically, a segmentation is likely to be correct when the segments have high probability in a large corpus of (mostly) clean text, in comparison with both (a) the original token, and (b)

other segmentations of that same token. We therefore apply a set of *likelihood ratios* to score candidate segmentations. The numerator quantifies the likelihood of a proposed segmentation, and the denominator quantifies the likelihood of the unsegmented token.

To describe our approach, we introduce the following notation. Let $w^{(t)}$ indicate token t from a corpus, where the tokenization is performed by simple whitespace pattern matching. We are concerned with the question of whether $w^{(t)}$ contains missing whitespace. Given a segmentation of $w^{(t)}$ such that i is the index of the first character in the second segment, we denote the segments as $w_{0,i}^{(t)}$ and $w_{i,\ell^{(t)}}^{(t)}$, where $\ell^{(t)}$ is the length of $w^{(t)}$ in characters.[3]

2.1 Non-contextual likelihood ratio

We first consider the probability of the bigram $(w_{0,i}^{(t)}, w_{i,\ell^{(t)}}^{(t)})$, in comparison with the unigram probability $w^{(t)}$:

$$r(w^{(t)}, i) = \frac{p_2\left(w_{0,i}^{(t)}, w_{i,\ell^{(t)}}^{(t)}\right)}{p_1(w^{(t)})}, \qquad (1)$$

where p_2 is a bigram probability, and p_1 is a unigram probability. These probabilities can be computed from n-gram counts,

$$p_2(u, v) = \frac{n_2(u, v)}{\sum_{(u',v')} n_2(u', v')} \qquad (2)$$

$$p_1(u) = \frac{n_1(u)}{\sum_{u'} n_1(u')}, \qquad (3)$$

where n_2 and n_1 are bigram and unigram counts, respectively. The denominator of p_2 is the count of all bigrams, and the denominator of p_1 is the count of all unigrams. Both are equal to the total size of the corpus, and they cancel in Equation 1. This makes it possible to perform segmentation by directly comparing the raw counts. However, in the contextualized models that follow, it will be necessary to work with normalized probabilities.

To use Equation 1, we first identify the segmentation point with the highest score, and then compare this score against a pre-defined threshold. The threshold controls the tradeoff between recall and precision, as described in § 4.

---

[1] https://www.accessible-archives.com. The dataset is described in a review article by Maret (2016).

[2] https://github.com/sandeepsoni/ whitespace-normalizer

[3] In our dataset, we do not encounter the situation in which a single token requires more than two segments. This problem is therefore left for future work.

In our experiments, the counts are obtained from Google n-grams (Michel et al., 2011). It is not essential that the corpus of counts be completely free of whitespace errors or other mistakes. As long as errors are independent and identically distributed across terms (in other words, each term is equally likely to have a segmentation error), the correct segmentation can still be recovered in the limit of sufficient data. This consideration prevents us from using the historical corpus, because it is possible that errors will be especially frequent for some terms, adding bias to the relevant n-gram counts.

2.2 Contextual likelihood ratio

The likelihood ratio based on word counts can be strengthened by considering additional context. Consider a term like *often*. According to Equation 1, we would be unlikely to segment *often* into *of ten*, since $p_1(often)$ exceeds $p_2(of\ ten)$, by a factor of 10-20 in the Google n-grams corpus.[4] Yet there are contexts in which segmentation is appropriate, such as the phrase *memory often years*.

We can resolve such cases by considering the additional context provided by the neighboring tokens $w^{(t-1)}$ and $w^{(t+1)}$:

$$r_c(w^{(t)}, i) = \frac{p\left(w^{(t)}_{0,i}, w^{(t)}_{i,\ell(t)} \mid w^{(t-1)}, w^{(t+1)}\right)}{p(w^{(t)} \mid w^{(t-1)}, w^{(t+1)})}. \tag{4}$$

We decompose these terms into trigram and bigram probabilities. The numerator can be expressed as:

$$\begin{aligned}
p&\left(w^{(t)}_{0,i}, w^{(t)}_{i,\ell(t)} \mid w^{(t-1)}, w^{(t+1)}\right) \\
&\propto p_3(w^{(t+1)} \mid w^{(t)}_{i,\ell(t)}, w^{(t)}_{0,i}) \\
&\times p_3(w^{(t)}_{i,\ell(t)} \mid w^{(t)}_{0,i}, w^{(t-1)}) \\
&\times p_2(w^{(t)}_{0,i} \mid w^{(t-1)}),
\end{aligned} \tag{5}$$

with p_3 and p_2 indicating trigram and bigram probabilities respectively. The denominator is similar:

$$\begin{aligned}
p&\left(w^{(t)} \mid w^{(t-1)}, w^{(t+1)}\right) \\
&\propto p_3(w^{(t+1)} \mid w^{(t)}, w^{(t-1)}) \\
&\times p_2(w^{(t)} \mid w^{(t-1)}).
\end{aligned} \tag{6}$$

In both the numerator and denominator, the constant of proportionality is $p(w^{(t+1)} \mid w^{(t-1)})$, which cancels from the likelihood ratio.

In the example above, the trigrams *memory of ten* and *of ten years* have relatively high conditional probabilities, and *memory often years* has a low conditional probability. This ensures that the appropriate segmentation is recovered.

Interpolation. The bigram and trigram probabilities in Equations 5 and 6 can be unreliable when counts are small. We therefore use interpolated probabilities rather than relative frequencies for p_3 and p_2:

$$\begin{aligned}
p_3(u \mid v, w) =& \alpha_3 \hat{p}_3(u \mid v, w) \\
&+ \beta_3 \hat{p}_2(u \mid v) \\
&+ (1 - \alpha_3 - \beta_3)\hat{p}_1(u)
\end{aligned} \tag{7}$$

$$p_2(u \mid v) = \beta_2 \hat{p}_2(u \mid v) + (1 - \beta_2)\hat{p}_1(u), \tag{8}$$

where $\hat{p}_n$ refers to the unsmoothed empirical n-gram probability, and $(\alpha_3, \beta_3, \beta_2)$ are hyperparameters. We manually set $\alpha_3 = 0.7, \beta_3 = 0.2, \beta_2 = 0.9$, and did not try other values.

3 Experimental Setup

We apply the segmentation techniques from the previous section to the Accessible Archives corpus, a dataset of manually digitized articles from newspapers in the nineteenth-century United States. As noted in the introduction, whitespace errors were introduced during the digitization process, likely by deleting newline characters when moving the files across operating systems. As a result, the dataset contains a relatively large number of concatenated terms, such as *andsaw, daythe, dreamsof, manufactureof, onlytwo, returningto, showsthe, theboys, thelevel,* and *thesea*.

To measure segmentation accuracy, two of the authors manually annotated a randomly-selected subset of 200 terms that occur in at least 5 contexts in the corpus. In each case, the annotator either provides the correct segmentation or indicates that no segmentation is necessary. The annotators indicated that 33 % of the terms needed a segmentation and agreed on all segmentation decisions, indicating that this problem is unambiguous for human readers. Although a high proportion of terms required segmentation, these terms were all concentrated in the long tail of the distribution of the terms by frequency. This indicates that the segmentation errors are spread across several terms in the corpus but are still rare and may not adversely affect the readability of the corpus. We tested the ability of likelihood ratio scores to recover the true

---

[4]From a web interface search of American books in the 19th century.

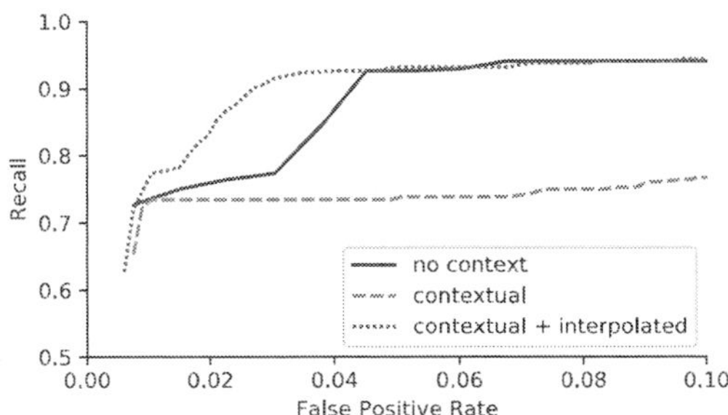

Figure 2: Performance of each method. The false positive rate is controlled by varying the threshold for segmentation.

segmentations. The evaluation is based on the following counts:

True positive: The system proposes a segmentation, and it matches the annotated segmentation.

False positive: The system proposes a segmentation, and either it does not match the annotated segmentation or the annotators marked the term as unsegmented.

False negative: A segmentation was annotated, and the system does not propose it.

True negative: A segmentation was not annotated, and the system does not propose one.

The **recall** is computed as $\mathrm{TP}/(\mathrm{TP} + \mathrm{FN})$, and the **false positive rate** is computed as $\mathrm{FP}/(\mathrm{FP} + \mathrm{TN})$.

4   Results

Results are shown in Figure 2 and in Table 1. The contextualized likelihood ratio obtains a recall of 0.768 at a false positive rate of 0.008, and a recall of 0.909 at a false positive rate of less than 0.029. Contextualization substantially improves the recall at low false positive rates, but only when used in combination with interpolated probabilities. This indicates that contextualization makes it possible to segment more aggressively without suffering false positives.

We also illustrate the strengths of each method through examples. Tokens like *Themotion, andprovided* and *wearthese* are correctly segmented as *The motion, and provided* and *wear these*. However, due to sparse counts in the trigram dictionaries, merely adding the context does not lead to correct segmentations in these cases without additionally using interpolation. On the other hand,

not relying on context leads to erroneous segmentations for tokens like *innumerous* (as *in numerous*), *Safeguard* (as *Safe guard*) and *Norice* (as *No rice*). Both contextualization and interpolation help in correcting these errors. Note that adding interpolation to the contextualization helps find a sweet spot between the more aggressive noncontextual model and the less aggressive contextual model.

All three methods are based on the calculation of likelihood ratio, which is crucial for their success. To show this, we additionally evaluate the performance for a rule-based baseline with the two rules described in § 2: we segment a token if it is out-of-vocabulary and some segmentation is in-vocabulary. When there are multiple valid segmentations, the segmentation with the largest second segment by length was chosen. The precision and false positive rate of this baseline is 0.24, 0.39 respectively. This shows the advantage of probabilistic segmentation over a deterministic dictionary-based alternative.

5   Related Work

Dataset "cleanliness" is an increasingly salient issue for digital humanities research. Difficulties with optical character recognition (OCR) were highlighted in a 2018 report to the Mellon Foundation (Smith and Cordell, 2018), which outlines an agenda for research and infrastructure development in handling such texts. A key point from this report is that *postprocessing* of noisily digitized texts will continue to be important, despite the obvious interest in improving the accuracy of OCR itself (e.g., Berg-Kirkpatrick et al., 2013).

Several papers tackle the more general problem of OCR post-correction. An early example is the work of Tong and Evans (1996), who employ bigram word counts and character transduction probabilities to score corrections by their logprobability. However, their approach cannot handle whitespace erorrs (which they refer to as "runon" and "split-word" errors). Another approach is to train a supervised system from synthetic training data, using features such as proposed spelling corrections (Lund et al., 2011). Dong and Smith (2018) propose an alternative unsupervised training technique for OCR post-correction, which builds on character-level LSTMs. In their method, which they call `seq2seq-noisy`, they build an ensemble of post-processing systems. On each ex-

False positive rate:	0.01	0.03	0.05	0.1
No context likelihood ratio	0.750	0.765	0.926	0.941
Contextual likelihood ratio	0.735	0.735	0.735	0.768
Contextual likelihood ratio + Interpolation	0.768	0.909	0.932	0.944

Table 1: Maximum segmentation recall at various false positive rates.

ample, a candidate output is produced by each system in the ensemble. They then select as noisy ground truth the system output that scores highest on a character-level language model trained on clean text from a New York Times (NYT) corpus, and use this noisy ground truth to train the other members of the ensemble.

Our paper approaches a special case of the general OCR post-correction problem, focusing specifically on whitespace errors, which Kissos and Dershowitz (2016) call *segmentation errors*. A key point is that these errors can and do arise even in texts that are manually keyed in, due to mishandling of file formats across operating systems. We are interested to test the applicability of general OCR post-correction systems to whitespace errors, but our results suggest that this problem can be addressed by the more lightweight solutions described here.

6   Conclusion

This paper describes an unsupervised approach for post-correcting whitespace errors, which are frequently present in digitized humanities archives. These errors can be resolved by considering two sources of information: character-level information about which surface forms are likely to be word tokens, and contextual information about which tokens are likely to appear in context. Both sources of information can be obtained from large-scale n-gram statistics, and combined using a straightforward likelihood ratio score. The resulting segmenter obtains high recall with a minimal rate of false segmentations. Tuning the interpolation coefficients on a validation set may improve performance further. Future work should test the applicability of these techniques in languages beyond English, and on other types of errors.

Acknowledgments

We thank the reviewers for their constructive feedback, as well as Georgia Tech computational linguistics lab members Ian Stewart, Sarah Wiegr-effe, and Yuval Pinter for a round of edits. In addition, we thank digital humanities lab members Bin Cao and Nikita Bawa for their early efforts in cleaning this corpus. The work also benefited from discussion with Ryan Cordell and David Smith. This research was supported by the Andrew W. Mellon Foundation under the auspices of Georgia Tech's Digital Integrative Liberal Arts Center. The initial work on this project was supported by the National Endowment for the Humanities, Office of Digital Humanities grant number HD-51705-13.

References

Taylor Berg-Kirkpatrick, Greg Durrett, and Dan Klein. 2013. Unsupervised transcription of historical documents. In *Proceedings of the 51st Annual Meeting of the Association for Computational Linguistics (Volume 1: Long Papers)*, pages 207–217, Sofia, Bulgaria. Association for Computational Linguistics.

Rui Dong and David Smith. 2018. Multi-input attention for unsupervised OCR correction. In *Proceedings of the 56th Annual Meeting of the Association for Computational Linguistics (Volume 1: Long Papers)*, pages 2363–2372, Melbourne, Australia. Association for Computational Linguistics.

Susanne Haaf, Frank Wiegand, and Alexander Geyken. 2013. Measuring the correctness of double-keying: Error classification and quality control in a large corpus of TEI-annotated historical text. In *Selected Papers from the 2011 TEI Conference*, volume 4. TEI.

Ido Kissos and Nachum Dershowitz. 2016. OCR error correction using character correction and feature-based word classification. In *IAPR Workshop on Document Analysis Systems (DAS)*, pages 198–203. IEEE.

Yuri Lin, Jean-Baptiste Michel, Erez Lieberman Aiden, Jon Orwant, Will Brockman, and Slav Petrov. 2012. Syntactic annotations for the Google Books Ngram Corpus. In *Proceedings of the ACL 2012 system demonstrations*, pages 169–174. Association for Computational Linguistics.

William B Lund, Daniel D Walker, and Eric K Ringger. 2011. Progressive alignment and discriminative error correction for multiple OCR engines. In *2011 International Conference on Document Analysis and Recognition*, pages 764–768. IEEE.

Susan Maret. 2016. Accessible archives. *The Charleston Advisor*, 18(2):17–20.

Jean-Baptiste Michel, Yuan Kui Shen, Aviva Presser Aiden, Adrian Veres, Matthew K. Gray, Joseph P. Pickett, Dale Hoiberg, Dan Clancy, Peter Norvig, Jon Orwant, Steven Pinker, Martin A. Nowak, and Erez Lieberman Aiden. 2011. Quantitative analysis of culture using millions of digitized books. *Science*, 331(6014):176–182.

David Smith and Ryan Cordell. 2018. A research agenda for historical and multilingual optical character recognition. `http://hdl.handle.net/2047/D20297452`, accessed February 2019.

Ray Smith. 2007. An overview of the tesseract ocr engine. In *Document Analysis and Recognition, 2007. ICDAR 2007. Ninth International Conference on*, volume 2, pages 629–633. IEEE.

Simon Tanner, Trevor Munoz, and Pich Hemy Ros. 2009. Measuring mass text digitization quality and usefulness: Lessons learned from assessing the OCR accuracy of the British Library's 19th century online newspaper archive. *D-Lib Magazine.*

Xiang Tong and David A Evans. 1996. A statistical approach to automatic OCR error correction in context. In *Fourth Workshop on Very Large Corpora.*

On the Feasibility of Automated Detection of Allusive Text Reuse

Enrique Manjavacas[1], Brian Long[2], and Mike Kestemont[1]

[1]University of Antwerp, CLiPS, {`firstname.lastname`}`@uantwerpen.be`
[2]University of Notre Dame, `blong2@alumni.nd.edu`

Abstract

The detection of allusive text reuse is particularly challenging due to the sparse evidence on which allusive references rely—commonly based on none or very few shared words. Arguably, lexical semantics can be resorted to since uncovering semantic relations between words has the potential to increase the support underlying the allusion and alleviate the lexical sparsity. A further obstacle is the lack of evaluation benchmark corpora, largely due to the highly interpretative character of the annotation process. In the present paper, we aim to elucidate the feasibility of automated allusion detection. We approach the matter from an Information Retrieval perspective in which referencing texts act as queries and referenced texts as relevant documents to be retrieved, and estimate the difficulty of benchmark corpus compilation by a novel inter-annotator agreement study on query segmentation. Furthermore, we investigate to what extent the integration of lexical semantic information derived from distributional models and ontologies can aid retrieving cases of allusive reuse. The results show that (i) despite low agreement scores, using manual queries considerably improves retrieval performance with respect to a windowing approach, and that (ii) retrieval performance can be moderately boosted with distributional semantics.

1   Introduction

In the 20th century, intertextuality emerged as an influential concept in literary criticism. Originally developed by French deconstructionist theorists, such as Kristeva and Barthes, the term broadly refers to the phenomenon where texts integrate (fragments of) other texts or allude to them (Orr, 2003). In the minds of both authors and readers, intertexts can establish meaningful connections between works, evoking particular stylistic

Reference (Vulgata, Ep 3,19) "scire etiam supereminentem scientiae caritatem Christi ut impleamini in omnem plenitudinem Dei"

"and to know the love (caritas) of Christ that is beyond knowledge, such that you'd be filled with all fullness of God"

Reuse (Bernard, Sermo 8, 7.l) "Osculum plane dilectionis et pacis, *sed dilectio illa supereminet omni **scientiae***, et pax illa omnem sensum exsuperat"

"It is a kiss of love and peace, but of that kind of love (dilectio) that is beyond any knowledge, and of that kind of peace that surpasses all senses."

Figure 1: Examples of allusive text reuse from the dataset underlying the present study.

effects and interpretations of a text. Existing categorizations (Bamman and Crane, 2008; Mellerin, 2014; Büchler, 2013; Hohl Trillini and Quassdorf, 2010) emphasize the broad spectrum of intertexts, which can range from direct quotations, over paraphrased passages to highly subtle allusions.

With the emergence of computational methods in literary studies over the past decades, intertextuality has often been presented as a promising application, helping scholars identifying potential intertextual links that had previously gone unnoticed. Much progress has been made in this area and a number of highly useful tools are now available—e.g. Tracer (Büchler, 2013) or Tesserae (Coffee et al., 2012). This paper, however, aims to contribute to a number of open issues that still present significant challenges to the further development of the field.

Most scholarship continues to focus on the de-

Proc. of the 3rd Joint SIGHUM Workshop on Computational Linguistics for Cultural Heritage, Social Sciences, Humanities and Literature, pp. 104–114
Minneapolis, MN, USA, June 7, 2019. ©2019 Association for Computational Linguistics

tection of relatively literal instances of so-called 'text reuse', as intertextuality is commonly – and somewhat restrictively – referred to in the field. Such instances are relatively unambiguous and unproblematic to detect using n-gram matching, fingerprinting and string alignment algorithms. Much less research has been devoted to the detection of fuzzier instances of text reuse holding between passages that lack a significant lexical correspondence. This situation is aggravated by the severe lack of openly available benchmark datasets. An additional hindrance is that the establishment of intertextual links is to a high degree subjective – both regarding the existence of particular intertextual links and the exact scope of the correspondence in both fragments. Studies of inter-annotator agreement are surprisingly rare in the field, which might be partially due to to the fact that existing agreement metrics are hard to port to this problem.

Contributions In this paper, we report on an empirical feasibility study, focusing on the annotation and automated detection of allusive text reuse. We focus on biblical intertext in the works of Bernard of Clairvaux (1090–1153), an influential medieval writer known for his pervasive references to the Bible. The paper has two main parts. In the first part, we formulate an adaptation of Fleiss's κ that allows us to quantitatively estimate and discuss the level of inter-annotator agreement concerning the span of the intertexts. While annotators show considerably low levels of agreement, We show that manual segmentation has nevertheless a big impact on the automatic retrieval of allusive reuse. In the second part, we offer an evaluation of current Information Retrieval (IR) techniques for allusive text reuse detection. We confirm that semantic retrieval models based on word and sentence embeddings do not present advantages over hand-crafted scoring functions from previous studies, and that both are outperformed by conventional retrieval models based on TfIdf. Finally, we show how a recently introduced technique, soft cosine, allows us to combine lexical and semantic information to obtain significant improvements over any other considered model.

2 Related Work

Previous research on text reuse detection in literary texts has extensively explored methods such as n-gram matching (Büchler et al., 2014) and se-

quence alignment algorithms (Lee, 2007; Smith et al., 2014). In such approaches, fuzzier forms of intertextual links are accounted for through the use of edit distance comparisons or the inclusion of abstract linguistic information such as word lemmata or part-of-speech tags, and lexical semantic relationships extracted from WordNet. More recently, researchers have started to explore techniques from the field of distributional semantics in order to capture allusive text reuse. Scheirer et al. (2016), for instance, have applied latent-semantic indexing (LSI) to find semantic connections and evaluated such method on a set of 35 allusive references to Vergil's *Aeneis* in the first book of Lucan's *Civil War*.

Previous research in the field of text reuse has also focused on the more specific problem of finding allusive references. One of the first studies (Bamman and Crane, 2008) looked at allusion detection in literary text using an IR approach exploiting textual features at a diversity of levels (including morphology and syntax) but collected only qualitative evidence on the efficiency of such approach. More ambitiously, Bamman and Crane (2009) approached the task of finding allusive references across texts in different languages using string alignment algorithms from machine translation. Besides the afore-mentioned work by Scheirer et al. (2016), the work by Moritz et al. (2016) is highly related to the present study, since the authors also worked on allusive reuse from the Bible in the works of Bernard. In their work, the authors focused on modeling text reuse patterns based on a set of transformation rules defined over string case, lemmata, POS tags and synset relationships: (syno-/hypo-/co-hypo-)nymy. More recently, Moritz et al. (2018) conducted a quantitative comparison of such transformation rules with paraphrase detection methods on the task of predicting paraphrase relation between text pairs but do not evaluate the method in an IR setup.

3 Dataset

The basis for the present study stems from the BiblIndex project (Mellerin, 2014), which aims to index biblical references found in Christian literature.[1] More specifically, we use a subset of manually identified biblical references from Bernard of Clairvaux which was kindly shared with us by Laurence Mellerin. The provided data consists of

---

[1] http://www.biblindex.mom.fr/

85 Sermons, totalling 199,508 words. The data came already tokenized and lemmatized. Bible references were tagged with a URL mapping to the corresponding Bible verse from the Vulgata edition of the medieval Bible in the online BiblIndex database. We extracted the online text of the Vulgata and used the URLs to match references in Bernard with the corresponding Bible verses. Since the online BiblIndex database does not provide lemmatized text, we applied an state-of-the-art lemmatizer for Medieval Latin (Manjavacas et al., (in press) to obtain a lemmatized version of the Vulgata. The resulting corpus data comprises a total of 34,835 verses totalling 586,285 tokens and amounting to a vocabulary size of 46,025 token types.

BiblIndex distinguishes three types of references: quotation, mention and allusion. While the links in the first two types are in their vast majority exact or near-exact lexical matches, the latter type comprises mostly references that fall into what is commonly known as allusive text reuse. Although our focus lies on the allusive category, Table 1 displays statistics about all these types in order to appreciate the characteristics of the task. As shown in Table 1 (last row), allusions are characterized by low Jaccard coefficients – in set-theoretical terms, the ratio of the intersection over the union of the sets of words of both passages. On average, annotated allusions share 6% of the word forms with their targets and 12% of the lemmata. In comparison, mentions and quotations have 25% or more tokens and 30% or more lemmata in common. The full distribution of token and lemma overlap for allusions shown in Fig. 2 indicates that more than 500 (65%) instances have at most 1 token in common; about more than 400 (50%) share at most 1 lemma.

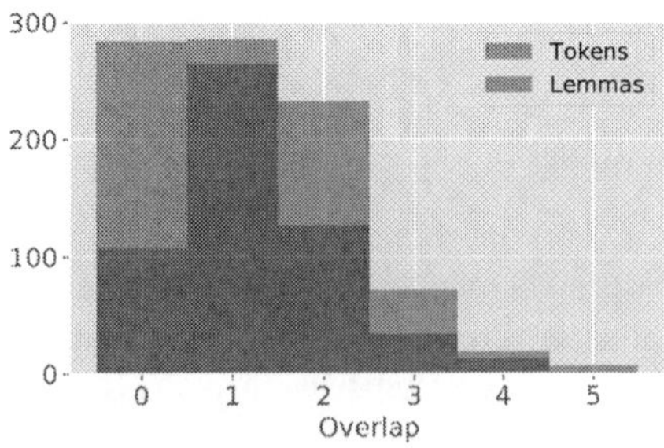

Figure 2: Histogram of token and lemma overlap between annotated queries and their Biblical references

4 Annotation

Conventional systems in text reuse detection typically work by segmenting texts into consecutive, equal-length chunks of texts, which are then used as queries to find cross-document matches. For (semi-)literal cases of reuse, this matching procedure yields good results and overlapping or adjacent matches can be easily merged into longer units of reuse. For allusive text reuse, such an approach seems unfeasible at the current stage, partially because the definition of the relevant query units is much harder to establish. As shown in Table 1, the annotated allusive references are mere 'anchors', consisting of single words or single multi-word expressions that cannot be easily used as queries. This is in agreement with pragmatic editorial conventions, which favour uncompromising signposting of references at anchor words over establishing particular decisions on the scope of the reference. However, from the point of view of the evaluation of IR systems, the provided editorial anchors must be turned into fully-fleshed, neatly delineated queries. In order to accomplish this, we have conducted an annotation experiment, which we will describe next.

4.1 Full dataset annotation

The aim of the annotation was to determine the scope of a biblical reference identified by the editors in text by Bernard. From an IR perspective, the annotation task consists of delineating the appropriate input query, given the anchor word in the source text and the corresponding Bible verse. An example annotation is shown in Fig. 1 where the anchor word provided by the editors is "scientiae" and the corresponding annotated query spans the subclause "sed dilection illa supereminet omni scientiae". Naturally, such references not always correspond to full sentences and often go over sentence boundaries.

The dataset was distributed evenly across 4 annotators, who worked independently through a custom-built interface. All annotators were proficient readers of Medieval Latin with expertise ranging from graduate student to professor. The annotators were familiar with the text reuse detection task and were given explicit instructions that can be summarized as follows: given a previously identified allusion between the Bernardine passage surrounding an anchor word, on the one hand, and a specific Bible verse on the other hand,

	Jaccard(token)	Jaccard(lemma)	Source length	Ref length	Count
Quotation	0.37 ($\pm$ 0.23)	0.37 ($\pm$ 0.22)	6.69 ($\pm$ 4.55)	15.12 ($\pm$ 5.99)	1768
Mention	0.26 ($\pm$ 0.18)	0.31 ($\pm$ 0.18)	7.47 ($\pm$ 5.52)	16.24 ($\pm$ 6.20)	3150
Allusion	0.02 ($\pm$ 0.04)	0.04 ($\pm$ 0.05)	1.10 ($\pm$ 0.85)	17.22 ($\pm$ 6.58)	876
Allusion (post)	0.06 ($\pm$ 0.07)	0.13 ($\pm$ 0.1)	6.86 ($\pm$ 4.83)		729

Table 1: Full dataset statistics for all link types originally provided by the editors. Last row shows statistics for allusive references in Bernard post annotation. We show Jaccard coefficients for original and lemmatized sentences, text lengths and instance counts.

annotate the *minimal textual span* in the Bernardine passage that is *maximally allusive* to the Bible verse. For the sake of simplicity, the interface only allowed continuous annotation spans and the annotated span had to include the pre-identified anchor token. Of a total of 876 initial instances, we discarded 147 cases in which annotators expressed doubts on the existence of the alleged reference or could not precisely decide the span. This decision was taken in order to ensure a high quality in the resulting benchmark data.

4.2 Inter-annotator agreement experiment

Determining the scope of an allusive reference is a relevant task for two reasons. Firstly, we expect this task to be reader-dependent, and thus highly subjective, given the minimal lexical overlap between the source and target passage. Measuring the agreement between annotators sheds new light on the overall feasibility of the task. Secondly, the resulting annotations allow us to critically evaluate the performance of existing retrieval methods under near-perfect segmentation conditions: if the correct source query is given, what is the performance of existing methods when attempting to retrieve the correct Bible verse in the target data?

Measuring inter-annotator agreement Inter-annotator agreement coefficients such as Fleiss's κ and Krippendorff's α are typically defined in terms of labels assigned to items in a multi-class classification setup (Artstein and Poesio, 2008). In the present case, however, the annotation involves making a decision on the span of words surrounding an anchor word that better captures the allusion and it is unclear how to quantify the variation in annotation performance. A naïve approach defined in terms of number of overlaping words has a number of undesirable issues. For example, since the annotations are centered around the anchor word, a relatively high amount of over-

lap is to be expected for short annotations. Moreover, disagreements over otherwise largely agreeing long spans should weigh in less than disagreements over otherwise largely agreeing small spans. Additionally, it is unclear how to quantify the rate of agreement expected under chance-level annotation, a quantity that needs to be corrected for in order to to obtain reliable and non-inflated inter-annotator agreement coefficients (Artstein, 2017). We have found that an extension of the Jaccard coefficient defined over sequences can help adapt Fleiss's κ to our case and tackle such issues.

Given any pair of span annotations, s and t, we can define overlap in a similar way to the Jaccard index, as the intersection (i.e. the Longest Common Substring) over the union (i.e. the total number of selected tokens by both annotators):

$$O = \frac{LCS(s,t)}{|s| + |t| - LCS(s,t)} \qquad (1)$$

Interestingly, this quantity can be decomposed into an agreement $A(s,t) = LCS(s,t)$ (number of tokens in common) and a disagreement score $D(s,t) = |s| + |t| - 2 \cdot LCS(s,t)$ (number of tokens not shared with the other annotator):

$$O = \frac{A}{A + D} \qquad (2)$$

The advantage of this reformulation is that it lets us see more easily how O is bounded between 0 and 1, and also that it gives us a way of computing the expected overlap score O_e by aggregating dataset-level A and D scores: $O_e = A_e/(A_e + D_e)$, with

$$A_e = \frac{\sum_{s,t} A(s,t)}{|s,t|}; D_w = \frac{\sum_{s,t} D(s,t)}{|s,t|} \qquad (3)$$

where $|s,t|$ refers to the number of unordered

annotation pairs in the dataset[2]. O_e can be thus interpreted as the expected overlap between two arbitrary annotators. The final inter-annotator agreement score is defined following Fleiss's:

$$\kappa = \frac{O_o - O_e}{1 - O_e} \qquad (4)$$

where O_o refers to the dataset average of Eq. 2.

Inter-annotator agreement results and discussion In order to estimate κ for our dataset, we extracted a random sample of 60 instances which were thoroughly annotated by 3 of the annotators. We obtain a $\kappa = 0.22$, which compares unfavorably with respect to commonly assumed reliability ranges. For example, values in the range $\kappa \in (0.67, 0.8)$ are considered fair agreement (Schütze et al., 2008). While our result remains hard to assess in the absence of comparable work, it is low enough to cast doubts over the feasibility of the task, which is in fact rarely explicitly questioned. The annotators informally reported that, against their expectations, the task was not straightforward and required a considerable level of concentration and interpretation. Such situation may be due to particularities of Bernard's usage of biblical language. Besides conventional, direct allusions, Bernard is also known for pointed use of single, significant allusive words, which are hard to isolate. Still it should be noted that in some instances inter-annotator agreement was high and, as Fig. 3(b) shows, in 22% of all pairwise comparisons even perfect. This suggests that there exist clear differences at the level of individual allusions. We now turn to the question how well current retrieval approaches perform, given manually segmented queries.

5 Retrieval Experiments

Given the small amounts of lexical overlap in the allusive text reuse datasets (c.f. Table 1), we aim to investigate and quantify to which extent semantic information can help improving retrieval of allusive references. For this reason, we look into 3 types of models. First, we look at purely lexical-based approaches. Secondly, approaches based on distributional semantics and, in particular, retrieval approaches that utilize word embeddings. Finally, we look at hybrid approaches that can accommodate relative amounts of semantic informa-

tion into what is otherwise a purely lexical model. From the retrieval point of view, all approaches fall into one of two categories: retrieval methods based on similarity in vector space and retrieval methods using domain-specific similarity scoring functions.

5.1 Lexical

Hand-crafted scoring function Previous work has devised hand-crafted scoring functions targeted at retrieving intertextual relationships similar to those found in Bernard (Forstall et al., 2015). The scoring function is used in an online retrieval system[3] and is defined by Eq. 5:

$$T(s,t) = ln\left(\frac{\sum_{w \in (S \cap T)} \frac{1}{f_{(w,s)}} + \frac{1}{f_{(w,t)}}}{d_s + d_t}\right) \qquad (5)$$

where $f_{(w,d)}$ refers to the frequency of word w in document d and d_d refers to the distance in tokens between the two most infrequent words in document d. Note that $T(s,t)$ is only defined for cases in which documents share at least 2 words, since otherwise the denominator cannot be computed. While this presents a clear disadvantage, it also lends itself to evaluation in a hybrid fashion with a complementary back-off model operating on passages with lower overlap. While originally $f_{(w,s)}$ is defined with respect to the query (or target) document, we observed such choice yielded poor performance (probably due to the small size of the documents), and, therefore, we use frequency estimates extracted from the respective document collections instead. We refer to this model as `Tesserae`.

BOW & TfIdf We include retrieval models based on a bag-of-words document representation (BOW) and cosine similarity for ranking. In a BOW space model, a document d is represented by a vector where the i_{th} entry represents the frequency of the i_{th} word in d. Beyond word counts, it is customary to apply the Tf-Idf transformation, that targets the fact that the importance of a word for a document is also dependent on how specific it is to that document. Tf-Idf for the i_{th} word is computed as the product of its frequency in d, denoted $Tf(w, d)$, and its inverse document frequency, $Idf(w, d)$, defined by Eq. 6:

$$Idf(w,d) = log\left(\frac{|D|}{1 + |\{d \in D : w \in d\}|}\right) \qquad (6)$$

---

[2] Such quantity is defined by $Nk(k-1)/2$, where N is the number of annotations and k the number of annotators.

[3] The retrieval system can be accessed at the following URL: http://tesserae.caset.buffalo.edu/

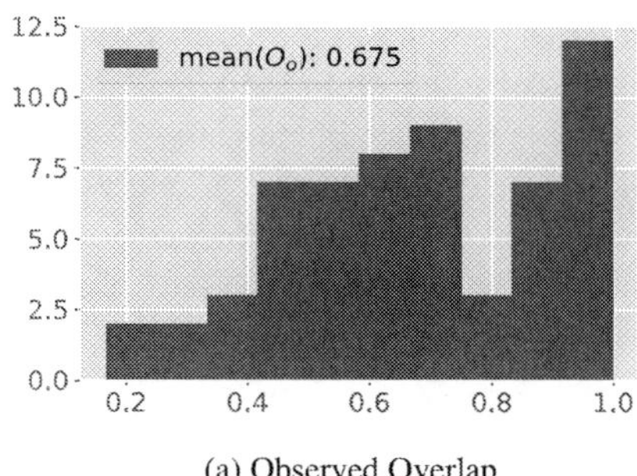
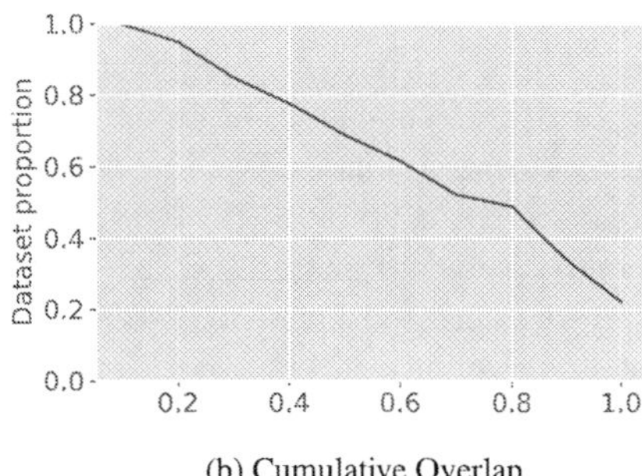

(a) Observed Overlap   (b) Cumulative Overlap

Figure 3: Observed overlap in the inter-annotator agreement experiments. On the left (a), we see the full histogram of O_o in the dataset ($N = 60$). On the right (b), we see the cumulative plot. We observe two modes in the histogram, perhaps indicating a qualitative difference in the dataset. One with high overlap scores close to 1.0 and another one at around 0.6 (close to the overall overlap mean).

We refer to these retrieval models as BOW and TfIdf. Given document vector representations in some common space, we can compute their similarity score based on the cosine similarity between such vectors:

$$cos(\vec{s}, \vec{t}) = \frac{\sum_i s_i t_i}{\sqrt{\sum_i s_i^2}\sqrt{\sum_i t_i^2}} \quad (7)$$

5.2 Semantic

We define a number of semantic models based on distributional semantics and, in particular, word embeddings. We use FastText word embeddings (Bojanowski et al., 2017) trained with default parameters on a large collection of Latin texts provided by (Bamman and Crane, 2011), which include 8.5GB of text of varying quality.[4]

Sentence Embeddings We use distributional semantic models based on the idea of computing a sentence embedding through a composition function operating over the individual embeddings of words in the sentence. The most basic composition function is averaging over the single word embeddings in the sentence (Wieting et al., 2015). We can take into account the relative importance of words to a given sentence using the Tf-Idf transformation defined in Section 5.1 and compute a Tf-Idf weighted average word embedding. We re-

fer to these models as BOW$_{emb}$ and TfIdf$_{emb}$ respectively.

Word Mover's Distance WMD is a metric based on the transportation problem known as Earth Mover's Distance but defined for documents over word embeddings. WMD has shown excellent performance in document retrieval tasks where semantics play an important role (Kusner et al., 2015). Intuitively, WMD is grounded on the idea of minimizing the amount of "travel cost" incurred in moving the word histogram of a document s into the word histogram of t, where the "travel distance" between words w_i and w_j is given by their respective distance in the embedding space $cos(w_i, w_j)$. Formally, WMD is computed by finding a so-called flow matrix $T \in \mathbb{R}^{V x V}$—where T_{ij} denotes how much of word w_i in s travels to word w_j in t—such that $\sum_{i,j} T_{i,j} c(w_i, w_j)$ is minimized. Computing WMD involves solving a linear programming problem for which specialized solvers exist.[5]

5.3 Hybrid

We look into methods that are able to encompass both lexical and semantic information.

Tesserae + WMD as backoff model (T+WMD) Since Tesserae score is only defined for document pairs with at least 2 words in common, it can be easily combined with other models in a backoff fashion. In particular, we evaluate this setup using WMD as the backoff model since it proved to be the

---

[4] All the relevant materials are available at the following URL: http://www.cs.cmu.edu/ dbamman/latin.html. We also experimented with an LSI retrieval model (Deerwester et al., 1990), similar to the one used by (Scheirer et al., 2016), but found it performed poorly on this dataset due to the small size of the documents in our dataset.

[5] We use the implementation provided by the pyemd package (Laszuk, 2017)

most efficient purely semantic model.[6]

Soft Cosine A more principled approach to combining lexical and semantic information is based on the soft cosine similarity function, which was first introduced by (Sidorov et al., 2014) and has been recently used in a shared-task winning contribution by (Charlet and Damnati, 2017) for question semantic similarity. Soft cosine generalizes cosine similarity by considering not only how similar vectors s and t across feature i but more generally across any given pair of features i, j. Soft cosine is defined by Eq. 8:

$$soft\_cos(\vec{s}, \vec{t}) = \frac{\sum_{i,j} S_{i,j} s_i t_j}{\sqrt{\sum_{i,j} S_{i,j} s_i s_j}\sqrt{\sum_{i,j} S_{i,j} t_i t_j}}$$

(8)

with $S \in \mathbb{R}^{V x V}$ representing a matrix where $S_{i,j}$ expresses the similarity between the i_{th} and the j_{th} word in the vocabulary. It can be seen that soft cosine reduces to cosine when S is taken to be the identity matrix.

Soft cosine is a flexible function since it lets us use any linguistic resource to estimate the similarity between words. For our purposes, matrix S can be estimated on the basis of WordNet-based semantic relatedness measures or word embedding based semantic similarity estimates. More concretely, we define the following two models. SC_{wn}, which uses a similarity function based on the size of the group of synonyms extracted from the Latin WordNet (Minozzi, 2010): $S_{i,j} = \frac{1}{|T_i \cap T_j|}$ where T_i refers to the set of synonyms of the i_{th} word. SC_{emb} which exploits word embedding similarity $S_{i,j} = max(0, cos(\vec{w_i}, \vec{w_j})$ over embeddings $\vec{w_i}, \vec{w_j}$. All soft cosine-based retrieval models are applied on $TfIdf$ document representations. In agreement with previous research (Charlet and Damnati, 2017), we boost the relative difference in similarity between the upper and lower quantiles of the similarity distribution by raising S to the nth-power.[7]

---

[6] We note that for this retrieval setup to be used in practice WMD and $Tesserae$ similarity scores must be transformed into a common scale. In the present paper, we assume an oracle on the lexical overlap with the relevant document and therefore the resulting numbers must be interpreted as an optimal score given perfect scaling.

[7] During development we found that raising S to the 5th power yielded the best results across similarity functions in all cases.

5.4 Evaluation

Given a Bernardian reference as a query formulated by the annotators and the collection of Biblical candidate documents, all evaluated models produce a ranking. Using such a ranking, we evaluate retrieval performance over the set of queries Q using Mean Reciprocal Rank[8] (MRR) (Voorhees, 1999) defined in Eq. 9:

$$MRR(Q) = \frac{1}{|Q|} \sum_{j=1}^{|Q|} \frac{1}{|R_j|}$$

(9)

Additionally, we also report $Precision@K$—based on how often the system is expected to retrieve the relevant document within the first k results—since it is a more interpretable measure from the point of view of the retrieval system user.

It must be noted that $P@K$ and MRR are not suitable metrics to evaluate a text reuse detection system on unrestricted data, since, in fact, most naturally occurring text is not allusive. However, the focus of the present paper lies on the feasibility of allusive text detection, which we aim to elucidate on the basis of a pre-annotated dataset in which each query is guaranteed to match to a relevant document in the target collection. The results must therefore be interpreted taking into account the artificial situation, where the selected queries are already known to contain allusions and the question is how well different systems recognize the alluded verse.

Results As shown in Table 2, the best model overall is SC_{emb}, achieving 21.95 MRR and 47.60 $P@20$, closely followed by another soft cosine-based hybrid approach: SC_{wn}. Interestingly, a simple $TfIfd$ baseline over lemmatized input results in strong ranking performance, surpassing all other purely lexical – including the hand-crafted $Tesserae$ – and all purely semantic models. In agreement with general expectations, all models benefit from lemmatized input and $TfIdf$ transformation (both as input representation in purely lexical models and as a weighting scheme for the sentence embeddings in purely semantic approaches). WMD outperforms any other purely semantic model, but as already pointed out, it compares negatively to the purely lexical $TfIdf$ baseline. The combination

---

[8] For clarity, we transform MRR from the original $[0-1]$ range into the $[0-100]$ range.

Metric	Lemma	Lexical			Semantic			Hybrid		
		BOW	TfIdf	Tesserae	BOW$_{emb}$	TfIdf$_{emb}$	WMD	SC$_{wn}$	SC$_{emb}$	T+WMD
MRR		11.85	16.42	12.39	8.54	9.59	13.68		21.41	17.01
	✓	15.07	19.51	13.36	9.82	11.13	14.07	19.75	**21.95**	16.18
$P@10$		20.16	30.59	19.20	15.50	18.11	24.14		37.31	29.22
	✓	27.30	34.43	25.79	16.87	20.99	25.38	35.25	**39.64**	31.14
$P@20$		25.38	35.94	22.22	20.44	24.14	27.85		44.31	33.61
	✓	34.16	43.35	30.86	22.63	26.20	31.28	44.44	**47.60**	38.27

Table 2: Retrieval results for all considered models grouped by approach type. All models are evaluated with tokens and lemmas as input except for SC_{wn} which requires lemmatized input. Overall best numbers per metric are shown in bold letters.

Metric	Lemma	Model		
		SC_{emb}	SC_{w2v}	SC_{rnd}
MRR		21.41	19.26	18.56
	✓	21.95	20.18	20.22
$P@10$		37.31	33.33	31.28
	✓	39.64	36.35	35.67
$P@20$		44.31	39.09	36.76
	✓	47.60	43.90	43.48

Table 3: Comparison of soft cosine using `FastText` embeddings (SC_{emb}), `word2vec` embeddings (SC_{w2v}) and a random similarity baseline (SC_{rnd}).

Metric	Lemma	Segmentation		
		Manual	Win-3	Win-10
MRR		21.41	13.41	13.98
	✓	21.95	14.67	14.69
$P@10$		37.31	25.79	25.10
	✓	39.64	25.93	26.47
$P@20$		44.31	31.41	31.41
	✓	47.60	32.78	34.57

Table 4: Comparison of best performing approach SC_{emb} across different segmentation types: manual and automatic window of 3 (Win-3) and 10 (Win-10) tokens to each side of the anchor word.

of $Tesserae$ with WMD as back-off proves useful and outperforms both approaches in isolation, highlighting that they model complementary aspects of text reuse.

In order to test the specific contribution of the similarity function used to estimate S, we compare results with soft cosine using a random similarity matrix (S_{rnd}) defined by Eq. 10:

$$S_{i,j} = \begin{cases} i = j & 1 \\ i \neq j & \sim \mathcal{N}(0.5, 0.05) \end{cases} \quad (10)$$

We also investigate the effect of the word embedding algorithm by comparing to SC_{emb} based on `word2vec` embeddings (Mikolov et al., 2013). As Table 3 shows, `FastText` embeddings, an algorithm known to capture not just semantic but also morphological relations, yields strong improvements over `word2vec`. Moreover, a random approach produces strong results, only underperforming the `word2vec` model by a small margins, which questions the usefulness of the semantic relationships induced by `word2vec` for the present task.

Finally, we test the relative importance of the query segmentation to the retrieval of allusive text reuse. For this purpose, we evaluate our best model (SC_{emb}) on a version of the dataset in which the referencing text is segmented according to a window approach, selecting n words around the anchor expression.

As Table 4 shows, results on manually segmented text are always significantly better than on automated segmentation. A window of 10-word around the anchor produces slightly better results than a 3-word window – more closely matching the overall mean length of manually annotated queries. This indicates the importance of localizing the appropriate set of referential words in context, while avoiding the inclusion of confounding terms. In other words, both precision and recall matter to segmentation, an issue that has been observed previously (Bamman and Crane, 2009).

Qualitative inspection To appreciate the effect of the soft cosine using a semantic similarity matrix, it is worthwhile to inspect a hand-picked selection of items which were correctly retrieved by SC_{emb} but not by $TfIdf$.[9] In Fig 4, the distributional approach adequately captures the antonymic relation between *visibilis* (‡) and *invisibilis* (†), which is reinforced by the synonymy between *species* (‡) and *imago* (†). Similar mechanisms seem at work in Fig 5, where the semantic similarity between vinery-related words increases the overall similarity score (*botrus*, *palmes*, *uva*, *granatus*).

‡ visibilis quaedam imago et species decoris eius
† qui est imago dei invisibilis primogenitus omnis creaturae

Figure 4

‡ botrum quem olim exploratores de israel in vecte ferebant
† pergentesque usque ad torrentem botri absciderunt palmitem cum uva sua quem portaverunt in vecte duo viri de malis quoque granatis et de ficis loci illius tulerunt

Figure 5

‡ descendentem vidi ille qui vidi
† dico enim vobis quod multi prophetae et reges voluerunt videre quae vos videtis et non viderunt et audire quae auditis et non audierunt
† et civitatem sanctam hierusalem novam vidi descendentem de caelo deo paratam sicut sponsam ornatam viro suo

Figure 6

Although the SC offers a welcome boost in retrieval performance, many errors remain. A first and frequent category are allusions that are simply hard to detect, even for human readers, often because they are very short or cryptic such as Fig 7, where despite increased semantic support—*cognovissent* being synonymous with *intellexerint*—the match is missed.

A second type of error occurs when less relevant candidates are pushed higher in the rank due to semantic reinforcements in the wrong direction. For example, in Fig 6 we have a query together with a wrongly retrieved match (*dico enim . . .*) and the true, non retrieved reference (*et civitatem . . .*). We observe that due to the high similarity of redundantly repeated perception verbs (*video*, *audio*), the wrong match receives high similarity whereas the true reference remains at lower rank.

6   Conclusions and Future Work

Our experiments have highlighted the difficulties of automated allusion detection. Even assum-

---

[9] In the examples, we display the relative contribution made by each term in a sentence to the total similarity score (darker red implies higher contribution). Queries are preceded by a double dagger (‡) and Bible references by a simple dagger (†).

‡ non intellexerint
† cum iustitiam dei cognovissent non intellexerunt quoniam qui talia agunt digni sunt morte non solum ea faciunt sed et consentiunt facientibus

Figure 7

ing manually defined queries, the best performing model could only find the matching reference within the top 20 hits in less than half of the dataset. Moreover, the retrieval quality heavily drops when relying on windowing for query construction. This aspect calls for further research into the problem of automatic query construction for the detection of allusive reuse.

Across all our experiments, purely semantic models are consistently outperformed by a purely lexical TfIdf model. Similarly, lemmatization boosts the performance of nearly all models which also suggests that ensuring enough lexical overlap is still a crucial aspect of allusive reuse retrieval. A similar reasoning helps explaining the superiority of $FastText$ over $word2vec$ embeddings, since the former is better at capturing morphological relationships – and lemma word embeddings suffer from data sparsity in the latter.

Overall, the hybrid models involving soft cosine show best performance, which indicates the effectiveness of such technique to incorporate semantics into BOW-based document retrieval and offers evidence that improvements in allusive reuse detection, however limited, can be gained from lexical semantics.

An interesting direction for future research is the application of soft cosine to text reuse detection across languages, leveraging current advances in multilingual word embeddings (Ammar et al., 2016) to extract multilingual word similarity matrices. Similarly, while the effect of adding semantic information from WordNet was less effective, it is still worth expanding the scope of semantic relationship beyond synonymy and exploring the usage of semantic similarity measures defined over WordNet (Budanitsky and Hirst, 2001).

Acknowledgments

We are indebted to Laurence Mellerin for providing us with the dataset and to Dinah Wouters, Jeroen De Gussem, Jeroen Deploige and Wim Verbaal for their help in curating the dataset and providing invaluable feedback and discussions.

References

Waleed Ammar, George Mulcaire, Yulia Tsvetkov, Guillaume Lample, Chris Dyer, and Noah A Smith. 2016. Massively multilingual word embeddings. *arXiv preprint arXiv:1602.01925*.

Ron Artstein. 2017. Inter-annotator agreement. In *Handbook of linguistic annotation*, pages 297–313. Springer.

Ron Artstein and Massimo Poesio. 2008. Inter-Coder Agreement for Computational Linguistics. *Computational Linguistics*, 34(4):555–596.

David Bamman and Gregory Crane. 2008. The logic and discovery of textual allusion. In *Proceedings of the Second Workshop on Language Technology for Cultural Heritage Data*.

David Bamman and Gregory Crane. 2009. Discovering Multilingual Text Reuse in Literary Texts. *Perseus Digital Library*.

David Bamman and Gregory Crane. 2011. Measuring historical word sense variation. In *Proceedings of the 11th annual international ACM/IEEE joint conference on Digital libraries*, pages 1–10. ACM.

Piotr Bojanowski, Edouard Grave, Armand Joulin, and Tomas Mikolov. 2017. Enriching word vectors with subword information. *Transactions of the Association for Computational Linguistics*, 5:135–146.

Marco Büchler. 2013. *Informationstechnische Aspekte des Historical Text Re-use*. Ph.D. thesis, Universität Leipzig.

Marco Büchler, Philip R Burns, Martin Müller, Emily Franzini, and Greta Franzini. 2014. Towards a Historical Text Re-use Detection. In *Text {Mining}*, pages 221–238. Springer.

Alexander Budanitsky and Graeme Hirst. 2001. Semantic distance in WordNet: An experimental, application-oriented evaluation of five measures. In *Workshop on WordNet and other lexical resources*, volume 2, page 2.

Delphine Charlet and Geraldine Damnati. 2017. Simbow at semeval-2017 task 3: Soft-cosine semantic similarity between questions for community question answering. In *Proceedings of the 11th International Workshop on Semantic Evaluation (SemEval-2017)*, pages 315–319.

Neil Coffee, Jean-Pierre Koenig, Shakthi Poornima, Christopher W Forstall, Roelant Ossewaarde, and Sarah L Jacobson. 2012. The Tesserae Project: intertextual analysis of Latin poetry. *Literary and linguistic computing*, 28(2):221–228.

Scott Deerwester, Susan T. Dumais, George W. Furnas, Thomas K. Landauer, and Richard Harshman. 1990. Indexing by latent semantic analysis. *Journal of the American Society for Information Science*, 41(6):391–407.

Christopher Forstall, Neil Coffee, Thomas Buck, Katherine Roache, and Sarah Jacobson. 2015. Modeling the scholars: Detecting intertextuality through enhanced word-level n-gram matching. *Digital Scholarship in the Humanities*, 30(4):503–515.

Regula Hohl Trillini and Sixta Quassdorf. 2010. A key to all quotations? A corpus-based parameter model of intertextuality. *Literary and Linguistic Computing*, 25(3):269–286.

Matt Kusner, Yu Sun, Nicholas Kolkin, and Kilian Weinberger. 2015. From word embeddings to document distances. In *International Conference on Machine Learning*, pages 957–966.

Dawid Laszuk. 2017. Python implementation of Empirical Mode Decomposition algorithm.

John Lee. 2007. A Computational Model of Text Reuse in Ancient Literary Texts. In *Proceedings of the 45th Annual Meeting of the Association of Computational Linguistics*, pages 472–479.

Enrique Manjavacas, Ákos Kádár, and Mike Kestemont. (in press). Improving lemmatization of non-standard languages with joint learning. In *Proceedings of the 2019 Conference of the North American Chapter of the Association for Computational Linguistics: Human Language Technologies, Volume 1 (Long Papers)*. Association for Computational Linguistics.

Laurence Mellerin. 2014. New Ways of Searching with Biblindex, the online Index of Biblical Quotations in Early Christian Literature. In Claire Clivaz, Gregory Andrew, and Hamidovic David, editors, *Digital Humanities in Biblical, Early Jewish and Early Christian Studies*, Digital Humanities in Biblical, Early Jewish and Early Christian Studies, pages 175–192. Brill.

Tomas Mikolov, Kai Chen, Greg Corrado, and Jeffrey Dean. 2013. Efficient estimation of word representations in vector space. *arXiv preprint arXiv:1301.3781*.

Stefano Minozzi. 2010. The Latin WordNet project. In *Akten des 15. Internationalen Kolloquiums zur Lateinischen Linguisti*, pages 707–716, Innsbruck. Institut für Sprachen und Literaturen der Universität Innsbruck Bereich Sprachwissenschaft.

Maria Moritz, Johannes Hellrich, and Sven Buechel. 2018. A Method for Human-Interpretable Paraphrasticality Prediction. In *Proceedings of the Second Joint SIGHUM Workshop on Computational Linguistics for Cultural Heritage, Social Sciences, Humanities and Literature*, pages 113–118.

Maria Moritz, Andreas Wiederhold, Barbara Pavlek, Yuri Bizzoni, and Marco Büchler. 2016. Non-literal text reuse in historical texts: An approach to identify reuse transformations and its application to bible reuse. In *Proceedings of the 2016 Conference on Empirical Methods in Natural Language Processing (EMNLP-16)*, pages 1849–1859.

Mary Orr. 2003. *Intertextuality: Debates and Contexts.* Polity Press.

Walter Scheirer, Christopher Forstall, and Neil Coffee. 2016. The sense of a connection: Automatic tracing of intertextuality by meaning. *Digital Scholarship in the Humanities.*

Hinrich Schütze, Christopher D Manning, and Prabhakar Raghavan. 2008. *Introduction to information retrieval*, volume 39. Cambridge University Press.

Grigori Sidorov, Alexander Gelbukh, Helena Gómez-Adorno, and David Pinto. 2014. Soft similarity and soft cosine measure: Similarity of features in vector space model. *Computación y Sistemas*, 18(3):491–504.

David A. Smith, Ryan Cordel, Elizabeth Maddock Dillon, Nick Stramp, and John Wilkerson. 2014. Detecting and modeling local text reuse. In *Proceedings of the ACM/IEEE Joint Conference on Digital Libraries*, pages 183–192.

Ellen M Voorhees. 1999. The TREC-8 Question Answering Track Report. In *TREC 8.*

John Wieting, Mohit Bansal, Kevin Gimpel, and Karen Livescu. 2015. Towards Universal Paraphrastic Sentence Embeddings. *CoRR*, abs/1511.0.

The Limits of Spanglish?

Barbara E. Bullock   Gualberto Guzmán   Almeida Jacqueline Toribio
The University of Texas at Austin
{bbullock,toribio}@austin.utexas.edu
{gualbertoguzman}@utexas.edu

Abstract

Linguistic code-switching (C-S) is common in oral bilingual vernacular speech. When used in literature, C-S becomes an artistic choice that can mirror the patterns of bilingual interactions. But it can also potentially exceed them. What are the limits of C-S? We model features of C-S in corpora of contemporary U.S. Spanish-English literary and conversational data to analyze why some critics view the 'Spanglish' texts of Ilan Stavans as deviating from a C-S norm.

1 Introduction

Code-switching (C-S), the alternating use of languages in a single conversation, is a vernacular practice of U.S. Spanish-English bilinguals. Latinx authors use C-S in their writing for various functions and at varying rates in addressing different readers. The occasional insertion of a Spanish word or expression into English language texts can appeal to monolingual and bilingual readers alike. Alternatively, the languages can co-occur in more complex patterns that engage only the most bilingual reader (Torres, 2007). The question then arises: What are the limits to the stylistic choices available to bilingual writers? To attempt to answer this question, we submit extracts of 'Spanglish' literature to experiments that allow us to model the features that identify the contour of an author's mixing. These results are, in turn, compared with naturally produced Spanish-English C-S conversation corpora.

C-S language data complicates NLP tasks like language identification, POS tagging, or language modeling (Solorio and Liu, 2008b,a; Solorio et al., 2014; Çetinoğlu et al., 2016; Barman et al., 2014; Vilares et al., 2016; Jamatia et al., 2015; Lynn et al., 2015; Elfardy et al., 2014; Molina et al., 2016; Rijhwani et al., 2017). Therefore, our experiments rest on language identification at the word level, coupled with analyses of syntactic and lexical features that do not require POS tagging. Our contributions are the following: (1) We compare the complexity of C-S in the prose of Ilan Stavans to that in other 'Spanglish' texts; (2) We introduce a new method of normalizing the probability of C-S in a corpus scaled according to the distribution of languages in a corpus; (3) We extract linguistic features of Stavans's writing – out-of-vocabulary items and syntactic transitions – and manually review them for grammatical analysis; (4) We assess the degree to which C-S in literature conforms to features that are attested in speech and that are predicted by linguistic principles and constraints.

2 Related Work

Research into C-S in spontaneously-produced and elicited spoken speech has offered insights into the social, cognitive, and structural dimensions of this multilingual phenomenon (Bullock and Toribio, 2009). The analysis of C-S in written discourse has garnered substantially less attention and, with some exceptions reviewed below (Montes-Alcalá, 2001; Callahan, 2004, 2002), it has centered largely on C-S in historical texts as a genre (Latin macaronic poetry, medieval Castilian Spanish-Hebrew *taqqanots* 'ordinances', personal letters) (Demo, 2018; Schulz and Keller, 2016; Miller, 2001; Gardner-Chloros and Weston, 2015; Swain et al., 2002; Nurmi and Pahta, 2004).

Spanish-English C-S is integral to the U.S. Latino experience, and Latino authors such as Gloria Anzaldúa and Junot Díaz, to name but two, have given authentic expression to this bilingual, bicultural reality and, in so doing, have brought legitimacy to literary C-S. The C-S crafted by Ilan Stavans stands as a point of contrast, a Spanish-English composite employed in rendering Spanglish renditions of *Don Quixote*, *Hamlet*, *Le Petit*

Proc. of the 3rd Joint SIGHUM Workshop on Computational Linguistics for Cultural Heritage, Social Sciences, Humanities and Literature, pp. 115–121
Minneapolis, MN, USA, June 7, 2019. ©2019 Association for Computational Linguistics

Prince, and The United States Constitution (excerpted in Example 1 below). The creative texts incorporate word-internal switches such as *joldeamos, unalienables, suddenmente*, which violate the Free Morpheme Constraint (Poplack, 1980), and *tinkleada*, whose phonotactic sequence of English syllabic [ɫ] followed by a Spanish bound morpheme is ruled out by the PF Disjunction Theorem (MacSwan, 2000). Stavans also employs the switching of lone function words, flaunting the Matrix Language Hypothesis (Myers-Scotton, 1997), which proscribes switching to a functional element and then immediately returning to the base language (Joshi, 1982). These properties led Lipski to characterize Stavans's Spanglish as "grotesque" (Lipski, 2004) and Torres to describe it as "unlikely" and "implausible" (Torres, 2005).

1. Nosotros joldeamos que estas truths son self-evidentes, que todos los hombres son creados equally, que están endawdeados por su Creador con certain derechos unalienables, que entre these están la vida, la libertad, y la persura de la felicidad. (Stavans, 2004)

2. Este asteroid ha sido glimpseado solamente una vez through un telescopio, y eso fue por un turco astrónomo en 1909. Él gave una impressive presentación de su discovery en una international astronomía conferencia. Pero nadie believed him por la manera en que él dessed up. Así es como son los grown-ups. Luckymente pa' el Asteroid B612, un Turco dictador made que sus people dressed con European estilo, on amenaza de death. Usando un very elegante traje, el astrónomo dio su presentatión again, en 1920. This time todos estaban convinced. (Stavans, 2017)

The parallel between literary and conversational C-S with respect to syntactic structure has been investigated. Callahan (2002; 2004) analyzed a corpus of 30 bilingual texts — novels and short stories published in the U.S. between 1970-2000 — totaling 2954 pages (word count unknown), with the goal of testing whether the Matrix Language Frame model (MLF), developed for oral speech, could be predictive of literary C-S. In broad terms, the asymmetric MLF model holds that one language provides the grammatical frame into which other-language material is inserted. Callahan manually annotated for Matrix language (ML) and Embedded language (EL) concluding that, in general, the C-S in the literary corpus can be accounted by the principles of the MLF model.

Human judges of automatically generated C-S have been shown to converge in their agreements that certain syntactic switches, such as the switching between subject pronoun and verb or between auxiliary and main verb, are dispreferred (Bhat et al., 2016; Solorio and Liu, 2008a). These findings are confirmed in linguistic research eliciting intuitions on constructed stimuli (Toribio, 2001). There are also observed directional effects in natural C-S, most notably with respect to the DET-N boundary; a switch generally follows a determiner in only one of the component languages (Joshi, 1982; Mahootian and Santorini, 1996; Blokzijl et al., 2017; Parafita Couto and Gullberg, 2017). In Spanish-English switches at this syntactic juncture, Spanish DET is consistently followed by an English bare noun regardless of which language is the ML (Bullock et al., 2018).

While we know much about the grammatical co-occurrence restrictions on intrasentential C-S, patterns of mixing in a broader sense remain to be explored. It is frequent to encounter claims that a vernacular is 'highly mixed' or to classify mixing according to a typology of complexity, e.g., from *insertion* to *alternation* or *congruent lexicalization*, where there is a single grammar into which words from more than one lexicon are inserted (Muysken, 2000). Metrics that aim to quantify C-S complexity in order to compare between corpora have been proposed to characterize the nature of language mixing (Das and Gambäck, 2014; Barnett et al., 2000; Gambäck and Das, 2016, 2014). In this paper we use and expand upon the metrics proposed by Guzmán et al. (2017), which are designed to quantify patterns of switching within and between corpora, to compare the C-S in the writings of Stavans against other literary works as well as against conversational C-S.

3   Methods

Four short extracts of stories rendered in Spanglish by Stavans, totaling 10,051 words, were downloaded from the web and converted from pdf format to text files. Additional data include the text of two other novels recognized for their sustained C-S: *Yo-Yo Boing!* by Nuyorican author Giannina Braschi (1998) and *Killer Crónicas: Bilingual Memories* by Chicana writer Susana

Chávez-Silverman (2004), both used by permission from the authors. Data representing natural, oral C-S include a Spanish-English transcription of a bilingual conversation in Texas (S7), collected and shared by Thamar Solorio (Solorio and Liu, 2008a) and a conversation, *maria40* (M40), extracted from the Miami Corpus, deposited in the Bilingual Bank (Donnelly and Deuchar, 2011). Each data set was processed using the word-level language identification system for Spanish-English available on github `https://github.com/Bilingual-Annotation-Task-Force/python-tagger` and described in Guzmán et al. (2016). In post-processing, punctuation and numbers were given the language tag of the previous token so that they were not counted as switches. Named Entities are tagged for Spanish or English within the language identification system used.

The sequence of language tags output from the system is used as input to the python script that calculates metrics for C-S (`https://github.com/Bilingual-Annotation-Task-Force/Scripts/blob/master/lang_metrics.py`): the M-Index (Barnett et al., 2000), or the ratio of languages represented in a corpus, bound between 0 (monolingual) and 1 (perfectly bilingual); the I-Index (Guzman et al., 2016), the probability of switching between any two n-grams, also bound by 0 (no switching) and 1 (switching at every token); and Burstiness (Goh and Barabási, 2008), which provides a probability distribution of how many tokens will appear in a sequence in a given language before a switch to another, bound between -1 (periodic) and 1 (aperiodic). These results of application of these metrics to our corpora are shown in Table 1.

3.1 Normalized I-Index

One of the drawbacks of the I-Index developed by Guzmán et al. (2016) is that it does not account for the underlying language distribution of a text. For example, a text with an M-Index of 0.01, i.e. a text dominated by one language, could never achieve an I-Index of 1 because there are insufficient tokens to incorporate more switching. In fact, the only way to reach an I-Index of 1, linguistic constraints on switching aside, is if the M-Index were near 1, or if the languages were almost equally distributed. As a result, values of the I-index are not directly comparable across corpora from different language distributions. To correct for this, we have developed an improved version of the I-Index normalized to account for these bounds. In a text of N tokens, with k languages, each with n_i tokens, then the following equation can be used to compute a normalized I-Index, which we will refer to as I_2:

$$I_2 = \frac{I - L}{H - L} \qquad (1)$$

where I represents the I-index described in (Guzman et al., 2016), and the lower and upper bounds, L and H, respectively, are defined by the following formulas:

$$L = (k - 1)/(N - 1) \qquad (2)$$

$$H = \min\left(\frac{2 \cdot (N - \max_i n_i)}{N - 1}, 1\right) \qquad (3)$$

The lowest amount of switching possible, L, outlined in Eq. 2 occurs when all n_i tokens of each language are concatenated together, leading to $k - 1$ switches between all monolingual chunks. However, the highest amount of switching possible, H, which we compute in Eq. 3, occurs if we alternate tokens from each of the languages and intersperse them between the tokens of the most common language. An issue that our I_2 presents is that, for a highly-skewed corpus, the difference between the H and L values is minuscule, which can cause numerical problems. In other words, this metric performs poorly for corpora where the vast majority (>95%) is in one language.

Note that our I_2 scales I according to the language distribution and allows for direct comparison across different corpora. An I_2 of 0 or 1 now corresponds to a text with the absolute minimum and maximum, respectively, of switching possible given a fixed underlying language distribution. This new metric, in a manner of speaking, controls for a varying M-Index. In fact, as a rough estimate, one can think of I_2 as being approximately equal to I/M, where M is the M-Index.

3.2 Results of Metrics

The three literary works (Stavans, *Killer Crónicas* and *Yo-Yo Boing!*) are distinguished from the conversations (M40, S7) by the M-Index, as seen in Table 1, indicating that the balance of languages in these texts is more even than in the conversations, where one language predominates (English in S7 and Spanish in M40). Within the literary corpora, the Stavans subcorpora stand out as having a higher probability of switching (I-Index) than the others, even more than *Killer Crónicas*, which is the most bilingual of all the datasets, with an M-Index of .99. This is reflected best by the Normalized I-Index, which is a valid measure of comparison here since none of the corpora are highly-skewed.

The quantitative models of these corpora indicate that the Stavans excerpts exhibit extreme switching relative to the other datasets. Contrary to prior work by Guzmán et al. (2016), the values of I_2 demonstrate that KC is not that much different from M40 and S7. The largest differences observed in I and I_2 are with the M40 and S7 corpora due to the skewed language distributions of the texts, which exaggerate the measurement of the amounts of switching.

A plot representing the densities of monolingual spans in the corpora, a visualization of Burstiness, is shown in Figure 1, where it can be seen that language mixing in Stavans and Killer Crónicas occurs more regularly throughout the text, whereas *Yo-Yo Boing!*, M40, and S7 show a long-tailed signal, indicating that C-S is a sporadic occurrence.

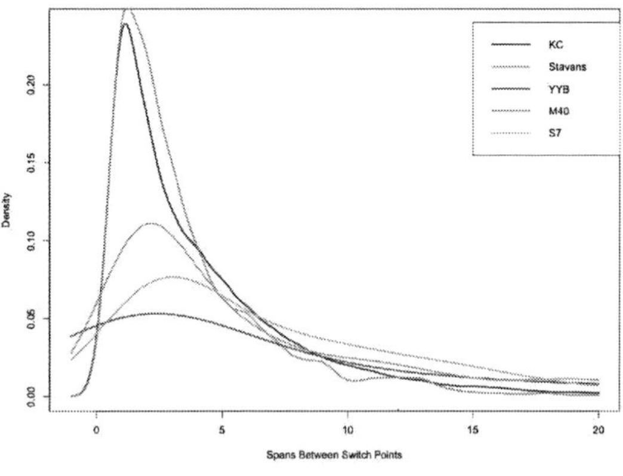

Figure 1: Span Densities

3.3 Lexical and Grammatical Analyses

As a second step toward modeling C-S, we compared the structural profiles of the Stavans extracts to *Killer Crónicas*, the texts in which C-S is the least bursty, to calculate the rate of word-internal switching. We filtered out words using the `aspell` command on Linux for English and Spanish. The mixed words were manually selected based on intra-word switching and NOT typographical errors, variable spellings (e.g., *cashe* to represent the Argentine pronunciation of *calle*), or non-words. We retained in our mixed-word list cross-linguistic phoneticizations such as *livin* in which English words are given a Spanish-like phonological representation. The results are given in Table 2 relative to the number of unique words in the corpora. The frequency of mixed words in *Killer Crónicas* is negligible relative to the proportion of the unique words in Stavans that are mixed. This difference is highly significant ($\chi^2 = 109.26$, df = 1, p-value < 2.2e-16) with a Cramer's-V test of .129 indicating a small effect size.

We investigated patterns of grammatical constraints by searching and tagging all subject pronouns and determiners in Spanish and in English according to their lexical entries (*la, the, yo, I,* etc.) and listing them alongside the word that followed in the text. We manually reviewed the lists of PRON + word and DET + word to eliminate any errors or any cross-linguistic homographs (e.g., Spanish *he* is an auxiliary verb). These were tabulated according to the language of the token and the language of the next word for each corpus. The proportion tables for DET-NOUN transitions is found in Table 3.

The asymmetry in directionality discussed above is evident in both literary corpora; Spanish determiners are more frequently found with English nouns than vice versa. However, Stavans shows a much higher mixing rate at this juncture, in general: .36 relative to .17 for *Killer Crónicas*: ($\chi^2 = 32.249$, df = 1, p-value < 1.356e-08) with a Cramer's-V test of .199 indicating a small effect size. The results for switching at the PRON-V juncture are shown in Table 4. While switching after a PRON is rare in *Killer Crónicas*, Stavans switches after a subject pronoun at a rate of about 13%, particularly if the pronoun is Spanish ($\chi^2 = 17.547$, df = 1, p-value < 2.803e-05) with a Cramer's-V test of .174). These analyses inform us that the Stavans corpora is qualitatively different from Killer Crónicas and distinguished by unusual C-S within words and across tightly knit syntactic boundaries.

Table 1: Metric results

Corpus	Length	Switches	M-Index	I-Index	I_2	Burstiness
Stavans	12405	4880	0.96	0.27	0.32	-0.03
Killer Crónicas	7002	2127	0.99	0.17	0.19	-0.06
Yo-Yo Boing!	75679	5339	0.97	0.04	0.05	0.36
M40	7638	1250	0.63	0.10	0.18	0.26
S7	8011	894	0.60	0.06	0.12	0.32

Table 2: Frequency of word-internal C-S

Corpus	Unique	Mixed	Freq
Stavans	4000	254	0.635
Killer Crónicas	2524	24	0.009

Table 3: Determiner-NP switching

	Stavans		*Killer Crónicas*	
Det	EnNP	SpNP	EnNP	SpNP
Eng	0.109	0.075	0.339	0.052
Span	0.278	0.538	0.050	0.560

Table 4: Pronoun-VP switching

	Stavans		*Killer Crónicas*	
Pro	EnVP	SpVP	EnVP	SpVP
Eng	0.474	0.099	0.653	0.005
Span	0.067	0.360	0.005	0.338

4 Discussion

We have observed that literary texts present more C-S than what is manifested in natural speech. However, different authors manifest different patterns of C-S, even when they employ more or less the same ratio of languages in their writings. While the M-index for the Stavans and *Killer Crónicas* corpora are nearly identical, demonstrating a near perfect balance of Spanish and English, with *Yo-Yo Boing!* close behind in terms of balance, the texts present distinct switching profiles. Specifically, Stavans, whose switching is criticized as unnatural, shows a higher probability of alternating between the languages, quantified by the I_2 and visualized as short spans of one language followed for short spans of the other. The C-S in Stavans also differs qualitatively from that in *Killer Crónicas*, the other literary text in our sample to show a similar anti-bursty distribution of C-S, in the preponderance of switching within the word (e.g., *adrifteando, astonisheado, askeó, wistfulmente*), switching at the DET-N boundary (e.g., *the casa*), and switching after PRON (*él slept*), all sites that are very rarely attested junctures of mixing in oral speech, and that are ruled out by predictive linguistic models.

Note that the effect of switching on functional words, such as pronouns and determiners, while in itself odd, will also lead to increased rates of C-S and to short language spans. Thus, we cannot know if it is the frequency of switching, the decision to switch after functional elements and within words, or a combination of these features that lead critics to characterize Stavans's 'Spanglish' texts in negative terms. In future work, we seek to determine whether there are expected constants of C-S for Spangish literature versus for natural speech. This will help determine the degree to which an observed C-S contour is an outlier.

We have presented methods for comparing between corpora that rest on multiple features easily gleaned from small corpora, but our conclusions can only be tentative. Language models that would permit direct comparisons of the statistical distribution of C-S between corpora would be desirable for establishing the limits of mixed vernaculars like so-called 'Spanglish'.

References

Utsab Barman, Amitava Das, Joachim Wagner, and Jennifer Foster. 2014. Code mixing: A challenge for language identification in the language of social media. In *Proceedings of the First Workshop on Computational Approaches to Code Switching*, pages 13–23.

Ruthanna Barnett, Eva Codó, Eva Eppler, Montse Forcadell, Penelope Gardner-Chloros, Roeland Van Hout, Melissa Moyer, Maria Carme Torras, Maria Teresa Turell, Mark Sebba, et al. 2000. The LIDES Coding Manual: A Document for Preparing and Analyzing Language Interaction Data Version 1.1–July 1999. *International Journal of Bilingualism*, 4(2):131–271.

Gayatri Bhat, Monojit Choudhury, and Kalika Bali. 2016. Grammatical constraints on intra-sentential code-switching: From theories to working models. *arXiv:1612.04538*.

119

Jeffrey Blokzijl, Margaret Deuchar, and M Carmen Parafita Couto. 2017. Determiner asymmetry in mixed nominal constructions: The role of grammatical factors in data from Miami and Nicaragua. *Languages*, 2(4):1–12.

Giannina Braschi. 1998. *Yo-yo boing!* Latin Amer. Literary Review Press.

Barbara E Bullock, Gualberto Guzmán, Jacqueline Serigos, and Almeida Jacqueline Toribio. 2018. Should Code-switching Models Be Asymmetric? *Proc. Interspeech 2018*, pages 2534–2538.

Barbara E. Bullock and Almeida Jacqueline Toribio. 2009. *The Cambridge handbook of linguistic code-switching*. Cambridge University Press.

Laura Callahan. 2002. The matrix language frame model and Spanish/English codeswitching in fiction. *Language & Communication*, 22(1):1–16.

Laura Callahan. 2004. *Spanish/English codeswitching in a written corpus*. John Benjamins Publishing.

Özlem Çetinoğlu, Sarah Schulz, and Ngoc Thang Vu. 2016. Challenges of Computational Processing of Code-Switching. In *Proceedings of the Second Workshop on Computational Approaches to Code Switching*, pages 1–11, Austin, Texas. Association for Computational Linguistics.

Susana Chávez-Silverman. 2004. *Killer Crónicas: bilingual memories*. Univ. of Wisconsin Press.

Amitava Das and Björn Gambäck. 2014. Identifying Languages at the Word Level in Code-Mixed Indian Social Media Text. In *Proceedings of the 11th International Conference on Natural Language Processing*, pages 378–387, Goa, India. NLP Association of India.

Šime Demo. 2018. Mining macaronics. In *Multilingual Practices in Language History: English and Beyond*, pages 199–221. De Gruyter Mouton.

Kevin Donnelly and Margaret Deuchar. 2011. The Bangor Autoglosser: a multilingual tagger for conversational text. *ITA11, Wrexham, Wales*, pages 17–25.

Heba Elfardy, Mohamed Al-Badrashiny, and Mona Diab. 2014. AIDA: Identifying code switching in informal Arabic text. In *Proceedings of The First Workshop on Computational Approaches to Code Switching*, pages 94–101.

Björn Gambäck and Amitava Das. 2014. On measuring the complexity of code-mixing. In *Proceedings of the 11th International Conference on Natural Language Processing, Goa, India*, pages 1–7. Citeseer.

Björn Gambäck and Amitava Das. 2016. Comparing the Level of Code-Switching in Corpora. In *LREC*, pages 1850–1855.

Penelope Gardner-Chloros and Daniel Weston. 2015. Code-switching and multilingualism in literature. *Language and Literature*, 24(3):182–193.

K-I Goh and A-L Barabási. 2008. Burstiness and memory in complex systems. *EPL (Europhysics Letters)*, 81(4):48002.

Gualberto A Guzmán, Joseph Ricard, Jacqueline Serigos, Barbara E Bullock, and Almeida Jacqueline Toribio. 2017. Metrics for Modeling Code-Switching Across Corpora. In *Interspeech*, pages 67–71.

Gualberto A Guzman, Jacqueline Serigos, Barbara E Bullock, and Almeida Jacqueline Toribio. 2016. Simple tools for exploring variation in code-switching for linguists. In *Proceedings of the Second Workshop on Computational Approaches to Code Switching*, pages 12–20.

Anupam Jamatia, Björn Gambäck, and Amitava Das. 2015. Part-of-speech tagging for code-mixed English-Hindi Twitter and Facebook chat messages. In *Proceedings of the International Conference Recent Advances in Natural Language Processing*, pages 239–248.

Aravind K Joshi. 1982. Processing of sentences with intra-sentential code-switching. In *Proceedings of the 9th conference on Computational linguistics-Volume 1*, pages 145–150. Academia Praha.

John M Lipski. 2004. Is "Spanglish" the third language of the South?: truth and fantasy about US Spanish. In *3rd Language Variation in the South (LAVIS III) conference, Tuscaloosa, AL*.

Teresa Lynn, Kevin Scannell, and Eimear Maguire. 2015. Minority language Twitter: Part-of-speech tagging and analysis of Irish tweets. In *Proceedings of the Workshop on Noisy User-generated Text*, pages 1–8.

Jeff MacSwan. 2000. The architecture of the bilingual language faculty: Evidence from intrasentential code switching. *Bilingualism: language and cognition*, 3(1):37–54.

Shahrzad Mahootian and Beatrice Santorini. 1996. Code switching and the complement/adjunct distinction. *Linguistic Inquiry*, pages 464–479.

Elaine R Miller. 2001. Written code switching in a medieval document: A comparison with some modern constraints. *Canadian Journal of Linguistics/Revue canadienne de linguistique*, 46(3-4):159–186.

Giovanni Molina, Fahad AlGhamdi, Mahmoud Ghoneim, Abdelati Hawwari, Nicolas Rey-Villamizar, Mona Diab, and Thamar Solorio. 2016. Overview for the second shared task on language identification in code-switched data. In *Proceedings of the Second Workshop on Computational Approaches to Code Switching*, pages 40–49.

Cecilia Montes-Alcalá. 2001. Written codeswitching: Powerful bilingual images. *Trends In Linguistics Studies AND Monographs*, 126:193–222.

Pieter Muysken. 2000. *Bilingual speech: A typology of code-mixing*, volume 11. Cambridge University Press.

Carol Myers-Scotton. 1997. *Duelling languages: Grammatical structure in codeswitching*. Oxford University Press.

Arja Nurmi and Päivi Pahta. 2004. Social stratification and patterns of code-switching in early English letters.

M Carmen Parafita Couto and Marianne Gullberg. 2017. Code-switching within the noun phrase: Evidence from three corpora. *International Journal of Bilingualism*, page 1367006917729543.

Shana Poplack. 1980. Sometimes I'll start a sentence in Spanish y termino en Español: toward a typology of code-switching. *Linguistics*, 18(7-8):581–618.

Shruti Rijhwani, Royal Sequiera, Monojit Choudhury, Kalika Bali, and Chandra Shekhar Maddila. 2017. Estimating code-switching on Twitter with a novel generalized word-level language detection technique. In *Proceedings of the 55th Annual Meeting of the Association for Computational Linguistics (Volume 1: Long Papers)*, volume 1, pages 1971–1982.

Sarah Schulz and Mareike Keller. 2016. Code-switching ubique est-language identification and part-of-speech tagging for historical mixed text. In *Proceedings of the 10th SIGHUM Workshop on Language Technology for Cultural Heritage, Social Sciences, and Humanities*, pages 43–51.

Thamar Solorio, Elizabeth Blair, Suraj Maharjan, Steven Bethard, Mona Diab, Mahmoud Ghoneim, Abdelati Hawwari, Fahad AlGhamdi, Julia Hirschberg, Alison Chang, et al. 2014. Overview for the first shared task on language identification in code-switched data. In *Proceedings of the First Workshop on Computational Approaches to Code Switching*, pages 62–72.

Thamar Solorio and Yang Liu. 2008a. Learning to predict code-switching points. In *Proceedings of the Conference on Empirical Methods in Natural Language Processing*, pages 973–981. Association for Computational Linguistics.

Thamar Solorio and Yang Liu. 2008b. Part-of-speech tagging for English-Spanish code-switched text. In *Proceedings of the Conference on Empirical Methods in Natural Language Processing*, pages 1051–1060. Association for Computational Linguistics.

Ilan Stavans. 2004. *Spanglish: The making of a new American language*. Harper Collins.

Ilan Stavans. 2017. *El Little Principe*. Edition Tintenfass.

Simon Swain, James Noel Adams, Mark Janse, et al. 2002. *Bilingualism in ancient society: Language contact and the written text*. Oxford University Press on Demand.

Almeida Toribio. 2001. Accessing bilingual code-switching competence. *International Journal of Bilingualism*, 5(4):403–436.

Lourdes Torres. 2005. Don Quixote in Spanglish: traducttore, traditore? *Romance Quarterly*, 52(4):328–334.

Lourdes Torres. 2007. In the contact zone: Code-switching strategies by Latino/a writers. *Melus*, 32(1):75–96.

David Vilares, Miguel A Alonso, and Carlos Gómez-Rodríguez. 2016. EN-ES-CS: An English-Spanish Code-Switching Twitter Corpus for Multilingual Sentiment Analysis. In *LREC*, pages 4149–4153.

Sign Clustering and Topic Extraction in Proto-Elamite[*]

Logan Born[1] **Kate Kelley**[2] **Nishant Kambhatla**[1]
loborn@sfu.ca kathryn.kelley@ubc.ca nkambhat@sfu.ca

Carolyn Chen[1] **Anoop Sarkar**[1]
nll-contact@sfu.ca anoop@sfu.ca

[1]Simon Fraser University
School of Computing Science

[2]University of British Columbia
Department of Classical, Near Eastern,
and Religious Studies

Abstract

We describe a first attempt at using techniques from computational linguistics to analyze the undeciphered proto-Elamite script. Using hierarchical clustering, n-gram frequencies, and LDA topic models, we both replicate results obtained by manual decipherment and reveal previously-unobserved relationships between signs. This demonstrates the utility of these techniques as an aid to manual decipherment.

1 Introduction

In the late 19th century, excavations at the ancient city of Susa in southwestern Iran began to uncover clay tablets written in an unknown script later dubbed 'proto-Elamite'. Over 1,500 tablets have since been found at Susa, and a few hundred more at sites across Iran, making it the most widespread writing system of the late 4th and early 3rd millennia BC (circa 3100–2900 BC) and the largest corpus of ancient material in an undeciphered script.[1]

Proto-Elamite (PE) is the conventional designation of this script, whose language remains unknown but was presumed by early researchers as likely to be an early form of Elamite. A number of features of the PE writing system are understood. These include tablet format and direction of writing, the numeric systems, and the ideographic associations of some non-numeric signs, predominantly those for livestock accounting, agricultural production, and possibly labor administration. Yet

the significance of the majority of PE signs, the nature of those signs (syllabic, logographic, ideographic, or other) and the linguistic context(s) of the texts remain unknown. It was recognized from the outset, due to the features of the script, that all the proto-Elamite tablets were administrative records, rather than historical or literary compositions (Scheil, 1905).

Texts are written in lines from right to left, but are rotated in publication to be read from top to bottom (then left to right) following academic practice for publishing the contemporary proto-cuneiform tablets. The content of a text is divided into entries, logical units which may span more than one physical line. The entry itself is a string of non-numeric signs whose meanings are for the most part undeciphered. Each entry is followed by a numeric notation in one of several different numeric systems, which quantifies something in relation to the preceding entry. This serves to mark the division between entries. An important exception exists in what are currently understood to be 'header' entries: these can present information that appears to pertain to the text as a whole, and are followed directly by the text's first content entry with no intervening numeric notation. A digital image and line drawing of a simple PE text along with transliteration are shown in Figure 1.

Although a complete digital corpus of PE texts exists (Section 2), it has not been studied using the standard toolkit of data exploration techniques from computational linguistics. The goals of this paper are threefold. By applying a variety of computational tools, we hope to

i. promote interest in and awareness of the problems surrounding PE decipherment

ii. demonstrate the effectiveness of computational approaches by reproducing results previously obtained by manual decipherment

---

[*]We would like to thank Jacob Dahl and the anonymous reviewers for their helpful remarks. This research was partially supported by the Natural Sciences and Engineering Research Council of Canada grants NSERC RGPIN-2018-06437 and RGPAS-2018-522574 and a Department of National Defence (DND) and NSERC grant DGDND-2018-00025 to the last author.

[1]New PE texts have been found as recently as 2006–2007, when excavations at Tepe Sofalin near Tehran uncovered ten tablets (Dahl et al., 2012).

Proc. of the 3rd Joint SIGHUM Workshop on Computational Linguistics for Cultural Heritage, Social Sciences, Humanities and Literature, pp. 122–132
Minneapolis, MN, USA, June 7, 2019. ©2019 Association for Computational Linguistics

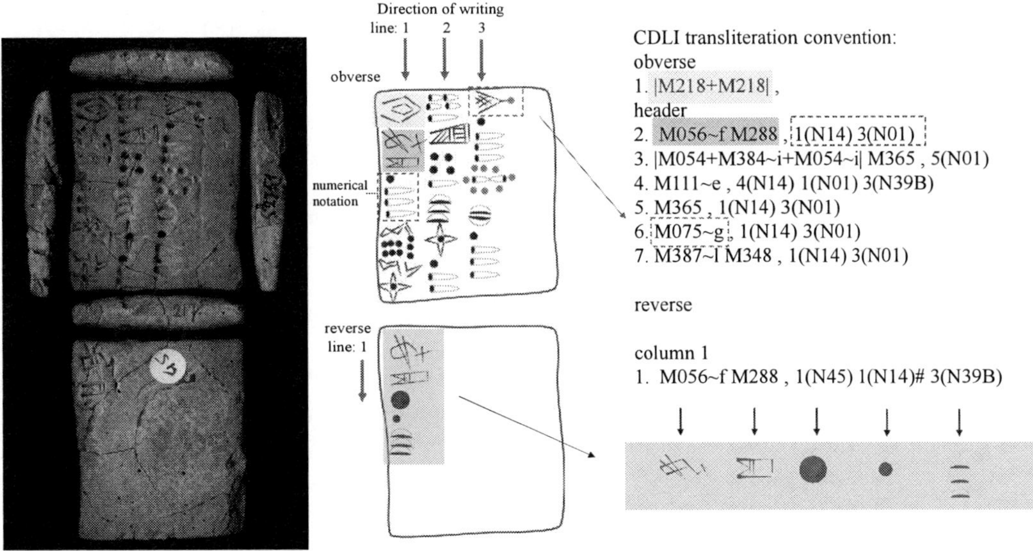

Figure 1: PE tablet *Mémoires de la Délégation en Perse* (MDP) 6, no. 217 (P008016; Scheil 1905). Digital image, line art, and transcription (called transliteration by the CDLI) from the Cuneiform Digital Library Initiative. Explanatory annotation added by current authors.

iii. highlight novel patterns in the data which may inform future decipherment attempts

We hope to show that interesting data may be extracted from the corpus even in the absence of a complete linguistic decipherment. To encourage further study in this vein, we are also releasing all data and code used in this work as part of an online suite of data exploration tools for PE.[2] Additional figures and interactive visualizations are also available as part of this toolkit.

2 Conventional Decipherment Efforts

Studies towards the decipherment of PE can be summarised by a relatively short bibliography of serious efforts (Englund, 1996).[3] Stumbling blocks to decipherment have included inaccuracies in published hand-copies of the texts, a lack of access to high-quality original images, and the associated difficulty in drawing up an accurate signlist and producing a consistently-rendered full transcription of the corpus. Members of the *Cuneiform Digital Library Initiative* (CDLI) have been remedying these deficiencies over the past two decades, and the PE script can now boast (i) a working signlist with a consistent manner of transcribing signs in ASCII, and (ii) an open-access, searchable database hosting the entire corpus in transcription, alongside digital images and/or hand-copies of almost every text.[4]

Historically, specialists of PE have operated on a working hypothesis that it may be, like later Sumerian cuneiform, to some extent a mixed system of ideographic or logographic signs alongside signs that may represent syllables. However, the level of linguistic content represented in both PE and proto-cuneiform has been called into question (Damerow, 2006), and the presence of a set of syllabic signs in PE is yet to be proven.

The strict linear organisation of signs in PE is the earliest such known to a writing system: proto-cuneiform arranged signs in various ways within cases (and sometimes subcases), and only in cuneiform from several hundred years later did scribes begin to consistently write in lines with one sign following the next. However, it is not clear to what extent the linear sign organization of PE reflects the flow of spoken language as in later writing systems.[5]

---

[2] https://github.com/sfu-natlang/pe-decipher-toolkit

[3] For the most complete and up-to-date bibliography, see Dahl 2019.

[4] http://cdli.ox.ac.uk/wiki/doku.php?id=proto-elamite

[5] Dahl (2019:83): "proto-Elamite texts are organized in an

Analysis of sign and entry ordering in the texts has also revealed some tabular-like organising principles familiar from proto-cuneiform. Longer sequences of signs can often be broken down into constituent parts appearing to follow hierarchical ordering patterns apparently based upon administrative (rather than phonetic/linguistic) principles, and hierarchies can be seen across entries as well (Hawkins, 2015; Dahl et al., 2018).

Traditional linguistic decipherment efforts have not yet succeeded in identifying a linguistic context for PE, though progress has been made, for example in positing sets of syllabo-logographic signs thought to be used to write personal names (PNs). We refer to Meriggi's (1971:173–174) syllabary as shorthand for these signs, as he was the first to identify such a set and his work has since been closely imitated (Desset 2016; Dahl 2019:85). Although he called it a syllabary, Meriggi was aware that the signs might not prove to be syllabic and that object or other signs might remain mixed in.

Continued efforts to establish the organizational principles of the PE script and to isolate possible syllable sequences or PNs may be advanced by computational techniques, which can be used to evaluate hypotheses much faster than purely manual approaches. In this endeavour it is necessary to remember that although early writing encodes meaningful information, that information may or may not be linguistic (Damerow, 2006). Although it is not known why PE disappeared after a relatively short period of use, one of several possibilities is that this relates to the way it represents information, perhaps providing a poorer, less versatile encoding compared to later cuneiform with its mixed syllabo-logography.

3 Data

All data in this work are based on the PE corpus provided by the CDLI. After removing tablets which only bear unreadable or numeric signs, this dataset comprises 1399 distinct texts. Most of these are very short: the mean text length is 27 readable signs, of which only 10 are non-numeric on average. Long texts do exist, however, up to a maximum length of 724 readable signs of which 198 are non-numeric.

Our working signlist (extracted from the tran-

scribed texts) contains 49 numeric signs and 1623 non-numeric signs. Of these, 287 are 'basic' signs, and 1087 are labeled as variants due to minor graphical differences. Sign variants are denoted by ∼, as in M006∼b, a variant of the basic sign M006. In an on-going process, analysis of the corpus aims to confirm whether sign variants are semantically distinct, or reflect purely graphical variation. Where the latter case is understood, the sign is given a numeric rather than alphabetic subscript, as in M269∼1. The remaining 249 non-numeric signs are compounds called complex graphemes which are made up of two or more signs in combination, as in |M136+M365|.

Future work is required to establish which sign variants are meaningfully distinct from their base signs; in the absence of such work, we have chosen to treat all variants as distinct until proven otherwise. Our models give interpretable results under this assumption, suggesting this is a reasonable approach. There are, however, cases where collapsing sign variants together would seem to affect our results, and we highlight these where relevant.

4 Analysis of Signs

4.1 Hierarchical Sign Clustering

Manual decipherment of PE has proceeded in part by identifying that some signs occur in largely the same contexts as other signs. This has produced groupings of signs into "owners", "objects", and other functionally related sets (Dahl, 2009). For example, M388 and M124 are known to be parallel "overseer" signs which appear in alternation with one another (Dahl et al., 2018:25).

In the same vein, we have investigated techniques for clustering signs hierarchically based on the way they occur and co-occur within texts. Our work considers three approaches to sign clustering: a neighbor-based clustering groups signs based on the number of times each other sign occurs immediately before or after that sign in the corpus; an HMM clustering groups signs based on the emission probabilities of a 10 state hidden Markov model (HMM) trained on the corpus; and a generalized Brown clustering groups signs as described in Derczynski and Chester 2016. By using three different clustering techniques, we can search for clusters which recur across all three methods to maximize the likelihood of finding those that are meaningful. This reduces the impact of noise in the data, which is especially useful

---

in-line structure that is more prone to language coding than proto-cuneiform..."

given the small size of the PE corpus.

4.1.1 Clustering Evaluation

We identified commonalities between our three clusterings using the following heuristic. Given a set of signs S, we found for each clustering the height of the smallest subtree containing every sign in S. If all of these subtrees were short (which we took to mean not larger than $2|S|$) then we called S a stable cluster.

In many cases, the stable clusters comprise variants of the same sign. This is the case for M157 and M157~a, which cluster together across all techniques and are already believed to function similarly to each other, if not identically.

One very large stable cluster consists of the signs M057, M066, M096, M218, and M371. This cluster is shown as it appears in each clustering in Figure 2. These signs belong to Meriggi's proposed syllabary (Meriggi 1971, esp. pp. 173–4) and are hypothesized to represent names syllabically (or logographic-syllabically; Desset 2016:83). Desset (2016:83) likewise identified "approximately 200 different signs" from possible anthroponyms, "among which M4, M9, M66, M96, M218 and M371 must be noticed for their high frequency." Desset's list differs from our cluster by only two signs, replacing M057 with M004 and M009. M004 and M009 group with other members of the putative syllabary in each clustering, but their position is much more variable across the three techniques. For M009 at least, this may indicate multivalent use: besides its inclusion in hypothesised PNs (e.g. Meriggi 1971:173; Dahl 2019:85), it appears in various different administrative contexts that don't appear to include PNs (e.g P008206) and as an account postscript (see below here and 5.3).

All three methods group the five signs in our cluster close to other suspected syllabic signs; however, since each technique groups them with a *different* subset of the syllabary, only these five form a stable group across all three methods. This may be due simply to their frequency, or they could in fact form a distinct subgroup within the proposed syllabary; future work may yield a better understanding of possible anthroponyms by trying to identify other such subgroups.

While this discussion has focused on the stable clusters for which we can provide some interpretation, others represent groups of signs with no previously recognised relationship, such as

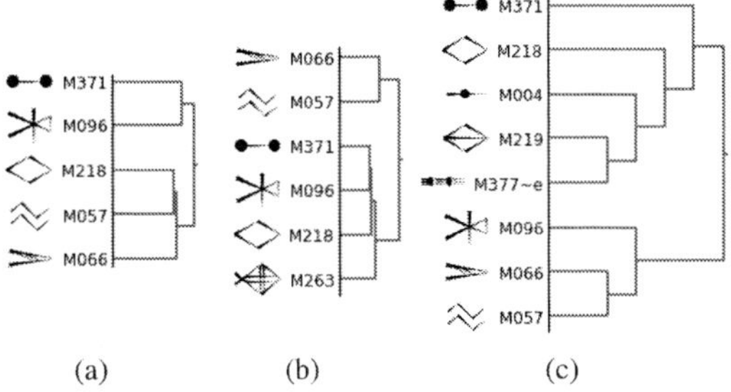

(a)   (b)   (c)

Figure 2: Detail of the (a) neighbor-based, (b) HMM, and (c) Brown clusterings showing signs possibly used in anthroponyms. M057, M066, M096, M218, and M371 are considered a stable cluster due to their proximity in all three clusterings.

M003~b and M263~a (Figure 3). M003(~a/b) are "stick" signs ($\smile$, $\frown$) understood in some PE contexts to denote worker categories (Dahl et al., 2018); they are graphically comparable to proto-cuneiform PAP~a-c ($\smile$) and PA ($\smile$), the latter of which can, in later Sumerian, indicate *ugula*, a work group foreman/administrator.

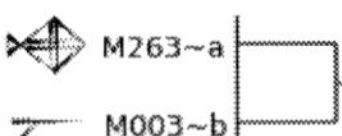

Figure 3: M003~b clusters identically with M263~a in all three techniques.

M263~a is one of a series of depictions of "vessels" ($\bowtie$), this particular variant appearing in 27 texts; notably the base sign M263 appears as a possible element in PNs (Dahl, 2019:85). Interestingly, M003~b and M263~a only appear together in a single text (P008727), one of a closely-related group of short texts[6] that each end in the administrative postscript M009 M003~b or M009 M003~c. It can also be noted that M263~1 occurs in another text belonging to this small group.

It thus remains for future work to interpret this and the many other stable clusters resulting from our work. These additional groupings are detailed in our data exploration toolkit, along with complete dendrograms for each clustering which are too large to include in this publication.

Although we have not performed a full study of the clusterings produced when sign variants are collapsed together, a preliminary comparison

---

[6] Available online at `https://cdli.ucla.edu/search/search_results.php?SearchMode=Text&requestFrom=Search&TextSearch=M009+M003`

125

suggests this is worth pursuing. For instance, a new cluster of small livestock signs arises in the neighbor-based clustering, comprising M367 ("billy-goat"), M346 ("sheep"), M006 ("ram"), and M309 (possible animal byproduct). Existing clusters, such as the stable cluster of syllabic signs, appear to remain intact, but a complete comparison of the techniques in this setting is warranted.

4.2 Sign Frequency and n-Gram Counts

Sign frequency is another useful datapoint for understanding the overall content of the corpus and for building a more nuanced understanding of sign use (Dahl, 2002; Kelley, 2018). Figure 4 shows the most common PE unigrams, bigrams, and trigrams. These counts exclude n-grams containing numeric signs or broken or unreadable signs (transcribed as X or [...]); n-grams which span the boundary between entries are also excluded. Note the sharp drop-off in frequency from the most frequent signs to the rest of the signary; in fact nearly half the attested signs (745 out of 1623) occur only once. Similar results were presented in Dahl 2002.

The most common unigrams include "object" signs and signs belonging to Meriggi's syllabary. The object signs are M288 (a grain container), M388 ("person/man"), M124 (a person/worker category paralleling M388), M054 (a yoke, usually indicating a person/worker category or animal), M297 ("bread"), and M346 ("ewe"). The syllabary signs are M218, M371 (which may double as an object sign/worker category), M387 (also a numeral meaning "100"), and M066.

The n-gram counts reveal the scale at which complex sequences of information are repeated across tablets. Over 1600 strings contain at least 3 non-numeric signs. Of these, only 11 trigrams are repeated at least 5 times across the corpus; two of these end in the "grain container" sign M288 and are therefore best parsed as undeciphered bigrams followed by an object sign. Following this, 52 other trigrams are repeated three or four times across the corpus, leaving the great majority (98%) of trigrams to appear only once or twice.[7] The most frequent trigram, M377~e M347 M371 (found 17 times per Figure 4), appears in no more than about 1.5% of the texts. Even among bi-

____

[7]This assumes that sign variants are meaningfully distinct, as is the working hypothesis among PE specialists. Collapsing variants together does not appreciably change these results, however, as it only increases most trigram counts by 1 or 2 instances. A similar result holds for bigram counts.

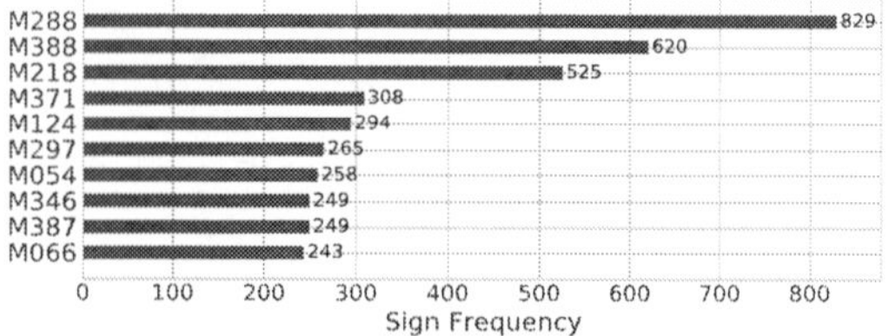

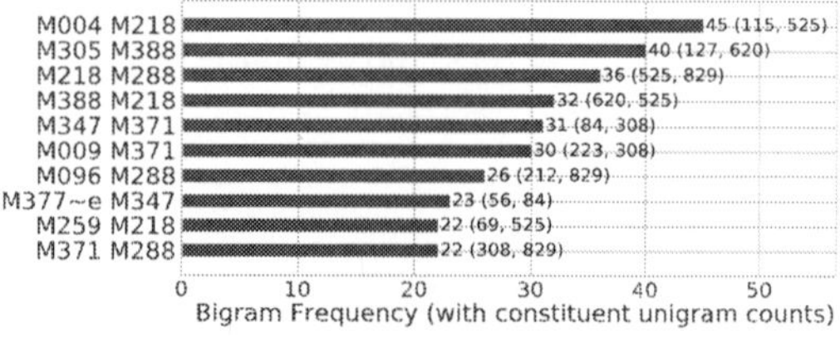

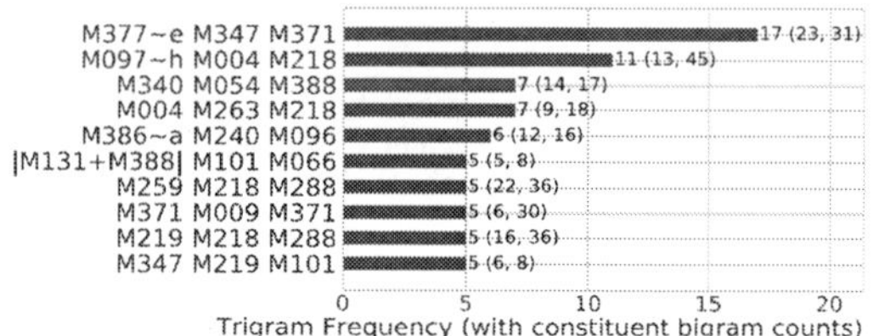

Figure 4: The 10 most frequent PE unigrams, bigrams, and trigrams (top to bottom). In parentheses are given the frequencies of the two unigrams comprising each bigram, and the two bigrams comprising each trigram: note that some frequent n grams are comprised of relatively infrequent $n - 1$-grams.

grams, the most common can only occur in up to 3.2% of texts.

External comparisons may help determine whether this is a meaningful degree of repetition, but such comparisons are not straightforward. Third millennium Sumerian or Akkadian accounting tablets are reasonable corpora to compare against, but these are available only in transliteration (using sign *readings*) while PE is transcribed (using sign *names*). This distinction makes n-gram counts from the two corpora incomparable without further work to transform the data.

Despite this, an impressionistic assessment of Ur III Sumerian administrative texts suggests that they are highly repetitious: information of wide importance to the administration (e.g. basic nouns, phrases describing administrative functions, month names, ruler names, etc.) occurs frequently. If one expects a similar pattern in the PE administrative record, our initial analysis suggests that trigrams (and perhaps bigrams) may not be a significant tactic for encoding these types of information, although unigrams might.

An n-gram analysis can also be used to begin exploring the frequency of suspected anthroponyms within the PE corpus. Dahl (2019:85) lists frequently-attested signs (10 instances or more) with "proposed syllabic values" obtained through traditional graphotactical analysis; Figure 5 presents the frequency of the most common bigrams and trigrams limited to this signset. This list fails to include what is thought to be the most commonly attested PN, M377~e M347 M371 mentioned above, since the middle sign, M347, is uncommon. Nonetheless the strings in this figure are more representative of possible PNs, since object signs which are understood to encode separate units of information have been weeded out. Overall we see that a small handful of 3-sign PNs are repeated at least 4 times across the corpus, but the majority appear 3 times or less. 2-sign PNs might be more frequent,[8] although some of the bigrams in the figure simply represent substrings from the trigrams. The ten most common bigrams all appear 13 or more times across the corpus, and the most frequent alone appears 45 times (M004 M218, including as part of a common trigram in Figure 5, accounting for 11 of its uses).

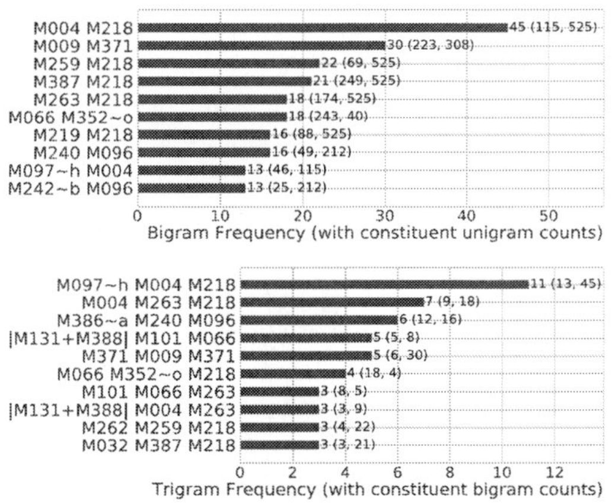

Figure 5: The 10 most frequent PE bigrams and trigrams (top to bottom), limited to signs in Dahl's (2019) syllabary. In parentheses are given the frequencies of the two unigrams comprising each bigram, and the two bigrams comprising each trigram.

Repeated n-grams, anthroponymic or otherwise, become increasingly rare for $n > 3$. No 4-gram or 5-gram appears more than 3 times; no

6-gram appears more than twice; and no 7-gram appears more than once. This low level of repetition indicates that common frequency-based linguistic decipherment methods may be ineffective on this corpus. We can, however, identify repeated strings which are similar to one another, if not exact copies, which may lead to insights about the function of certain PE signs and sign sequences. For example, the only two 6-grams which occur multiple times in the corpus differ from one another by only a single sign:

M305 M388 **M240** M097~h M004 M218
M305 M388 **M146** M097~h M004 M218

A further variant appears once in the corpus:

M305 M388 **M347** M097~h M004 M218

Traditional graphotactical analysis parses the first of these strings as follows:

- Institution, household, or person class: M305
- Person class: M388
- Further designations of the individual: M240 M097~h M004 M218

Side-by-side comparison of these 6-grams raises the question of whether the third sign in each sequence (M240, M146, and M347 respectively) is yet another classifier preceding a stable PN M097~h M004 M218, or may reflect a PN pattern in which the first element (perhaps a logogram?) can alternate.

Although there are no repeated 7-grams or 8-grams, there are three pairs of 7-grams which differ by only a single sign, and one such pair of 8-grams. We hope that by exploring sign usage within such strings, future work will be able to identify new sign ordering principles and possibly reach a more controlled set of signs that may represent anthroponyms. Such a list would offer a better (if still slim) chance at linguistic decipherment. Our data exploration toolkit provides an interface for fuzzy string matching to facilitate further investigation of strings like these.

5 LDA Topic Model

Latent Dirichlet Allocation (LDA; Blei et al. 2003) is a topic modeling algorithm which attempts to group related words into topics and determine which topics are discussed in a given set of documents. Notably, LDA infers topical relationships solely based on rates of term co-occurrence, meaning it can run on undeciphered texts to yield information on which terms may be related. Note, however, that topics may be semantically broad, and

---

[8] However, according to Desset's (2016) traditional analysis of 515 hypothetical anthroponymic sequences, "250 (48.5 %) were made of 3 signs, 118 (22.9 %) of 4 signs, 83 (16.1 %) of 2 signs, 38 (7.3 %) of 5 signs, 15 (2.9 %) of 6 signs, 8 (1.5 %) of 7 signs and 3 (0.5 %) of 8 signs."

one must be careful not to infer too much about a sign's meaning simply from its appearance in a given topic. LDA differs from the other clustering techniques we have considered in that it also provides a means for grouping tablets based on the topics they discuss, which may reveal genres or other meaningful divisions of the corpus.

We induced a 10-topic LDA model over the PE corpus. We chose a small number of topics to make the task of interpreting the model more manageable; fewer topics make for fewer sets of representative signs to analyze. Furthermore, with 10 topics the model learns topics which are mostly non-overlapping (Figure 6), meaning there are few redundant topics to sort through. We note, however, that model perplexity drops sharply above 80 topics, and topic coherence peaks around 110 topics; future work may therefore do well to investigate larger models.

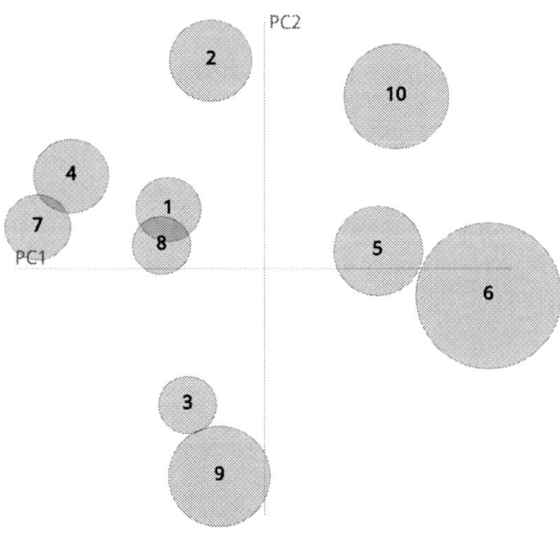

Figure 6: Intertopic distance (measured as Jensen-Shannon divergence) visualized with LDAVis (Sievert and Shirley, 2014) using two principal components (PC1 and PC2). Larger circles represent more common topics.

The following sections begin to elaborate on the topics which we can most easily interpret, although space constraints prohibit full analysis of each individual topic. Our data exploration toolkit provides additional details including information about topic stability using the stability measure introduced by Mäntylä et al. (2018).

5.1 Topic 1

The most representative signs for this topic are M376 and M056∼f. M376 has been speculated to represent either a human worker category or cattle; M056∼f is a depiction of a plow (, comparable to the proto-cuneiform sign for plow, APIN). This is an intriguing connection as a sign-set for bovines has not yet been identified in PE, despite the clear cultural importance of cattle suggested by PE cylinder seal depictions (Dahl, 2016). More interesting still is the fact that M376 and M056∼f never occur in the same text. Their inclusion in the same topic implies that they simply occur in the presence of similar signs (though not as direct neighbors of those signs, since they do not group together in the neighbor-based clustering). Topic modelling in this case has brought to light tendencies in the writing system that may have been intuitively grasped but would be difficult to quantify manually.

5.2 Topic 3

The signs M297∼b and M297 are both highly representative of this topic. This is interesting as the relationship between these two signs has been uncertain (Meriggi, 1971:74). M297∼b was hypothesised to indicate a "keg" by Friberg (1978). It is an "object" sign that almost always appears in the ultimate or penultimate position of sign strings; it sometimes appears in the summary line of accounts followed by numerical notations that quantify amounts of grain or liquids. Friberg suspected such texts referred to ale distributions. Ale is thought to have been a staple of the PE diet at Susa. Meriggi suggested M297 may indicate "bread", but he also included it in his syllabary; it is the 6th most common sign in PE, appearing in 145 texts, and M297∼b is the 31st most common appearing in 66 texts. Yet topic 3 is the dominant topic in only 85 texts, suggesting that the LDA model has identified a particular subset of the accounts that refer to M297 or M297∼b. Also of note is the fact that M297∼b occurs in topic 3 at a significantly higher rate than M297, despite being rarer in general—a much higher percentage of the overall uses of M297∼b appear in this topic (around 75%) than do the overall uses of M297 (less than 15%).

5.3 Topics 4 and 7

The texts included in topics 4 and 7 successfully reproduce aspects of Dahl 2005 with reference to the genres of PE livestock husbandry and slaughter texts. Dahl was able to decipher the ideographic meaning (if not phonetic realization) of signs for female, male, young, and mature sheep and goats and some of their products, beginning with the key observation that proto-cuneiform UDU (⊕, "mixed sheep and goats") is graphically comparable to M346 (✳). The most representative signs in topic 4 are M346 ("ewe") and M367 ("billy-goat").

While almost every instance of M346 is representative of topic 4, it is assigned to topic 5 in the atypical text P272825 (see 5.4). Several other typical livestock context uses of M346 belong to topic 7. Topic 7 was the most stable topic across 30 repeated runs in our topic stability evaluation. The most predictive sign for this topic is M009 (═), which is also representative of topic 4 (and appeared in Section 4.1.1). The most representative texts in this topic include a few nanny-goat herding texts; many more texts in this topic have no known association with livestock or animal products, though a few (e.g. P009141 and P008407) do bear seal impressions depicting livestock.

5.4 Topic 5

The reason that the LDA model groups these 144 texts is not immediately apparent to the traditional PE specialist. An odd feature of the topic is that M388 ("person/man") is considered the most representative sign, but the most representative *text* is a simple tally of equids that never uses M388, and in fact uses few non-numerical signs overall. This may be due simply to noise in the model: M388 may be a kind of "stopword" which crops up in unrelated topics due to its high frequency. That said, an intriguing feature is that a significantly larger proportion of the texts in this topic bear a seal impression than do texts in the other topics. Seal impressions are unknown to the LDA model, and their presence suggests that it is at least possible the model has identified similarities in tablet content not easily observed through traditional analysis. The atypical "elite redistributive account" (Kelley, 2018:163) P272825, which is also sealed, is associated with this topic. This text has around 116 entries using complex sign-strings, fifteen of which include M388.

5.5 Topic 6

The ten most representative signs for topic 6 include the five of Meriggi's possible syllabic signs that grouped most stably in our clustering evaluation (see 4.1.1). Nine of the ten are also included in Meriggi's syllabary, excluding only

M388, the second most representative sign in the topic. M388 has been key to the identification of possible PNs, since it tends to appear just before longer sign strings and, through a series of arguments drawing on cuneiform parallels, may function as a Personenkeil (a marker for human names; Damerow and Englund 1989; Kelley 2018:222 ff.). The texts of topic 6 are of diverse size and structure, but do tend to include many traditionally identifiable PNs.

5.6 Topic 10

This topic also confirms existing understanding of a PE administrative genre, namely that of "labor administration" (Damerow and Englund, 1989; Nissen et al., 1994). The most representative signs are the characteristic "worker category signs" described in the very long ration texts discussed by Dahl et al. (2018:24–23), and indeed all of those texts appear in this topic, in addition to a variety of other identifiable labor texts of somewhat different (but partially overlapping) content.

5.7 Remaining Topics (2, 8, and 9)

Initial assessments also suggest promising avenues of analysis for topics 2, 8, and 9. Topic 2 is heavily skewed towards M288 ("grain container"), the most common PE sign;[9] its third most representative sign (M391, possibly meaning "field") may suggest an agricultural management context for some texts in this topic. Topic 8 is strongly represented by |M195+M057|. This is an undeciphered complex grapheme, frequently occurring as a text's second sign after the "header" M157. In topic 9, the two most representative signs are M387 and M036 (possibly associated with rationing). Since the LDA model is not aware of the numeric notation between entries, it is interesting that the bisexagesimal numeric systems B# and B appear prominently in this topic, whether or not M036 (associated with those systems) appears: see particularly P009048 (the text most strongly associated with this topic) and P008619.

5.8 LDA Summary

The preceding sections confirm that the LDA model largely learns topics which traditional PE

---

[9] A remarkable 37.3% of the topic's probability mass is allocated to this sign, compared to just 2.5% for the second most predictive sign (M157, the "household" header sign). No other topic is so skewed: only topic 4 comes close, with 20.3% of its mass assigned to M346 ("sheep").

specialists recognise as meaningful. Our brief interpretations of the topics serve only to highlight the amount of potentially fruitful analysis that still remains to be done. It also remains to see what topics arise when sign variants are collapsed together: preliminary results suggest that topics resembling our topic 6 and topic 10 are still found, but new topics also appear which have no clear correlates in the model discussed in this paper.

6   Related Work

Meriggi (1971:173–174) conducted manual graphotactic analysis of PE (and later linear Elamite) texts, for example by noting the positions in which certain signs could appear in sign-strings. Dahl (2002) was the first to use basic computer-assisted data sorting to present information on sign frequencies, and Englund (2004:129–138) concluded his discussion of "the state of decipherment" by suggesting that the newly transliterated corpus would benefit from more intensive study of sign ordering phenomena. Apart from the use of Rapidminer[10] to perform simple data sorting in Kelley 2018, no publications have yet described any effort to apply computational approaches to the dataset.

Computational approaches to decipherment (Knight and Yamada, 1999; Knight et al., 2006), which resemble the setup typically followed by human archaeological-decipherment experts (Robinson, 2009), have been useful in several real world tasks. Snyder et al. (2010) propose an automatic decipherment technique that further improves existing methods by incorporating cognate identification and lexicon induction. When applied to Ugaritic, the model is able to correctly map 29 of 30 letters to their Hebrew counterparts. Reddy and Knight (2011) study the Voynich manuscript for its linguistic properties, and show that the letter sequences are generally more predictable than in natural languages. Following this, Hauer and Kondrak (2016) treat the text in the Voynich manuscript as anagrammed substitution ciphers, and their experiments suggest, arguably, that Hebrew is the language of the document. Hierarchical clustering has previously been used by Knight et al. (2011) to aid in the decipherment of the Copiale cipher, where it was able to identify meaningful groups such as word boundary markers as well as signs which correspond to the same plaintext symbol.

Homburg and Chiarcos (2016) report preliminary results on automatic word segmentation for Akkadian cuneiform using rule-based, dictionary based, and data-driven statistical techniques. Pagé-Perron et al. (2017) furnish an analysis of Sumerian text including morphology, parts-of-speech (POS) tagging, syntactic parsing, and machine translation using a parallel corpus. Although Sumerian and Akkadian are both geographically and chronologically close to PE, these corpora are very large (e.g. 1.5 million lines for Sumerian), and are presented in word level transliterations rather than sign-by-sign transcriptions. This makes most of these techniques inapplicable to PE. Our study is more similar in spirit to Reddy and Knight (2011), as the Voynich manuscript and PE are both undeciphered and resource-poor, making analysis especially difficult.

7   Conclusions

We have shown that methods from computational linguistics can offer valuable insights into the proto-Elamite script, and can substantially improve the toolkit available to the PE specialist. Hierarchical sign clustering replicates previous work by rediscovering meaningful groups of signs, and suggests avenues for future work by revealing similarities between yet-undeciphered signs. Analysis of n-gram frequencies highlights the level of repetition of sign strings across the corpus as a point of further research interest, and also reveals sets of similar strings worth examining in detail. LDA topic modelling has replicated previous work in identifying known text genres, but has also suggested new relationships between tablets which can be explored using more traditional analysis. The methods we have used are by no means exhaustive, and there remain many more approaches to consider in future work. Particularly in a field populated by a small handful of researchers, the faster data processing and ease of visualization offered by computational methods may significantly aid progress towards understanding this writing system. We hope that our data exploration tools will help facilitate future discoveries, which may eventually lead to a more complete decipherment of the largest undeciphered corpus from the ancient world.

---

[10]https://www.rapidminer.com/

References

David M. Blei, Andrew Y. Ng, and Michael I. Jordan. 2003. Latent Dirichlet allocation. *Journal of Machine Learning Research*, 3:993–1022.

Jacob L. Dahl. 2002. Proto-Elamite sign frequencies. *Cuneiform Digital Library Bulletin*, 2002/1.

Jacob L. Dahl. 2005. Animal husbandry in Susa during the proto-Elamite period. *Studi Micenei ed Egeo-Anatolici*, 47:81–134.

Jacob L. Dahl. 2009. Early writing in Iran, a reappraisal. *Iran*, 47(1):23–31.

Jacob L. Dahl. 2016. The production and storage of food in early Iran. In M.B. D'Anna, C. Jauß, and J.C. Johnson, editors, *Food and Urbanisation. Material and Textual Perspectives on Alimentary Practice in Early Mesopotamia*, volume 37, pages 45–50. Gangemi Editore.

Jacob L. Dahl. 2019. Tablettes et fragments proto-élamites / proto-Elamite tablets and fragments. *Textes Cunéiform Tomes XXXII Musée de Louvre*.

Jacob L. Dahl, Laura Hawkins, and Kate Kelley. 2018. Labor administration in proto-Elamite Iran. In Agnès Garcia-Ventura, editor, *What's in a Name? Terminology related to the Work Force and Job Categories in the Ancient Near East*, pages 15–44. Alt Orient und Altes Testament 440. Ugarit Verlag: Münster.

Jacob L. Dahl, M. Hessari, and R. Yousefi Zoshk. 2012. The proto-Elamite tablets from Tape Sofalin. *Iranian Journal of Archaeological Studies*, 2(1):57–73.

Peter Damerow. 2006. The origins of writing as a problem of historical epistemology. *Cuneiform Digital Library Journal*, 2006/1.

Peter Damerow and Robert K. Englund. 1989. *The Proto-Elamite Texts from Tepe Yahya*. Bulletin (American School of Prehistoric Research). Peabody Museum of Archaeology and Ethnology, Harvard University.

Leon Derczynski and Sean Chester. 2016. Generalised Brown clustering and roll-up feature generation. In *Proceedings of the Thirtieth AAAI Conference on Artificial Intelligence*, AAAI 2016, pages 1533–1539. AAAI Press.

François Desset. 2016. Proto-Elamite writing in Iran. *Archéo-nil. Revue de la société pour l'étude des cultures prépharaoniques de la valée du Nil*, 26:67–104.

Robert K. Englund. 1996. The proto-elamite script. In Peter Daniels and William Bright, editors, *The world's writing systems*. Oxford University Press, Oxford, UK.

Robert K. Englund. 2004. The state of decipherment of proto-Elamite. *The First Writing: Script Invention as History and Process*, pages 100–149.

Jöran Friberg. 1978. *The Third Millennium Roots of Babylonian Mathematics I-II*. Göteborg Dept. of Mathematics, Chalmers University of Technology, Göteborg, Sweden.

Bradley Hauer and Grzegorz Kondrak. 2016. Decoding anagrammed texts written in an unknown language and script. *Transactions of the Association for Computational Linguistics*, 4:75–86.

Laura F. Hawkins. 2015. A new edition of the Proto-Elamite text MDP 17, 112. *Cuneiform Digital Library Journal*, 1.

Timo Homburg and Christian Chiarcos. 2016. Akkadian word segmentation. In *Tenth International Conference on Language Resource Evaluation (LREC 2016)*, pages 4067–4074.

Kate Kelley. 2018. *Gender, Age, and Labour Organization in the Earliest Texts from Mesopotamia and Iran (c. 3300–2900 BC)*. Doctoral dissertation, University of Oxford.

Kevin Knight, Beáta Megyesi, and Christiane Schaefer. 2011. The Copiale cipher. In *Proceedings of the 4th Workshop on Building and Using Comparable Corpora: Comparable Corpora and the Web*, pages 2–9. Association for Computational Linguistics.

Kevin Knight, Anish Nair, Nishit Rathod, and Kenji Yamada. 2006. Unsupervised analysis for decipherment problems. In *Proceedings of the COLING/ACL on Main Conference Poster Sessions*, COLING-ACL '06, pages 499–506, Stroudsburg, PA, USA. Association for Computational Linguistics.

Kevin Knight and Kenji Yamada. 1999. A computational approach to deciphering unknown scripts. In *Proceedings of the ACL Workshop on Unsupervised Learning in Natural Language Processing*.

Mika Mäntylä, Maelick Claes, and Umar Farooq. 2018. Measuring LDA topic stability from clusters of replicated runs. In *Proceedings of the 12th ACM/IEEE International Symposium on Empirical Software Engineering and Measurement*, ESEM '18, New York, NY, USA. ACM.

Piero Meriggi. 1971. *La scrittura proto-elamica. Parte Ia: La scrittura e il contenuto dei testi*. Accademia Nazionale dei Lincei, Rome.

Hans J. Nissen, Peter Damerow, and Robert K. Englund. 1994. *Archaic Bookkeeping: Writing and Techniques of Economic Administration in the Ancient Near East*. University of Chicago Press.

Émilie Pagé-Perron, Maria Sukhareva, Ilya Khait, and Christian Chiarcos. 2017. Machine translation and automated analysis of the Sumerian language. In

Joint SIGHUM Workshop on Computational Linguistics for Cultural Heritage, Social Sciences, Humanities and Literature, ACL, pages 10–16. Association for Computational Linguistics.

Sravana Reddy and Kevin Knight. 2011. What we know about the Voynich manuscript. In *Proceedings of the 5th ACL-HLT Workshop on Language Technology for Cultural Heritage, Social Sciences, and Humanities*, pages 78–86.

A. Robinson. 2009. *Lost Languages: The Enigma of the World's Undeciphered Scripts*. Thames & Hudson.

Jean-Vincent Scheil. 1905. Documents archaïques en écriture proto-élamite. *Mémoires de la Délégation en Perse*, 6:57–128.

Carson Sievert and Kenneth Shirley. 2014. LDAvis: A method for visualizing and interpreting topics. In *Proceedings of the Workshop on Interactive Language Learning, Visualization, and Interfaces*, pages 63–70. Association for Computational Linguistics.

Benjamin Snyder, Regina Barzilay, and Kevin Knight. 2010. A statistical model for lost language decipherment. In *Proceedings of the 48th Annual Meeting of the Association for Computational Linguistics*, pages 1048–1057. Association for Computational Linguistics.

Author Index

Association for Computational Linguistics
209 N. Eighth Street
Stroudsburg, Pennsylvania 18360

ISBN 978-1-5108-8779-4